CAN SOMEBODY

SHOUT

AMEN!

PATSY SIMS

St. Martin's Press,
New York

Design by M. Paul

D. 29024

Library of Congress Cataloging-in-Publication Data

Sims, Patsy.
    Can somebody shout amen!   *88 - B4411*

    1. Revivals—United States—History—20th century.
    2. United States—Church history—20th century.
    I. Title.
    BV3773.S56   1988   269'.24'0973   87-27955
    ISBN 0-312-01397-3

First Edition
10 9 8 7 6 5 4 3 2 1

For Mel Berger,
Robert Cashdollar, Iris Day,
and Kathleen Hall Jamieson,
with love and appreciation for
making this book possible.

CONTENTS

ACKNOWLEDGMENTS

During the course of writing this book, I can truthfully say I have been through hell and high water: my cat Sam lost a leg; she, the manuscript, and I got caught in a flash flood of—appropriately enough—the Jordan River (the one that runs through Virginia); I went through three publishers and four editors; and my computer's printer seemed to konk out every time I attempted to meet a deadline and finally died while I was trying to get the final manuscript to New York. In the end, the project was possible only because of the help of a cast and crew that would rival a Cecil B. DeMille production. I am hesitant to start giving credits, for fear of accidentally overlooking someone and because such a list would probably run longer than the manuscript itself. However, there are some I simply must single out for help I can never possibly repay.

My thanks go to my literary agent, Mel Berger, for being my friend, booster, and sounding board; to my various editors—Thomas Dunne, Richard Marek, Michelle Salcedo, and especially Elizabeth Backman, who did combat far beyond the call of duty; to Kathleen Hall Jamieson, my academic mentor, unflagging patron, and with whom almost all things became possible; to the University of Maryland for its supportiveness, especially to my thesis committee, Roger Meersman, Andrew Wolvin, and Charles Kauffman; to Shirley Strum Kenny, who has since moved on to Queens College, for believing in me sight unseen; to Rebecca Farwell and Emily LeRoy, who in addition to their work on the computer helped me make many a dash to the post office; to Paul Darby, Frank Vacca, and Joe Velletri, who came to my aid every time the drat printer went on the fritz; and most especially to Bob Cashdollar, Iris Day, and Dottie Vann, for providing everything from advice on the manuscript to Kleenex when absolutely nothing worked but tears.

For sharing background information, technical advice, anecdotes, and clippings, I am grateful to many scholars, journalists, and other specialists as well as to the institutions and publications with which they are affiliated. They are far too numerous to name, but I am especially grateful to Charles Conn, official Church of God historian; Wilma Dykeman, Tennessee state historian; J. Wayne Flynt of Auburn University; David Edwin Harrell, Jr., of the University of Alabama; Loyal Jones, director, Appalachian Center, Berea College; James Auchmutey of the *Atlanta Constitution*; Michelle Scott Hancock and Jim Jones of the *Fort Worth Star-Telegram*; Louise Lione of the *Charlotte News & Observer*; Peter Geiger and Stuart Warner of the *Akron Beacon Journal*; Darrell Sifford of the *Philadelphia Inquirer*; Susan Tifft of *Time* magazine; Adon Taft of the *Miami Herald*; and freelance writer Caren Goldman Ritter. Many libraries and archives were generous in their help. I am especially indebted to the Library of Congress and its loan division and American Folklife Center.

My special thanks to the MacDowell Colony, where I thought I had written the last word in this book; to the PEN American Center, for financial aid at an especially critical moment; and to Marty Harding and the Brambles—Barbara, Chris, Bill, and Toby—for providing me with hideaways. I wish also to thank the National Endowment for the Arts and the District of Columbia for grants that, while not for this project, nevertheless advanced and enabled me to continue as a writer. I must also mention Visa, MasterCard, and American Express, which have shown about as much faith in me as anyone and without whom this and all my other books would have not been possible.

I would also like to thank Albert E. Brumley & Sons, V. B. (Vep) Ellis, William J. Gaither, and Songs of Calvary for permitting me to use some of their copyrighted lyrics.

And to the evangelists, their workers, and members of the audiences, my deep appreciation for the cooperation and sharing that ultimately was the making of this book.

INTRODUCTION

In the sanctuaries of my growing up, those proper churches on the Main Streets of the South, tents and tabernacles were as off limits as the abandoned house next door. I don't remember being told this, directly, in so many words. It was more a feeling I absorbed, from intonations, insinuations, association—that there were strange goings-on under the canvas flaps. Incredible things not unlike the sideshows at the Southeast Texas State Fair. I harbored a special fascination for Harry's Tabernacle in Beaumont. I don't know why. I don't even recall what, if anything, Mother ever said about it, other than the name. And maybe it was simply that—the name—that set it apart from the First Methodist or Calder Avenue Baptist Church. Or maybe it was the way she said it. For whatever reason, while I was never scared of the dark, the mere mention of Harry Hodges Tabernacle gave me the shivers. One night when Mother came home and said she had had a flat tire outside Harry's Tabernacle, the incident and its proximity to the clapboard structure seemed, in the telling, to somehow be related. Perhaps that was only the workings of a child's mind, but I think not nor do I think I was or am unique. Many folks, I would venture to say, have long attached a vague sort of strangeness to tents and so-called Holy-Roller churches. And certainly I was no different.

Every summer along the back roads of the South, the tents would appear—some larger than others but always bearing placards promising

SIGNS—WONDERS—MIRACLES. I have no idea how many I have passed in my lifetime, always curious about what went on under the canvas. Yet I never ventured inside a revival tent or into one of what we Southern Baptists viewed as the "off-brand" churches so often associated with them, churches that over the years managed to move to our side of the tracks and in some cases even go "uptown." Finally, in June 1981, I decided to take a look. I packed my tape recorder and a supply of cassettes, and embarked on what I thought would be a two-year project but somehow managed to grow into three, then four, eventually almost six.

When I started out, I'm not sure I could have pronounced *glossolalia*, let alone know what it meant. My knowledge of evangelists was limited to Billy Graham and "Angel" Martinez, whose name I vaguely remembered from long-ago revivals at Beaumont's First Baptist Church. I quickly discovered I was equally in the dark about what Pentecostals were and did and exactly what constituted an honest to goodness old-time revival.

What I had expected to find and what I went looking for was a Sunday-evening–type service—not quite so formal as the morning worship but with a string of sin-and-repentance hymns, finger-jabbing-burn-in-hell sermons, and wrenching invitations that would make a saint feel guilty about not going to the altar. My original idea was to concentrate on one evangelist, following a revival from the planning stages through the actual services, returning to the area six months later to see what had happened to the people who had been healed or "saved."

Before I got on the road, I called my sources throughout the South to gather the names of possible subjects—no easy feat as most evangelists are independent and go their own way. I headed first to the Baltimore Civic Center for a revival conducted by R. W. Schambach. After sitting through four hours of gospel rock and what struck me as more a one-man theatrical performance than a sermon, I concluded that this wasn't a real revival and went back to my sources. Then I heard about how H. Richard Hall had been on the sawdust trail for almost forty years, and I was certain I had found my man. But when his sermon was only slightly less unorthodox than Schambach's, I set out for Knoxville, Tennessee, to look into a two-week revival being conducted by H. Wayne Simmons. Only after I had accumulated enough material for several fair-size volumes did I come to understand that the rambunctious music, the humorous biblical vignettes, the noisy services with everyone running around the tent shouting and trying to pray out loud at once indeed constituted an old-time revival—Pentecostal-style—and differed only in decibels from what transpired week after week in those strange-named little churches.

When Richard Hall found out during our first meeting that I had never been around Pentecostals, he let me know I was in for an experience. Patiently he tried to explain the differences between the Assemblies of God, the Church of God, the Church of God of Prophecy, and the United Pentecostals, assuring me, "You don't understand this now, but you will. You'll be an expert before you're finished." I can't take credit for the latter, but I can attest to the accuracy of another prediction he made: that I would end up with far more than a book would hold.

Indeed, that first three-day revival back in April 1981 was the beginning of an odyssey, an experience, an education. Between then and now I attended almost fifty services conducted by fifteen evangelists—Pentecostals, all—with audiences ranging from fifty to almost five thousand. Before, after, and in between, I taped interviews with twenty-two revivalists, thirty-one of their workers and close relatives, fifty-five members of the audiences, and thirty "experts," and carried on less formal conversations with dozens more. I worshiped, conversed, and broke bread with them, ending up with 225 hours of taped services and interviews and enough cartons of written notes, newspaper clippings, magazine articles, and copies of the evangelists' own slick publications to start a sizable archive. And I can't begin to estimate the many books, chapters, pages, words I have read on almost every conceivable aspect of revivalism—the history, music, miracles, money.

What I discovered—and what I explore in this book—is a world more fascinating than I ever imagined, one dominated by men who are colorful, compelling, and not just a little unorthodox. These men of God sprang out of a tradition that dates back almost two hundred years, to the Great Revival, a series of no-holds-barred attacks on sin that laid the groundwork for revivals as we know them today. It was, in fact, out of them that the word *revival* first came into use among ministers seeking to restore an earlier piety, when their fellow Americans had more respect for God and men of the cloth.

The Great Revival, roughly from 1798 to 1810, was not the first on the American continent. In the 1740s the Great Awakening had swept the eastern seaboard. But the meetings among the sin-hardened settlers in Kentucky, western Virginia, the Carolinas, and Tennessee were different. On the frontier, Puritan services lost some of their formality. The pioneers lived hard and died hard, and their conversion was in keeping with their rugged life-style. They were brought to their knees, crying, shouting, leaping, by a group of equally rough-hewn preachers who, historian Bernard A. Weisberger wrote, converted sinners with "the same quick-triggered zest their neighbors directed against the British, or land speculators, or excise men."

To get to these revivals, families traveled as far as a hundred miles by wagon, horse, or foot, trips that sometimes took more than a week. And they came for the same reasons many revivalgoers today attend: to visit with neighbors, to be entertained by rousing services, to find respite from their drab, hard lives, to experience a miracle. The largest, most historically important meeting took place on August 6, 1801, when a crowd variously estimated at from twelve to twenty-five thousand gathered at Cane Ridge, near the present city of Lexington, Kentucky.

By the time the Great Revival ended, it had established a model for the revivals that followed. Then—as now—the services were emotionally charged, with plain, unpolished preaching by men who for the most part had no formal theological training. In a nation that had held to the Calvinistic doctrine of predestination, these traveling evangelists spread the more democratic Arminian theology of salvation for all who believed, which has dominated revival preaching ever since. Conversion, once an intensely private and personal experience, now came about publicly and under excruciating emotional pressure. While along the coast conversion was an exercise of the mind, on the frontier it was more likely to be an exercise of the body.

In the middle of the nineteenth century, when Darwinism was challenging creationism and the agrarian society was losing ground to urbanism, the emphasis of revivals shifted from converting sinners to reaffirming the "saved" in a world that seemed both bewildering and indifferent. But while the revivals held even more strongly to the fundamental truths of the Bible, they nevertheless borrowed from the very world their followers distrusted so much. When revivals ventured into the industrial age, they did so under the guidance of Dwight L.

Moody, a former Boston shoe salesman who moved to Chicago in 1856 at age nineteen. Moody became the first revivalist to spend lavishly ($30,000 for an eight-week crusade in Philadelphia in 1875) and to use the tools of modern persuasion—publicity, organization, and advertising—to attract audiences. He set still another precedent for future revivalists: the role of the evangelist as God's "right-hand" man. As Weisberger observed, "To thousands of his converts, God must have looked uncannily like Dwight L. Moody."

By the turn of the century, commercialism had come to revivalism. As evangelists were increasingly forced to compete for audiences with baseball, motion pictures, and other forms of entertainment, the services became more folksy and entertaining, with an emphasis on audience participation. Sermons evolved into dramatic, often humorous monologues, and the song services became lively and frankly entertaining, with the chorister—or "front man"—gaining new prominence. To justify the growing labor and expense that went into a revival, evangelists placed even more emphasis on mass conversions, and the success of a crusade came to be measured by the "cost per convert"— a figure arrived at by dividing the cost of the services by the number converted.

No one prodded the move into contemporary America more than William A. Sunday. Beginning in 1911, the former baseball player refined the publicity and organizational machinery set in motion by Moody, and in an era when "old-time" religion could no longer count on a captive audience he successfully vied for attention with film stars, heads of state, World War I heroes, even big-time gangsters. With Billy Sunday behind the pulpit, revivalism became a combination of big business and showmanship. Alternately funny and abrasive, Sunday—in the words of one historian—"skipped, ran, walked, bounced, slid and gyrated" across the platform. Although capable of conventional preaching, he preferred biblical vignettes, which remain popular with today's evangelists. Every story became a dramatic performance with Sunday acting out all the parts. He was at his best when he reduced the Bible to everyday vernacular, as he did in relating the Devil's temptation of Christ: "Turn some of these stones into bread and get a square meal!" he mimicked. "Procure the goods!"

Billy Sunday soon attained celebrity status because, according to Weisberger, "religion had no spokesman more clearly cut out for popularity and wealth in the dawning age of bally-hoo." Literally hundreds of thousands shook his hand to reaffirm their embrace of Christ as their savior, and the press accorded those handshakes the same front-page prominence they gave breaking news of the day. Sunday perpetuated and refined the role of the revivalist both as God's anointed and as entertainer. His reward was wealth. During his heyday, the "freewill" offerings—collected from audiences specifically for Sunday's personal use—averaged $80,000 a year, a million dollars by the height of his career. No longer was the revivalist to be denied worldly prosperity— a fringe benefit that by the 1980s reached gaudy excesses, as evidenced by Jim and Tammy Bakker's air-conditioned doghouse and vintage $62,000 Rolls-Royce.

In 1920, however, revivalism began to decline, and even Billy Sunday, approaching sixty, no longer could fill tents and his custom-built coliseums with tens of thousands of people. While Sunday had done much to modernize the old-time revival, eventually he too could not compete with radio, movies, automobiles, and other new wonders. For thirty years no one would command the crowds and the attention of a Billy Sunday. When revivals did make a comeback after World War II, they were the work of numerous independent associations that came in a variety of sizes and styles and, according to historian David Edwin Harrell, Jr., "lived or died with the charisma of the evangelist." Unlike their Presbyterian and Methodist predecessors of the Great Revival days, these evangelists were Pentecostal with only a few Baptists—most notably Billy Graham—staging crusades. The best known were Oral Roberts, Asa Alonzo Allen, William Branham, and Jack Coe. For the most part, these revivalists—even the lesser known—were imposing, compelling men, carrying on in the tradition of Billy Sunday. But each had his own personality, his own style.

Roberts, the son of a Pentecostal minister, launched his own ministry in 1947 when he was twenty-nine and quickly became the giant of the sawdust trail. He was tall, handsome, with a "smattering" of college that set him apart from most of his brethren. Among his many talents was an abundant skill for organizing. While his tent meetings may have seemed a bit uncouth to outsiders, within Pentecostal ranks they were models of decorum, and it came as little surprise when in March 1968 he joined the more prestigious Boston Avenue Methodist Church in Tulsa. By the 1980s, however, his more extreme money-raising tactics—likened by many to spiritual blackmail—made Roberts an embarrassment to some who had once envied and admired him.

By contrast, William Branham was a meek, mild-mannered little man with a halting, boring delivery. Nevertheless, he captivated his audiences with accounts of his constant communications with God and angels. As word of his legendary healing powers spread, his staff was hard pressed to find halls large enough to accommodate the crowds. His followers were so certain Branham was "the man sent by God" that after he was killed in an automobile accident in December 1965 they stored his embalmed body in a funeral home attic, convinced that on Easter he would rise from the dead.

The most flamboyant of the era were A. A. Allen and Jack Coe. Both were dynamic and equally controversial. Coe was a large, hulking man with "a raucous wit and reckless boldness," second only to Roberts as the real hero of the people. He loved a good fight and particularly hard cases. As a testimonial to his healing successes, he strung supposedly discarded crutches and canes across the platform of his tent. Then in February 1956 the mother of a three-year-old polio victim claimed her son's legs were irreparably damaged because Coe had instructed her to remove the child's braces, and the evangelist was arrested in Miami for practicing medicine without a license. After a highly publicized two-day trial, the charges were dropped. Ten months later the thirty-nine-year-old faith healer was dead—the victim of polio.

A smaller man, sometimes likened in appearance to Jimmy Cagney playing George M. Cohan, Allen had no less of a platform presence. He was a superb fund-raiser and an even better entertainer, singing, strutting, and performing one-man Bible extravaganzas. Like Coe, he thrived on controversy and difficult cases—especially attempted resurrections. Even his arrest in 1955 for drunken driving did not lessen his popularity. In the eyes of many, he was the top-most tent revivalist to hit the sawdust trail since the days of Billy Sunday.

As in the past, one of the primary roles of the new revival—under the leadership of Roberts, Allen, Branham, and Coe—was to fill the needs of the emotionally barren poor and dispossessed and to ease the insecurities of a generation growing up in "cultural anonymity." From 1947 to about 1958, faith healing was the central theme. While salvation was preached and speaking in tongues encouraged, the drawing card and high point of each service was the miracle, that special moment when the revivalist attempted to heal the sick, cast out devils, and raise the dead. In the late 1950s when the audiences and offerings began to dwindle, some evangelists dropped out but many looked for ways to broaden their appeal. In some ministries the promise of financial prosperity for the believers became the most advertised miracle. Increasingly the emphasis shifted to entertainment, with musical skills as important to the ambitious revivalist as knowing how to preach. Song services grew longer and livelier with quartets and choristers backed by ensembles of guitars, drums, pianos, organs, and amplifiers. By the 1970s many revivalists had moved into auditoriums and civic centers or onto television and radio. But whether they remained in tents or went indoors, most continued to draw upon the models of their itinerant evangelistic ancestors.

Today revivalists—or "one-man denominations," as they have been called—still manage to fill auditoriums and tents and affect the thinking of many poor as well as middle-class American Protestants who feel lost and estranged in an increasingly complicated world. For these seemingly disinherited, the revival continues to offer not only religious fulfillment but also a source of entertainment, a sense of belonging, a feeling of worth—they are, after all, God's chosen people. Through ostensibly extemporaneous sermons and pronouncements, the revivalists are able to influence their followers' emotions, beliefs, and financial contributions. A mere laying on of hands can elicit a commitment or a cure or even render a person unconscious.

It is a power some evangelists have not always wielded ethically and honestly, a trust not always responsibly met. H. Richard Hall talked openly about what he called the "seamy side" of revivalism. "That might strike you as strange, but there is a bad side," he told me during our first interview. "We have one of the brethren that is now in prison." That aspect of tents and tabernacles was not news to me nor, do I think, to many Americans. The history of evangelism has been riddled with conduct that at times has rivaled such fictional portrayals as *The Scarlet Letter* and *Elmer Gantry*. During the "roaring twenties" the glamorous, flamboyant Aimee Semple McPherson—dubbed the "Queen of Heaven"—was accused by authorities of faking her own kidnapping to cover up a tryst with a married employee. And in 1976 the television ministry of Billy James Hargis came crashing down after a national magazine quoted students—male and female—who claimed to have had sex with the Oklahoma fundamentalist.

Still other evangelists have had legal skirmishes ranging from somewhat innocuous charges of disturbing the peace to more serious allegations of drunken driving, income-tax evasion, and practicing medicine without a license. The particular revivalist Brother Hall referred to was serving a twelve-year prison sentence for allegedly conspiring to commit arson and assault. His frequent scrapes with the law—mostly over the use of alcohol and drugs—had gained him the reputation as "the naughty boy of the evangelistic set."

This tainted image was reinforced by the sex-and-money scandal that forced Jim and Tammy Bakker to abandon their multimillion-dollar spiritual empire in March 1987 and led to an unholy free-for-all with rival evangelists slinging charges of sexual improprieties, lust for power, and greed. Long before that episode, the Bakkers, who worked their way up from a tent, were no strangers to controversy and ridicule—even from their fellow brethren. In the midst of one revival I attended, when the somewhat frenzied evangelist went on a tirade about ungodly attire, he made no effort to disguise the target of his attack. "Can you picture Mary, the mother of Jesus, lookin' like that little hussy down in North Carolina!" he shouted. "That little Jezebel on television!"

At the time the same evangelist was awaiting the outcome of his appeal of a 1984 conviction for income-tax evasion for which he had been fined $20,000 and sentenced to five years in prison. His own holdings were said to include a fleet of fancy cars, a Learjet, a private landing strip, a guitar-shaped swimming pool, and properties in Texas, Tennessee, and Alabama—some of them bought under an assortment of assumed names and all courtesy of his estimated 150,000 followers.

Most of those believers continued to stick by him, likening his conviction to the crucifixion of Christ, a common response among the adherents of the more flamboyant men of the cloth who find themselves at odds with the law. In the eyes of the believers, these men have direct lines of communication with God and are empowered by Him. Who can question what the evangelists say or do if their instructions and authority come from Above? Who can say God did or didn't tell one to buy a Jaguar and another to build a rococo amusement park?

After almost six years of observing evangelists and faith healers, I—

like a good many people—concluded that these men of God are not necessarily all good. But who are the sincere, the honest, and who are the charlatans, the Elmer Gantrys? I cannot and would not venture an opinion—or play "God," so to speak.

From the outset, my goal has been to enable the reader to venture into the tents and tabernacles of America and vicariously experience an old-time revival. To get to know, as I did, the evangelists and the people in the audiences, to understand who they are and why they are drawn there.

Over the years revivalists—especially faith healers—have been the butt of jokes and ridicule or the object of blind, unquestioning adoration. My hope has been to offer an unbiased rendering, to show the good and the bad, the strengths and the weaknesses, by allowing the people and events to speak for themselves. My aim was not to write the definitive history of revivalism but rather to explore human needs and feelings and an institution that is so much a part of American and religious heritage. Most of all, I wanted to write a book in which the reader could hear the soaring hallelujahs and feel the sinking despair of those whose miracles never come.

It has not been easy to strike that balance or to put into words what I saw, heard, experienced. It is no easier to translate sights, sounds, human emotions into words or to capture a moment than it is to be truly unbiased and fair. How do you re-create the excitement of a middle-age woman, recently delivered from sin, as she waits to have her Bible autographed? Or describe the courage of another who lost her gamble with faith healing, yet goes valiantly to the operating table to have her second leg removed, still believing in God and His great capacity to care and to cure?

At the very least, I hope I have succeeded in taking the reader with me inside the tents and tabernacles and the lives of America's revivalists.

CAN SOMEBODY

SHOUT

AMEN!

THE BEGINNING . . .

Dirt-gray from its more ordinary burdens, heaped now with sawdust, the dump truck lumbered through the fairgrounds entrance, across the blacktopped parking lot, to the grassy expanse where the men waited and where the truck's gears ground and groaned and its bed tilted, emptying the golden shavings. Three times the truck made the trip, appearing, disappearing, reappearing again out of some far recesses of the park. Sixteen men and boys watched the comings and goings, shifting nervously, excitedly, as they awaited yet another of those male-ordained rituals of proving their strength again or for the first time. It was Monday, a workday, but they had chosen instead to go about "the Lord's business" and they were impatient to begin. The seconds weighed like minutes, hours, forever almost, and then came the announcement: *"Here comes the preacher!"* His humble bobtailed truck bore no promises of SIGNS—WONDERS—MIRACLES or JESUS SAVES, yet it carried itself with no less pride. Immediately activity surrounded it. The men, in teams and as a team, emptied the truck and its low-slung trailer with a quiet importance, moving quickly, efficiently. Soon the lot was measured, a precise site agreed upon, and tools and equipment were spread out in place, on the ground. Thick rolls of caramel-color canvas. Two center poles, prone and thirty feet apart. Assorted poles, spikes, chains, and bright-yellow cables plaited into neat, loose braids. Even unassembled, in the eyes of the evangelist it loomed mightily, like a canvas cathedral. The one God had given him in a vision.

"This is the tent God wanted us to have," he proclaimed. "It's a beautiful tent. One of the most beautiful tents you'll *ever* see!"

He moved into the midst of the men to help, for putting up the tent was as much a part of his "calling" as preaching the gospel and praying for the sick. The yellow braids were unraveled and the ropes attached near the top of a center pole. As four men lifted the column, pushing from behind, others pulled the ropes in a three-way tug-of-war. Slowly, sluggishly, the pole ventured up.

"How does that look?" one man called to a bystander.

"Needs to go this way, just a hair."

"Okay, give 'em a little slack and let 'em pull it out," the man instructed his team. To a teenage boy across from him he yelled, "Tighten up over there!" He craned his neck and watched the pole rising. "Give 'em just a *lit*tle slack." The pole continued its upright journey, its movement becoming barely noticeable, then ceasing. When the guylines had been secured and the process repeated, the canvas was unrolled and its thirty-foot sections laced together and hooked to the center poles. Now the men formed an assembly line. At even intervals around the canvas's edge teams placed stakes and chains and the shorter side poles. Another group followed with sledgehammers, rhythmically slamming the giant nails into the red earth. In the distance thunder rumbled nearer, and the men hurriedly inserted the side poles. As two men disappeared under the flattened cloth, the others stepped back, expectant. The air was still. Winches squeaked, and slowly, cautiously, the canvas rose—waist high, shoulder level, pausing at half-mast while the poles were adjusted. Again the winches squealed and the canvas inched upward, until it took the full shape of a tent. And the men, as one, cried, *Praise the Lord!*

Then the work continued on into the night, late into the next day: sickling, mowing, wiring, carting-in chairs and amplifiers and drums and organs and sawdust a wheelbarrow at a time. Always there was the waiting—for the electrician and the fire inspectors to give their nod, for all the parts, the eight months' preparations to come together. Finally the men left to shower and shave and dress and join womenfolk and children for their long-awaited revival.

REVIVAL!

CHAPTER I

H. WAYNE SIMMONS:
Climbing God's Ladder

By late afternoon a thunderstorm had passed through the Knoxville area and gone. The ominous gray clouds had arrived quickly, unexpectedly, delivering rain and a strong, mean wind that billowed and badgered the canvas which in turn yanked and pulled at the sturdy mooring chains. For more than half an hour the storm tormented the tent before moving on to the east, leaving behind a swamp of mushy earth and puddles that now reflected a cloudless sky. A middle-age woman ventured out, silently surveyed the damp tent, and, with the evening service little more than an hour away, began deepening a shallow ditch that bordered the canvas. In baggy slacks, a scarf tied about her head, she sang low and lively and to herself so that only scattered notes and phrases drifted beyond the glow of excitement that surrounded her. As she worked, cars began to circle the grassy area and park—one or two at first, their numbers steadily increasing and the passengers, as they headed past the woman, exchanging a "Praise the Lord!"

The tent itself reminded me of a modest Sistine Chapel, its underside embellished with red-and-blue stripes. Three sections of folding chairs, in a semicircle, faced the low-slung trailer that served as a platform. At one end of it was a spinet piano; at the other, a home organ with none of the graceful gold pipes common to more stately edifices. A simple pine lectern stood center stage.

Aside from muddy water that seeped through the sawdust, the tent's interior was neater than I had expected, perhaps because as a beginning evangelist H. Wayne Simmons conducted only two or three revivals a summer, usually within driving distance of his home in nearby Maryville, and because he himself was meticulously groomed. Throughout the two-day chore of putting up the tent, his dark hair had been precisely combed, the cuffs and collar of his Western-cut shirt as stiffly starched as they were tonight with his three-piece suit and tie. He was good-looking in the way a country-singing star is attractive, a likeness that had been particularly striking in the unfaded jeans and freshly polished boots he worked in. Of average size and build, he was friendly yet reserved, in a manner that seemed more ill at ease than aloof. Even now, seated on the platform rattling a tambourine, he was visibly nervous, his body taut.

At thirty-eight, Wayne Simmons was not unlike many young men bent on working their way to the top. He appeared eager to impress, ambitious to succeed. But for him the top was the highest rung on God's ladder, to become another Oral Roberts or R. W. Schambach, even a Pentecostal Billy Graham. Over the years he had worked at assorted jobs: barbering, painting houses, managing a dry cleaner's, clerking at a supermarket. Yet long before he felt "called," he had known these were merely stopovers on his way to the sawdust trail. Shortly after he was saved, he had worked briefly with two other evangelists and for a time conducted services under a small, dilapidated tent someone had given him. After he became disillusioned with those he viewed as hypocritical churchgoers and returned to a secular job, he still nursed a strong conviction that God wanted him to preach— a conviction he wrestled with for ten years before yielding. Then, for two years before he quit his job as sales representative for a meat-packing firm, he held weekend revivals in area churches. Now, in addition to pastoring Praise Temple Assembly of God in Maryville, he preached extended revivals, some as long as two weeks.

On this June evening in 1981, Simmons was embarking on what he referred to as the Southeastern National Camp Meeting. In the 1950s and 1960s, before audiences and many of the evangelists themselves were lured away by television, Knoxville had been a mecca for tent revivals that drew overflow crowds for weeks and months at a stretch. The town was less than two hundred miles from Cane Ridge, Kentucky, where in August 1801 a throng estimated at from twelve to twenty-five thousand gathered for the Great Revival. Pentecostalism itself had its beginnings a hundred miles away at the turn of the century. Today the nearby hills and hollows remained populated with what outsiders sometimes derisively referred to as "Holy Roller" churches, and if a tent-revival circuit existed, it was in that area where Tennessee, North Carolina, Virginia, and West Virginia converge. Knoxville itself no longer shared the enthusiasm of some of its smaller, rural neighbors. Here in the city, tents were a thing of the past, a dying bit of Americana that could not compete with television and the attractions at Gatlinburg.

But Wayne Simmons was out to change that. For years he had dreamed of staging revivals on a par with those conducted by the late A. A. Allen and William Branham, revivals that attracted page-one headlines and standing-room-only crowds. He had devoted eight months to turning that dream into reality: finding a suitable location, lining up speakers and musicians, obtaining permits, mailing circulars, drumming up publicity, raising money. In selecting Chilhowee Park Fairgrounds for the two-week revival, Simmons had gotten about as close to the heart of downtown Knoxville as he could with a tent. The park was located a scant three miles from the business district, bordering both sides of a busy thoroughfare cluttered with supermarkets, service stations, and fast-food outlets. To one side, beyond the chain-link fence, a small assortment of amusement rides stood rusting and immobile; to the other, where the tent was located, the land was open except for a miniature golf course, a stand of restrooms, and a silver fighter plane.

The tent stood alone on a large island of grass surrounded by a wide asphalt running track on which the cars parked. The rush-hour traffic had thinned, and the now-gentle murmur of passing cars became inseparable from the sound of percussions and of a piano and organ. A medley of fast, loud Pentecostal hymns lured the people and entertained them as they arrived. The gathering reminded me of a Wednesday-night prayer meeting, the crowd seemingly drawn from local churches. Some in suits and Sunday attire, others in shirtsleeves and housedresses, the people appeared to be plain, solid, laboring-class folks—men, women, and children of all ages. As they waited, they visited among themselves, excited by the music and the novelty of the tent, seemingly as eager to have a good time as they were to worship.

From the platform, the piano scampered through a few bars of another song, joined first by the organ, then by cymbals and drums, and finally the deep-thumping electric bass, with the piano and guitar alternately taking the lead like butterflies playing tag. Sometimes the beat was a lively one-two, sort of a gospel swing; other times, a slower spiritual waltz. The attitudes of neither the pianist nor the organist betrayed the calisthenics of their fingers and feet, for their torsos were erect, their expressions somber. The pianist was a fragile, angelic-looking young woman, her cheeks, lips, and eyelids painted the same delicate pastels as her floral-print dress. The organist was tall, lean, with trim hair, and a thin mustache. He wore around his neck a large silver cross, and seemed serious beyond his twenty-six years. Both he and the pianist had been reared Pentecostal, and performing at revivals was an avocation they took as seriously as their regular jobs.

Wayne Simmons encouraged the musicians with his tambourine and a sporadic, controlled *"Thank Ya, Jesus!"* In spite of the infectious liveliness of the music and his familiarity with the audience, the young evangelist remained tense, edgy, apart from his more relaxed wife and his brother Jerry, who were seated with him on the platform. The first night of a revival was always the hardest. Wayne Simmons knew that, and yet he suffered, alone. His left hand raised, his eyes squinched shut, he mumbled a private petition to God as a heavyset man stepped to the lectern, waiting for the music to stop before summoning the crowd, "Let's stand and invite the presence of the Holy Spirit into our midst!" He gestured grandly, orchestrating a clatter of wood as the people rose. But before he could begin, the congregation grew noisy, talking, moaning, offering a hundred prayers aloud, at once, over-whelming the invocation and the piano's soft ripples and trills. No heads bowed; instead, the people raised their hands and their eyes upward, oblivious to all that was around them. Only a scattered *Lord!* or *Jeeeesus!* was discernible in the cacophony. Then the voices died away, and the man offered a lone, clear *"Amen!"*

Jerry Simmons rested his electric guitar against the piano and hurried toward the pulpit. Except for a brief rebellion after high school, he had sung and played musical instruments in church since he was ten. Now, in addition to his supervisory position at the same meat-packing company where his brother once worked, Jerry played the organ at Praise Temple, managed Wayne's evangelistic association, and fre-quently led the singing at his revivals. He and Wayne Simmons bore little resemblance. At forty, Jerry had straight blond hair and was more relaxed than his ambitious younger sibling, taller, broader, a stature that fitted the supportive role he had assumed. He felt no rivalry toward his brother and willingly contributed his time, talent, even money to boost the ministry.

Tonight he and Dickie Dixon would share the responsibility of stoking the people's emotions in preparation for the sermon. In many ways the success of the revival rested on the audience as much as it did on Wayne Simmons, for it was its responsiveness that would fuel and encourage his performance. In spite of the vigorous musical overture and the fact that many were members of Praise Temple, the people were somewhat staid and unresponsive by Pentecostal standards, and Jerry Simmons leaned across the pulpit, ready to meet the challenge.

"How many love Jesus tonight?" he cried out.

A few murmured *I do,* faintly, without enthusiasm.

Undaunted, his volume rising, Jerry continued to prod. "If you love Him, let's *glo*-ri-fy Him! Hallelujah! How many of you got the *victr'y* tonight? How many *looove* Him tonight?" Scarcely waiting for the anemic response, he plunged full speed into song. "*I heard an old, old sto-ry, how my Saviour came from glory . . .*" The musicians and the congregation followed close behind. "*How he gave His life on Cal-va-ry . . .*" Like a metronome, Jerry Simmons's hand marked time, and the tent vibrated with the quickened tempo. "Hallelujah!" he shouted above the music. "If you got it, *sing* it!" Then his voice slid into the chorus. "*Ooooooh, there's vic-to-ry in my Je-sus . . .*" Over and over the words were repeated, as they had been so many times before, until the lyrics became sacred reflexes the people sang by rote. "*. . . We'll sing and dance the vic-to-ry.*"*

For almost an hour Jerry and Dickie Dixon took turns leading the singing, delivering short monologues that were at once inspirational and humorous, entertaining the people as they warmed them up for Wayne Simmons's appearance. In a style reminiscent of that developed by chorister Charles Alexander at the turn of the century, Dixon called to the organist, "Play it, Grady!" and then, like a human pogo stick,

---

sprang across the platform. He was a short, round man of thirty-two who had grown up on the revival circuit with his parents and now juggled building houses with evangelizing. His gyrations were in sharp contrast to his austere suit, and his folksy language and imagery echoed that of rural black ministers I had heard. Never still, he bounced and bent, shaking his head and tossing his hair as he sang and delivered minisermons.

"Oh, glooo-ry, I've got revival in my soul!" he shouted. "Oh, yes! I've been *down*, but when I'm down I know Jesus is with me, and when I'm up I know He's with me too, *hallelujah*, and when I roll outta bed in the morning if I got a headache, I say, Devil, I'm not gonna have your ol' headache. God made this day for *me*! and I'm gonna enjoy it! *Hallelujah!*"

A bald man on the front row whooped, "*Hallelujah!*"

And Dickie Dixon bounded on. "We're children of *God!*—Can you say hallelujah! *HalleluuuuuJAH!*" The word sailed across the audience like a yo-yo that glides out slowly, smoothly, then quickly reels back into itself. "I'm a child of *God! hallelujah*, washed in the blood, filled with heaven's Holy Ghost! I got something in my soul that puts a *click* in my heels, hallelujah, and lets me know I'm goin' *home*, can you say amen! I don't know about you, but I'm ready for *reviiiival!*" His tone soared, then softened. "Somebody said, Sing your song, so I'm gonna do it. It's entitled 'I'll Fly Away,' 'cause one glad morning when I was a kid—oh, ever since I was big enough to chew on the altar rail—and that's where I cut my teeth—I heard the saints of God sing that old song. I've seen Gran'ma standin' with tears in her eyes and sing and you'd believe she could *alllll*most see Jesus." His voice shimmied. "The song has been sung for almost twenty years that I've heard it, but that lets me know it's just that much more *reeeal*, hallelujah! I can go home tonight and lay down in bed and shut my eyes and wake 'em up again and be in a city with streets of *puuuure* gold, *halleluuuuuuJAH!* Oh, I get excited about that! I've only flown on an airplane once, and I loved it to death. I wasn't scared. Got on that thing and the landing gear wouldn't operate and ever'body was sweating and turning—Lord, what's gonna happen next? and I was just grinning from ear to ear and looking out the window enjoying the scenery." He chuckled, then grew serious and filled with awe. "That's the highest I've ever been. But oh, one day I'm gonna go past the Milky Way, *hallelujah!* They think they've got some pictures from satellites and rocket ships, but wait'll you see the picture my *eyes* take of this old world as I'm going to *Glory*, halleluuuuJAH! 'Cause I'm gonna fly away." Without pause his speech merged into song, "*oooOOOOOOovoooooooh some glad morning when this life is o'er, I'll fly away . . ."*

While Dixon strutted back and forth across the platform, Wayne Simmons nodded and tapped his toe to the beat, yet he moved with the self-consciousness of someone who knew he was being watched. Again he squinted and his lips slowed to a different tempo before he rejoined the congregation. Outside, the sunlight had faded into a soft lavender as the crowd continued singing and a black woman, accompanied only by the piano, offered a slow, gospel rendition of "Oh, How I Love Jesus."

It was completely dark by the time Wayne Simmons approached the pulpit, and the people, eager for him to begin, shifted and settled in their seats. When the tent was quiet, his voice ventured thin and uncertain. "Do you know how to touch Jesus?" he asked. When the audience failed to respond, he inhaled and proceeded cautiously. The people waited expectantly as the evangelist nervously searched for common ground, commiserating with their hurts and fears, and warning them about holy hucksters "who play on your feelings to receive an offering." His voice reached and maintained a raspy screaming level.

"Now I will bust the Devil wide open in this meeting," he said. "I *hate* commercialized religion."

Finally a soft, flat amen rose from the audience, and his brother Jerry yelled, "Preach on!"

Wayne Simmons stepped back from the lectern, heartened. "I have one purpose in mind in this meeting, and that's to touch God that I may touch your life and God may touch you," he said. "Only *God* can perform a *di*-vine miracle in your life! And I believe *Go-odd* has something for us tonight." He leaned across the pulpit. "How many believe God will touch you?"

Yes, Jesus! the congregation agreed, reserved.

"On June the thirteenth when the last amen is said under this old

---

*"I'll Fly Away." Copyright © 1932, in *Wonderful Message*, Hartford Music Co., owner. Copyright © 1960, by Albert E. Brumley & Sons, renewal. All rights reserved. Used by permission.

tent," Simmons declared, "I'm going to walk away a different man. Amen?"

Only a few amens rose from the crowd.

Simmons challenged, "How many's going to walk away a different person?"

Again the response was weak.

"I'm going to ask again," he said forcefully, "How many of you believe God enough that He will touch you where no man can touch you?"

The crowd applauded lightly and murmured a unison of faint amens. Otherwise the tent was bedtime still. The children, having passed beyond restlessness, napped or leaned against their parents. Outside, streetlights defined the thoroughfare, and a yellow neon flashed on and off at a nearby business. An occasional car circled slowly, then disappeared into the night.

Wayne Simmons looked out over the audience, his knuckles white from gripping the lectern. His eyes narrowed. "We'll have some old-fashioned Holy Ghost, Devil-chasing, God-healing revival, because America *needs* old-fashioned, down-to-earth, Pentecostal, heaven-touching revivals to call sin by name and tell people there is still a God that can touch people's hearts and mend their broken lives!"

"*Come on!*" his brother Jerry prompted.

"*Praise the name of the Lord!*" Wayne Simmons thundered. He flipped open a black Bible, and the sound of turning pages rustled through the tent. "There are two settings in the fifth chapter of Mark," he said, proceeding to read aloud: "And then Jesus immediately knowing in Himself that virtue had gone out of Him turned Him about in the press and said, *Who* touched my clothes?" His speech gathered momentum as he read the familiar passage, scarcely hesitating between the last verse, a brief prayer, and his sermon. For almost an hour he alternately paraphrased the scriptural account of Jesus and Jairus and cited modern-day parallels, tying together the past and the present with the refrain "Who touched me?" As he preached, he paced back and forth, one hand grasping a microphone, the other pointing to heaven or hell or dabbing his forehead with a folded handkerchief. His face reddened, yet his delivery seemed more dramatic than his message, the words and phrases emphasized beyond their importance. There was none of the self-assurance he had exhibited while putting up the tent, and he was visibly and verbally nervous. The audience responded with polite applause, timid amens, but for the greater part of the sermon Simmons seemed to be preaching to himself, and he struggled to draw the people into the service. Finally, with jacket removed, necktie loosened, he attacked the stalemate head-on, likening today's congregations to the crowds that thronged Jesus. "Ever'body likes to get close to the preacher, especially on Sunday morning, and they can look so sanctimonious," he said accusingly before returning to the biblical account. "And you know there were a lot of people this particular day who were just along for the noise. They were just there because the crowd was there."

"Come on!" Jerry Simmons called out, and several members of the audience chimed in, *That's right!*

Detecting a spark of enthusiasm, Wayne Simmons grinned. "You know, it's foolish to go to church because the crowd goes to church!" he shouted with new confidence.

That's right!

"It's foolish to go to church because they have good singing!"

That's right!

"It's foolish to go to church because—wellll, my neighbor's going to church." Simmons's voice grew stern. "You need to go to church because *you* want to worship God in spirit and in truth!"

The audience came alive with applause, and Jerry Simmons cried, *"Yes!"*

Now Wayne Simmons and the audience fed one another, his performance and their responsiveness growing in intensity, in volume. The sermon was no longer a monologue but rather an exchange between him and the people.

"God will touch *any*one!" he shouted. "He will heal the cancer! He will open the blind eye!"

A barrage of *AMEN*s interrupted Simmons, and he drew tall, his words somersaulting through the air. "God will touch the home where people need to be touched in their personal lives. You see, it's not the problem that we talk about so much. It's not that particular place where the severe pain is. It's the problem we don't talk about."

Yes!

"It's the nights we cry behind closed doors when no one is looking!"

Yes!

"It's when you become open and honest and sincere with God and say, O, God, I hurt! I feel! I am in des-per-a-tion!" His voice softened. "Your deepest hurt is after midnight when it's all silent. Amen?"

Thank You, Jesus!

"Aren't you glad Jesus touches, heals, and delivers?" Simmons asked cheerfully. "Praise God, He was a deliverance preacher." Again he smiled. "I love that terminology: Jesus Christ, a deliverance preacher. Amen?"

Praise the Lord!

"Oh, I thank God that His blood reaches to the highest mountain, and it'll go down to the gutter!" he cried, his pitch once again escalating to a screaming level. "I serve a God that gave His only begotten Son that loves the prostitute! the harlot! and He'll turn her life around and He'll call her 'Daughter'!"

A wave of praise swept across the tent as Simmons pounded home his message of God's love for the lowly on up to the wealthy and powerful. "You see, Jesus has compassion for the people that are in the business world, can you say amen! God loves the president of the company you work for. So many old fogies they say, Well, it's a sin to have money. You can't live right and have money," he whined. "Honey, you give me a million dollars," he boomed, "and I'll *show* you whether I can live right and have money!"

Simmons looked out over the tittering audience. When he resumed, his voice was calm. "It may seem that ever'body else is getting the blessing of God, but, neighbor, I want you to know God still has your name printed in His mind, and *God* has never forgotten *you*. In your darkest moment He says, Only believe!" He stepped back from the lectern, glowing. "What a God!" he sighed. "What words of power and authority! When the Devil tells you that you are defeated, that you must *diiiiie*, God says, I—still—heal! I still have an arm that's outstretched down to humanity that will pick him up and set him on a plane with Jesus Christ." Simmons paused. "Have you ever come to the end of the road? Which one of you is going to touch Jesus tonight? Some of you will walk away empty-handed because your mind is not made up to touch Jesus. You see, my mother's here. My wife's here. My brother, the musicians, but I must press my way through and touch *Him*."

The piano began playing quietly as Simmons continued. "God can reach to the highest and reach down and get the lowest at the same instant and bring them together, hallelujah. Come on," he urged, "slip your hands up. Let's believe God for a miracle right now."

Softly, her lyrics almost inaudible, the soloist sang, *He touched me! Oh, He touched meeeeee*, as Wayne Simmons prayed aloud. "Jesus, these people standing before me tonight, Lord, need a miracle." *Oh, He touched me!* "Lord, some have come to the end of the line, but, Jesus, I know You're going to touch them tonight." *But oh what joy that filled my soooooooul . . .* "I come against doubt, fear, and disbelief in Your life, in the name of Jesus Christ, may God touch you." *. . . and ma-ade me whooooole.*

A short man with receding hair stepped forward onto a rectangle of green felt that covered the area between the platform and the chairs. Then a plump woman in red hurried down the aisle, followed by another member of the audience and still another until the mat was crowded. Simmons called for the ministers and counselors, and a dozen men and women came forward and paired off with the people who had responded to the altar call. An elderly man approached a woman holding an infant, whispered something to the mother, and then placed his hand firmly on the child's head. Next to him, as another minister began to pray for her, the woman in red fell backward onto the sawdust and lay motionless except for her quivering lips. All around, the counselors laid hands, with sometimes two and three reaching out to the same person until there was a tangle of arms and people and touching. *. . . and ma-ade me whole.**

Wayne Simmons was alone when I arrived the second evening an hour before the service. In dark trousers and white dress shirt, he hummed along with a vocal recording of "T'is So Sweet to Trust in Jesus" as he busied about the tent, tugging on chains, realigning chairs. "This is what we call 'seating evangelistically,' " he explained, spacing the chairs five or six inches apart. "The first night we never put 'em this close. In other words—" He placed a chair a foot away from the rest. "Like so."

"Why?" I asked.

"Fills the tent up!" he chuckled mischievously. "It's like icing on a cake. If you don't have much, you spread it out thin and it'll cover the cake. Then as the crowd grows, why, you just keep scooting the chairs closer together and adding more." One hundred fifty people had attended the night before, he estimated. Not all were members of Praise Temple. Many were folks he had never seen. The tent could hold more than eight hundred chairs, and he talked excitedly about the prospects of carloads arriving from Texas and Indiana by week's end.

Sun streamed through the entrance, where the flaps had been raised. The tent, dried by several hours' sun, billowed, its top gently rising and settling with the late-afternoon breeze. Simmons studied the gentle rise and fall of the canvas. "Tents have a personality of their own," he said. "It's been wet and drawed up real tight, and now it's dried and relaxed."

"Like you?" I joked, observing that he too seemed more at ease, relieved that opening night was behind him.

He laughed good-naturedly, then went on, a tinge of pride in his voice. "You have to watch 'em for signs of something going wrong. Like I found a lot of ropes loose around here on the side today, where they just worked loose."

"From the wind?"

"Right."

High winds had destroyed the tent of another evangelist several months earlier, the second he had lost in two years. For Simmons, the thunderstorms that had been whipping through the area each day threatened a similar fate. He had bought the tent a year ago for $15,000, which he continued to pay off in monthly installments. Even if the canvas were to be ripped to shreds, he would remain liable for the debt. There was no such protection as tent insurance. Nevertheless, Simmons was philosophical. "You don't stop because a tent blows down," he said. "You just salvage what you can and go on."

At sixty-by-ninety feet, Simmons's tent was certainly not the most impressive in the evangelistic field in terms of size. Yet he regarded it with a pride only another tent revivalist could understand. In 1951 the late A. A. Allen poetically referred to his first tent as "an eagle with outstretched wings against the good, clean, cotton-white clouds." Twenty years later Allen confessed, "None of the tents I've had since, even the gigantic one I have now that is so large no stretch of canvas in the world can compare with it in size and seating capacity, has meant as much to me as that first tent." He had, he later wrote in his autobiography, "longed for it as I had longed for new shoes when I was a youngster." Allen's feelings were not unique. During the 1950s and 1960s, the heydays of the healing and charismatic revivals, evangelists frequently vied with one another to own the largest tent. Shortly after Oral Roberts paid $65,000 for one that could seat 7,500, rival Jack Coe ordered a slightly larger tent and then, in the evangelistic monthly *The Voice of Healing*, published this notice:

A letter from the Smith Manufacturing Co., Dalton, Ga., declares that according to his measurements the Coe tent is by a slight margin the largest Gospel tent in the world. Since Oral Roberts [also] has a prayer tent 90' by 130' Brother Roberts has the largest amount of tent equipment. Both the Coe and Roberts tents are larger than the Ringling Brothers big top.

On another occasion, Coe wrote in his own publication, *Herald of Healing*:

I bought my present tent to accommodate the crowds attending my meetings . . . When evangelists make statements about the size of their tents, they could dispel much of the controversy by giving the actual length and width. Then people would not feel that someone was telling a lie or exaggerating. I'm not saying this to belittle or condemn some other evangelist, but many have claimed that we are exaggerating when others beside myself state that they have the world's largest tent. If they do . . . I praise God for it! If they will write me, telling me the size of their tent . . . I will print this information in my magazine, admitting that mine is only the second or third largest.

It was one of Coe's earlier tents that A. A. Allen first bought. In 1960 he too joined the race to have the biggest and best, boasting that his latest acquisition was both the world's largest tent and the only one made of vinyl. Several years later, after still bigger acquisitions, Allen announced in his *Miracle Magazine* that God had instructed him to cut one of his discarded tents into strips and offer them—for a price

—to the "partners" in his ministry. He quoted God as telling him: "Don't you know that this tent is saturated and impregnated with My Power? I want you to cut these strips of canvas into little prayer rugs and send them to your friends who are partners in this ministry." For a pledge of one hundred dollars, a "Power Packed Prayer Rug" would be sent by return mail; smaller, wallet-size pieces—called "Prosperity Blessing Cloths"—were also available for smaller contributions.

Wayne Simmons's tent had belonged to Ralph Duncan before his election to the Tennessee State Legislature in 1978. It came with a bobtailed truck and 150 folding chairs. Although in its seventh season, the canvas was neither faded nor worn, and its lifespan would be determined, Simmons explained, by the care it received and whether it was erected in an industrial area where pollution would eat at the cloth. As he continued his last-minute inspection, he jerked at a yellow guy line. "The tent doesn't have a rope in it," he boasted. "It's all made out of aircraft cable and chains." Again he checked the tension. "Most of the old tent system was ropes, and they would draw up when they got wet and you would have to reground the stakes."

Finding the right tent had been a long, costly ordeal, one that had taught Simmons, the hard way, to follow God's advice. The summer before, when he scheduled his opening revival, he had planned to use a tent that belonged to Dickie Dixon's father, who now was a missionary in Mexico. After buying quarter poles and announcing the meeting in nearby LaFollette, Simmons and Dickie Dixon learned that the tent had already been sold by the co-owner to someone else. Then, in a long-distance telephone conversation, Simmons arranged to buy another tent he had seen a few months earlier, only to discover when he drove to Georgia to pick it up that the seller had removed the flaps and replaced the side poles with two-by-fours. "The whole deal was sour," Simmons complained now. "Nothing was right about it." He shook his head. "But if I had listened to God—see, I wanted a vinyl tent. I had prayed and prayed about the thing, and God had showed me a canvas tent—the *exact* tent I've got now—in a vision. If I had just listened to the Spirit, I wouldn't have lost the money I spent for Brother Dixon and me to go to Georgia, because this tent is what God wanted me to have. It's a beautiful tent. One of the most beautiful tents you'll ever see, and I saw it just as clear as day in prayer."

"How did you feel when you closed the deal in Decaturville and knew you had your own tent?" I asked.

Wayne Simmons laughed. "I knew I owed a lot of money!"

"Were you excited?" I pressed. "Did you feel sort of like a boy with his first car?"

"Yes," he said thoughtfully. "Or I felt after it was over, I guess I felt more of a humbleness before God, that I was seeing the will of God come to pass. I felt very honored that He would place me in the realm of all this equipment when some preachers struggle for years and seemingly they can never get anything going for them. Their church is not a success, as we would term it, numerically and financially, and I don't believe that's God's will. I believe God's will is for a pastor or an evangelist to succeed."

"Had you always wanted a tent, or was this something you felt only recently?" I asked.

"I felt it for years," he answered.

"You couldn't afford one?"

"It wasn't God's time," he insisted. "After you fall off the cliff enough you pretty soon learn not to get up there and slip off again. You learn to really seek the will of God. I know I'll miss God tomorrow, and I'm sure I *will* miss God somewhere along the line, but I've learned some wisdom, and that is to have some patience and wait on Him."

Although people had begun to arrive for the service, Simmons continued his rounds, checking the stakes, dusting off the organ. Just inside the entrance he hurriedly looked over the bookstand, straightening its selection of key rings, Bibles, and recordings by the Simmons Evangelistic Team and by Jimmy Swaggart, a television revivalist from Baton Rouge and a first cousin of country-rock singers Jerry Lee Lewis and Mickey Gilley. "We try to keep things nice and clean," Simmons said as he rearranged the taped sermons. "You notice all the poles are painted, which they *weren't* when I bought the tent. But this just adds to it. It makes it neat. And we try to keep our equipment nice because I like to look like I know where I'm going whether I know or not." He chuckled, then grew serious. "We're saying as Christians we are better than the world. Therefore I should keep my tent as first class as I can. God's not shoddy and we shouldn't be shoddy either. Heaven's not going to be a shoddy place."

It was almost starting time, but Simmons was wound up. "Here's a lady that's living her life as a prostitute. Here's somebody in the business world—they're used to money. They're used to things first class even though they have a drinking problem. And you're standing up there telling them Jesus is the answer, and you have a tent that looks like it's about to fall apart and everything's in disarray and your truck's beat and battered and paint's peeling off of it. Well, they say, if Christ does you that way I don't want it. A lot of people fall out with an evangelist staying in a good motel, having a decent car. But that's *all* an evangelist has is a place to sleep and a car, and he should have something nice!"

During the past three days at least two dozen people had turned out to help with the revival: digging holes for the center poles, mowing the grass, vacuuming the platform, bringing sandwiches for those too busy to break for lunch. Nevertheless, Wayne Simmons looked at the accumulating crowd and shook his head. "The evangelistic crowd, they have no idea what it takes to put a crusade in motion," he complained. "They think all there is to it is playing an organ, setting a piano up there, and," he said mockingly, "we're here to hear some good music, have a good time. They don't know that it costs hundreds and thousands of dollars."

"How much *does* a meeting like this cost?" I asked.

"About six thousand dollars."

"That's including rent, insurance, salaries, and the mailings?"

"Right. If we get anything above that we can pay some on the equipment, the tires and truck and gasoline and all that." While Simmons said he drew his salary from Praise Temple, not from the evangelistic association, proceeds from the revival offerings would be used to pay Dickie Dixon, the musicians (including Simmons's son Rodney, the drummer), and his sixteen-year-old daughter Tywanna who ran the bookstand.

Simmons had left a good-paying job to become an evangelist, he emphasized. With his knowledge of the business world, he was confident he could be financially comfortable, if not wealthy. And he would have a lot fewer headaches. As a beginning revivalist, he often felt he was shouldering the responsibilities of the world. But he was finally beginning to see some change. Later in the summer he would be conducting a revival in Cookeville, midway between Knoxville and

Nashville. Already the local pastors were sharing the workload, and the local newspaper had promised advance coverage. "*Here* I've had to do all the push myself," he said. "I've had to *buy* all my time. I've had to *buy* newspaper ads. I've had to spend my own money to do mail-outs. In the last year and a half the newspaper and the radio and just different news media have begun to pick up, and that helps. People may not agree with that, but how would they have known to assemble around Christ without His disciples? Do you know what they were?"

"You mean their occupations?"

"I mean *after*, not before they started following Christ," he clarified. "Some people said, Well, they went along with Christ to lay hands on 'em and to cast out devils and to see the people come to Jesus. Maybe so. I do agree they had a ministry. But you know what they were?" Simmons answered for me. "He had a P.R. man. He had a sound man. He had an advertising manager. Did He not? They went into a city before He got there and noised it abroad and even got the Upper Room set up for Him to come. That was His evangelistic team. A lot of people don't see that. They say, Well, if God wants me to be anything He'll promote me. That's a bunch of junk. They'll *never* get anywhere."

All week long Wayne Simmons fretted about the weather, in private conversation and during the services. The every-afternoon thunderstorms had turned the grounds to mud and confined the crowd to only the very faithful. A stable hundred, some evenings a few more. After a particularly vindictive wind whipped through the area, almost yanking the tent from its moorings, Simmons accused the Devil of trying to destroy the revival and God's work. "The thing had already begun to lift off the ground," he told the audience that night, "and when you get one lifting off the ground, honey, you just wave 'bye, 'cause it's done gone." With an air of excitement, he related how God had miraculously spoken to a man traveling on the freeway, telling him to go to the aid of Jerry Simmons who was struggling single-handedly to save the tent. "It'd already started lifting off on this end," Wayne Simmons said, pointing to his right. "Now, don't anyone be afraid," he reassured the people who had come in spite of the continuing rain. "It's secure. This thing doesn't have rope in it. It has aircraft cable, and one—just *one*—strand of this cable could lift your car and two or three more." At another service he urged members of the congregation to stand on the wettest spots under the tent as he prayed to God, "Let it be beautiful. Let it be pretty. Stay the rain just for a few hours and a few days." In the midst of his petition, pleas—some in English, some in unknown tongues—boiled up from the crowd and blended and brewed into what sounded like a verbal magic potion, with one dominant voice punctuating, "*Let it dry, Lord, let it dry.*" But to no avail.

By Monday of the second week, planks straddled the puddles to form walkways from the parking areas to the tent. Inside, the sawdust was incapable of absorbing all the water, and pools surfaced among the chairs. When I arrived shortly before noon, Wayne Simmons and Joe Miles were attempting to move the bobtailed truck from the rear of the tent where it had been bogged down since the revival's start. The truck's motor struggled and strained, its big tires spinning helplessly, slinging a spray of mud. Simmons leaned out the driver's window and looked first at the whirling wheels, then at Miles. He let up on the gas while Joe Miles dumped a shovelful of sawdust onto the muddy tracks. Again Simmons gunned the motor, and the tires slipped and spun, deepening the ruts.

Joe Miles shook his head knowingly. A minister since 1939, he pastored Scott Street Assembly of God in Knoxville, but he too had been a tent revivalist when he was younger, heartier. He was small, almost a miniature of a man, in his sixties, with curly, graying hair. In spite of the heat and the task at hand, he wore a white dress shirt and a tie, for he had interrupted his weekly visits to the hospitalized members of his congregation. Most nights he was seated in the audience, and many days he showed up at the tent to help. He did so both out of friendship and commiseration. Carefully he spread shavings in front of the rear tires. "Okay," he signaled Simmons, "now don't let up." The elder preacher stepped back, rested his forearm on the shovel's handle, and concentrated on the wheels. Simmons revved the engine, then floored the gas pedal. The tires spun in their tracks, slipping each time they seemed on the verge of freeing themselves. Simmons refused to let up on the gas. He tensed his muscles, as if by doing so he could liberate the tires. Suddenly the truck lunged forward, but even then he would not stop and went speeding, looping, loping across the grass. As a teenager he had been fascinated by fast cars and motorcycles. Up until his ministry began to consume his leisure time, he had worked on his own automobile: changing the oil, tuning the motor, tinkering. "The Indianapolis 500 used to thrill my heart as a boy," he had confessed during one of our interviews. "I always liked the old Offenhauser race cars." He still yearned to own a Dusenberg, and he remembered every feature of his first cars as vividly as he knew his children's freckles and moles.

Joe Miles watched the truck romp around the grounds and grinned. "It takes a strong spirit to hold a tent meeting," he said. "A *strong* man."

Under the tent, a man with a thatch of white hair was seated at the piano studying the keyboard. Jane Felker stood behind him, hands on her hips, grimacing. "Somebody played too hard and broke a key," she complained. The broken note came as little surprise to me. Each night one gospel group or another had performed loud, rambunctious music, usually accompanied by a pianist who fiercely pounded the ivories. Yet Jane Felker worried as if she personally were responsible. "It's not ours," she said. "Rose Music Company *just* loaned it to us." But the repairman himself seemed unconcerned as he mended the injured key, then prepared to leave, admonishing her not to let anyone play the piano until that evening's service, until the glue dried. As he drove away, she cupped her hand over her eyes to shield them against the noonday glare. The sky was a blinding blue, not yet cluttered with the clouds that would without fail deliver that afternoon's rain. The bobtailed truck pulled onto the blacktop and stopped, and Wayne Simmons hopped out, wiping sweat from his forehead with his bare hand. He strode across the boards into the tent's shade and surveyed the platform, the bookstand, the semi-circle of folding chairs, taking note of a bit of mud caked on the loud-speakers, a chair out of place. Jane Felker stood at his side, watching, listening, as he reminded her to rake the sawdust and to line up the chairs vertically as well as horizontally. He would have his brother Jerry stop by later with furniture polish.

A sense of importance swelled within Sister Felker, tickling her lips, brightening her eyes. All that morning and for the rest of the afternoon, the tent would be *her* responsibility. She was, I estimated, in her late forties, although she seemed worn beyond those years from rearing eight children and keeping up with her husband, a cobbler by trade, who had his own "storefront" ministry. Everything about her seemed tired, haggard. Her baggy slacks and her cotton shirt hinted of many washings and dryings, and her hair, pulled into a careless ponytail, was thin and straggly. Yet there was an inner richness, a spirit that danced in her eyes and in her voice.

When the two of us were alone, she bubbled with childlike exuberance. "I'm so thrilled to be able to stay with the tent," she said. "There hasn't been anything that I could do for the Lord for a long time." She looked around her, exhilarated by the mere sight of the tent and its furnishings. After Wayne Simmons was unable to recruit volunteers to stay with the tent, he had offered to pay the Felkers to spend the nights there and guard the equipment. Jane stayed on most days without remuneration, although the prospect of earning extra money while doing a good turn clearly excited her. She and her husband planned to drive to Missouri for a ministerial conference. The additional income would help buy gas.

Bill Felker was a tall man, with thinning hair, a full, bushy mustache, and dark-rimmed glasses. He was immensely outgoing, singing lustily during the services and always stepping forward as soon as Reverend Simmons summoned ministers for the altar call. As the days passed, he and his wife had become part of what I considered "the regulars." This small nucleus of individuals could be counted on to do whatever was needed to keep the revival going and dutifully appeared each night in the same seats, as if they had season tickets.

Besides running a shoe shop, Bill Felker bought time on a local radio station for his own weekly religious broadcast. Although I had heard him referred to as "Reverend Felker," I was uncertain as to the exact nature of his clerical role because many members of the audience introduced themselves as lay preachers or evangelists. Now when I asked, Jane Felker proudly explained, "He ministers wherever the door is open. That's his call, to evangelize. Wednesday nights we go down to Wayne's and Sundays we go to Scott Yancey's."

"Does he go to help like he has here, or does he preach?" I asked.

She shook her head. "As far as preaching, lately he hasn't, but his shoe shop's his pulpit. He preaches in there all day long. He's reaching people in there, and it's getting the Word out." She leaned forward confidingly. "There's more to the Gospel than just getting behind the pulpit," she said firmly. "You've gotta live it."

As we talked, I squirmed in my folding chair, the flat wooden variety without a curved seat. Sitting in one throughout the three-to-four-hour services was a test of endurance, and I saw nothing more comfortable than the piano bench and a lone lawn-type lounge to sit on, let alone spend the night.

"Where do y'all sleep?" I puzzled.

"We took the pillows off the couch, and C.B.'s been sleeping up there on the platform," she said. "Bill sleeps in the van, and I've got a lounge. That lounge over there you take to the beach?" She pointed to the lawn chair. "I don't lay down," she whispered secretively. "I just set there and keep my eyes open to see what's going on."

"Do you lower the flaps at night?"

"Halfway, because you want light," she said knowledgeably. "You want people to be able to see there's somebody in here. That it's not easy pickings." The day the tent was going up Wayne Simmons had told me about the twenty-four-hour security. I understood why after the musical instruments and the sound system arrived, and after hearing Dickie Dixon recall the time he and his parents returned to find their tent cut to shreds by vandals.

When I asked how Jane Felker passed her days, she glanced around the deserted tent. "I was just looking this morning to see what I had to do," she said, still taking stock. "I've been wanting just to get alone with God. Just me and God, my Bible and prayer, and yesterday I was rebuking myself. I said, You turkey, you're reading but you're not praying," she scolded herself. "I've been here *all* week and I hadn't been praying. So yesterday I was sitting in the back corner over there, and I just got to reading, got to thinking about it—the Word, you know—and I just started crying and praising the Lord, speaking in tongues." Her voice filled with wonder. "And I was speaking a different language than I usually speak."

"In tongues?" I asked, referring to the unintelligible "language" so often uttered by Pentecostals during moments of religious ecstacy.

She nodded. "They say God gives you *your* prayer language, and I've never really been satisfied with how I sound when I'm speaking in tongues because I sound to me like gibberish," she said. "When you're speaking a language, you stop and you pause and there's inflection and your words don't all roll together. I figured maybe it's because I'm not as educated as I should be. But education has nothing to do with speaking in tongues."

At the services, I had heard various people—including Wayne Simmons—speak in what the apostle Paul referred to as "the tongues of men and of angels." Although regarded by Pentecostals as the first indication, or "evidence," that someone has received the baptism of the Holy Ghost, I had been told that speaking in tongues was not a one-time occurrence. The Spirit-filled individual continued to be a channel for glossolalia in prayer and in praise. While the wordlike sounds seemed meaningless, there was a cadence that reminded me of a Romance language. On more than one occasion I had wondered if the speaker knew what he or she was saying. When I asked Jane Felker if the utterances could be repeated at will, without the person being in the Spirit, she answered no. "You don't know what you're saying," she explained, "because it's as the Spirit gives utterance. We don't control it. We don't know the language."

"So how can you pause if the Spirit doesn't lead you to pause?" I proposed.

Jane Felker stopped, baffled. "I don't know," she laughed. "That's a good question."

"But you say you do sound different at times?"

"Yes. There's a boy, a friend of ours, and it makes you wonder, because for the most part he just says, Sha-ma-ma-ma-ma. Like that. Then another time he'll—I don't know what it is, but I got to talking like him one night, and I said, Well, Lord, I guess Randy is real. Because I got to talking like he was talking and I *couldn't* stop! I'd wanta change it and uh-uh, it came back the way Randy talked. It sounded like an Indian dialect."

In the early years of their marriage, she and Bill Felker had been active Presbyterians, with her husband serving as a church elder. Then in 1967, shortly after he was healed at one of R. W. Schambach's revivals, they began attending a Pentecostal church. "My husband had the baptism a long time before I did," she said with admiration. "I didn't know what it was and when you don't know what something is, you don't know if you want it or not. When he received the baptism he spoke in tongues for four hours. He spoke *continuously*, never slowed up, and finally about four o'clock in the morning he said, Gimme a cup of coffee. Then I never heard another word in English until about five. He talked all night long. All night. That was in July, and then I received it in November. I was carrying a baby and my husband, he used to tease me. He'd say, You don't want to get this Holy Ghost while you got that baby inside a you." She laughed in retrospect. "So the baby was born in August and I received the baptism in November. But it's made a difference in our lives."

"Do you remember how you felt?"

She sighed. "The baptism of the Holy Ghost, it's another step up the ladder. If you'll remember when you received salvation, oh what a joy it was in your life! That burden was lifted because you'd given it all to Jesus. Okay, when you get the baptism of the Holy Ghost, it's the same thing, except it's another step up the ladder because the baptism of the Holy Ghost is to the believer what salvation is to the sinner. A whole new world is opened up to you."

"What about when you fall out or are slain in the Spirit—how do you feel when that happens?" I asked, remembering the individuals I had seen appear to pass out during the altar call, falling backward without any attempt to break their fall and without apparent ill effects. Some merely lay there; others, their lips quivering, seemed to be praying. Jane Felker's face brightened with awe as I posed the question. "It's just like going down on a feather bed," she said. "It's beautiful. You don't get hurt. In the natural if you'd fall from straight up to back like that, you'd have a headache, a knot on your head and everything else. But I've fallen flat backward, just straight down on a concrete floor, and *nothing!*"

"It doesn't hurt?"

"No!"

"What sensation do you feel?" I asked. "Are you aware of other people around you, or are you totally alone?"

"There's two differences," she explained authoritatively. "You can be *down* under the power, and you can be *out* under the power. I have never had the blessing of being out. Out, you hear nothing whatsoever around you. When you're down, you are aware of it, that you're going down and you feel it. It's just like—" She grappled for the right words. "You can feel the power of God just closing in around you and dooooown you go." One leg of her folding chair began to sink into the soft, wet earth, and she laughed at the coincidence. "That was pretty appropriate."

"And then when you're lying down there—" I started.

"God deals differently with different people. There may be something you need in your life that He'll deal with you about at that time."

"He'll be talking to you about it?"

"Or you may be talking to Him," she said. "Sometimes He speaks to you when you're down, sometimes He doesn't. Sometimes you have visions when you're down, sometimes you don't. It's just like anything else in life—we're all different. And God works with us as all different individuals. But it's beautiful."

"Is it relaxing?"

"Oh, definitely. You know in Acts it says, These people are not drunk as you would suppose. Sometimes when you get up, you can't stand up. You're liiiimp." Her voice wobbled, to illustrate.

Some people I later spoke to doubted the experience was always genuine. One veteran Pentecostal evangelist observed: "I think people get pent up and they get pressed down and go this way for years and really what happens is they come to the place where they totally unload, and when they do there has to be an in-rush of exuberance. They just turn aloose everything." But now when I asked Jane Felker, she sighed. "It is a beautiful feeling. Really, going down under the power will do you more good than a good night's sleep."

Vivian Simmons's late-model compact sped through the rolling countryside, winding past wild roses, an occasional house, and fields of young corn. Like her husband, she had been raised in the Maryville area, and she drove fast and with familiarity, scarcely slowing as she turned from one road onto another. She was short and bouncy with a turned-up nose and tightly curled brown hair. Her parents had called her "Go," a nickname that was as appropriate at age thirty-four as it was in childhood. As a youngster, the "going" had been to the Baptist church, to Sunday services and Wednesday-evening prayer meetings and, afterward, to the Humdinger Drive-in. Now it was to keep up with two teenage children and to travel to those places in and near Tennessee where her husband held revivals. She had met me on Alcoa Highway to lead the way through the maze of roads that ended at the small subdivision of split-level houses where she and Wayne Simmons lived. The two had met when she was fourteen and he was seventeen, and married a year later. Except for brief periods in Atlanta and Fort Worth, they had remained in and among these hills. Her father had worked in a quarry; Wayne's, at the Aluminum Company of America and as an independent Pentecostal minister, pastoring on weekends. Although both families were rigid fundamentalists in their discipline, the Simmonses were especially strict, forbidding their two sons to attend movies and county fairs or even to participate in sports. When

Wayne Simmons was twelve he rebelled, continuing to attend church but doing what he now characterized as "the whole catalog—except drink." By the time he was seventeen he had held a gun on several people and had thrown a poker at his brother Jerry, piercing his cheek.

"I had just gone crazy in my mind," he speculated as the three of us sat in their living room. "If God hadn't saved me, I would have either been in the pen or killed someone. One time my Dad had bought a muffler and the thing went bad and he was going to take it back. And I said, Well, I'll go with you. I was fifteen, I guess. So I stuck my thirty-two automatic under my belt with a full load, and my thought was this: If that guy gives him any static, I'm gonna blow him to hell. I mean, that was my mind. I'm just going to blow him to hell." He laughed, a short, dry, uneasy laugh. "Just hardcore."

"How long did this period of your life last?" I asked.

His forehead creased. "From twelve to seventeen," he estimated, "but it had been building up for years. It just seemed like there was something dark always following the Simmons family, that there was always a curse. Someone missing or something. I remember hearing them tell about someone in the family—a cousin or whatever—throwing a baby to the hogs. And my grandfather fell ten stories on the elevator and every bone in his body broke. My stepgrandfather evidently was murdered. Never did show up. And my uncle was murdered. Picked up a fifteen-year-old boy and a twenty-five-year-old man and they murdered him. Just seemed like the family was gripped by the Devil."

The tales of a misspent youth seemed incongruous coming from the soft-spoken man who sat across from me now. This Wayne Simmons punctuated his conversations with "Praise the Lord!" and addressed his family with tenderness in his facial expression and his voice. Although he was dressed casually in slacks and a white bush shirt, he differed little from the always-serious man I had watched perform under the tent.

"My parents, they tried to teach me right," he hastened to add, "and it's had an influence—what they taught me—on my life. I had a praying mother, a praying dad, and a lot of times I would slip in late at night and hear Mother praying, but nobody could reach me and really lead me to Christ. I remember I wanted help so bad—" He agonized even now. "I wanted help, but I didn't want help. I didn't know how to *find* help. I knew of no one I could really turn to. I

couldn't talk to anybody." He sipped some iced tea. "By this time I
was into motorcycles, and a certain evangelist I had been listening to
on radio by the name of A. A. Allen—he always touched my heart. I
would turn him on and just weep, and I had planned, when he came
to Atlanta—it was the nearest point—I had planned to ride that motorcycle there and find help *some* way."

"Did you go?"

He glanced toward his wife. "No, I met one of her friends who
invited me to Victory Baptist Church, and then I met *her* a few services
later. It was a *di*vine act of God that brought me to that church."

A grandfather clock's rhythmic, hypnotic tocks punctuated Wayne
Simmons's re-creation of that snowy night in February 1961 when he
was "born again." "When they started to give the altar call I said I'm not
staying for this *thing*, and I went outside. I couldn't leave because I had
brought a couple of friends and they wouldn't come out. The preacher
was talking to this one boy, and I said to myself, They're gonna get him
in there and get him religion and then we can't go to the dance. We'd
always go to church and then to a dance. You know, kinda mix it up a
little bit. You gotta keep on the good side of both of them, the Lord *and*
the Devil, at that time, isn't that right?" He chuckled uneasily. "It went
on and on and it became so cold that I thought, I'll go back and see
what's going on. So I went in and sat down on the back pew, and Ted
Raby came back, and all he had to say to me was, Don't you want to give
your heart to the Lord? That's all it took. The Lord changed me that
night just from one person to another."

Simmons' was seventeen and a senior in high school at the time.
After graduation, he enrolled in barber's college, and nine months later
married. He cut hair and stocked supermarket shelves until he and
Vivian moved to Atlanta. There they attended a Pentecostal church
and his "apprenticeship" into the ministry began. "A friend of our
pastor was going to have a tent meeting in Carrollton, Georgia, and
he asked us to help," he recalled. "We didn't know *what* God wanted
us to do. We just knew that God wanted us to work for Him in some
way. I felt the call of the ministry, but yet I had never announced it."

Had Vivian Simmons been aware of his feelings? Wayne Simmons
answered for her. "At this point she didn't know *anything*. *No* one
really knew how I felt. But one night during this meeting, after it had
been going on some days, a good friend of mine was sitting near the

rear of the tent and she began to write. She said God was giving her something. After the service she came and said, God told me to write this down and give it to you. And it said, Wayne is my boy—Tell him to be very patient and wait on me, that I am going to use him in due time, but to be patient." Amazement filled Simmons's voice even now. "And you know when He said to be patient, that could mean six months or, like Moses, be forty years—"

His wife cut in, "Don't you still have that paper?"

"I have it somewhere," he acknowledged, then continued the story. "We had a good meeting there, and Charles Sanford, the evangelist, asked me to go with him on the road and be the music director, or song leader. Boy, I was all excited. I said, Man, *yes* I'll go. I wanta do something for the Lord." Simmons exuberantly recalled the incident. "I had just been saved and, boy, I was ready to run the race! So we headed out to Savannah, Georgia. We got the tent up, got started, and I might say it was a disastrous time. Here were two kids trying to save the world! I was nineteen at the time and he was eighteen. I didn't know where I was going, and he didn't either. I hadn't even read the Bible through," he confessed. "Of course, I was *just* leading the singing at the time, but I did feel this call on my life. The crowds were low. Finances were low. There was about six of us—including the man staying with the tent— and we got down, *all* we had was one can of salmon between us. That was *all* we had to eat. This was just the hard times."

"But we were really enjoying it!" Vivian said brightly.

And Simmons agreed. "We had a ball! We didn't have any money, but we had God!"

Before the Savannah meeting ended, wind destroyed the tent, and Vivian and Wayne Simmons returned to Maryville. "I went to painting some houses—she and I." He nodded toward his wife. "We painted a motel and we painted houses and within maybe a month or two we got to putting it together again and I told Sister Simmons that I *did* feel the call of God on my life." He hesitated, then admitted, "I was overanxious. I didn't listen to what God told me in Carrollton through this lady, and she was a lady of God. I should have stayed put under a senior pastor or a minister and learned from him and studied, but I didn't, and therefore it cost me many good years of my life. But I said, Well, praise the Lord, if God's called me to preach, I'm gonna preach! And somebody gave me an old tent. Thirty by sixty. Just a small job. And we sewed on that thing and got it all patched up and we threw it up in Newport, Tennessee, and *it* was a disaster." He shook his head slowly. "I'll be honest with you. It didn't work. So I pulled back to a li'l ol' place called Lonsdale in Knoxville, on a li'l ol' lot, and *it* failed miserably."

"How many people came?"

"Well, the crowd was all right," he said, hedging, "but I was just so green. I didn't know what I was doing. It wasn't God's time for me."

By this point Wayne Simmons had learned to wait. He returned home in time to attend a seventeen-week tent revival being conducted by Texas-based evangelist Dan Goodin, who offered him a job before leaving town. For the next two years the Simmonses traveled with Goodin and in between meetings ran his Fort Worth headquarters. "We did the printing. We did the mail-outs. We did the precrusade work, the radio work. I wasn't doing any preaching, any ministering," he emphasized. "I was learning."

"You were behind the scenes?" I clarified.

"Well, but also I would take the fore part of the service. The singing. The announcements. And then I would introduce him—"

"In the tent ministry we call it 'front,' " Vivian Simmons explained.

Her husband nodded. "Yeah, 'front man'—that's the term used in evangelistic circles. Who's your front man? Is he good?" he illustrated. "Anyway, all of this was very helpful to me. It was very rich background, but still I became discouraged. By nineteen sixty-six I thought, well, maybe I had missed God. Maybe I'm *not* called to preach. And then I began to look at people's lives, and this old thing began to gnaw on me again: Well, if that's God, I don't want to have anything to do with it. So I quit."

For the next ten years he attended church and sang in a gospel trio but never once discussed the ministry—not even with his wife. Yet all the while he privately agonized over his calling, frequently spending his lunch hour alone in the church, crying and talking to God. "Not one minute's rest did I ever get," he said now of those years. "God just seemed to speak to me every second: You are to preach for Me. I have called you to preach." Vivian Simmons sat quietly, studying her husband as he recalled the anguish. "I would wake up three or four o'clock every morning, and the call of the ministry was right before me. I had this key to the church, and I remember this one particular time I had come to the end of the line. I would weep and cry alone.

And God said, Son, you're either going to say yes, or tell Me flat no, that you're not going to do what I've called you to do." Simmons faced me squarely. "I mean, it wasn't a figment of the imagination," he said firmly. "I'm saying that God *spoke* to me."

"You heard His voice?"

Simmons nodded. "I felt this thing so strong I believe—and I stand in the fear of God then and now—that if I would've said no and went in rebellion, I believe I would be backslid today." Beyond the front window a hibiscus swayed with the gentle breeze, but in the quiet living room, the grandfather clock sounded like the beat of a swollen heart. "This happened in the Assembly of God church in Knoxville," he reiterated. "This particular day I went in and I said, God, I don't know how to begin. I don't even know how to tell my wife I *know* You've called me. But God, if You think I can do it and You're calling me—if You will just open the door and help me, I'll do my best. I'll give it all I've got. And I left the church. I just left it in the Lord's hands."

Several months passed before Simmons finally shared his struggles with Vivian and the pastor of their church. Still he could not gather the courage to announce his calling. For weeks he prayed and fasted, but even after telling the minister he would make his public declaration the next Sunday, Simmons wrestled with the thought of actually doing it. As the time approached he grew increasingly anxious. That Friday, after a sleepless night, he told his wife he wanted to rest awhile longer and remained in bed to pray. "She left the room, and it wasn't five minutes till the presence of God just seemed to fill the room," he recalled. "I went into a vision and I was running out of this church. I ran out into the church property, the grassy area, and I just sat down with my head down between my knees and I said, O, God, I *can't*! I just can't!" His voice rehearsed all the emotions he had felt on that long-ago morning. "It was *so* real. It was a visitation from Jesus Christ *Himself!* I saw from my right, walking from the church, a man dressed in white. I never did see His face. Just from His shoulders down. But I remember I was crying with all that was within me, uncontrollably, and He put His arms around me and just held me for the longest. He said, It's gonna be all right. Said, Now you stop your crying. He said, I'll remove every fence from around you." Simmons explained, "All around this church was a high fence six to eight feet tall. And very methodically, very casually, taking His time, He rolled the fence completely off the posts, and He threw this whole large roll of fencing into this field. And He came back and He said, I've removed the fence from around you. Now go back and tell them you're called to preach."

Two weeks later Simmons preached his first sermon. That was September 1975. For the next two years, like his father and so many Pentecostal ministers, he held weekend revivals at nearby churches while continuing to work for the packing house. In 1977 he finally quit his secular job and evangelized full time until founding Praise Temple a year later.

Since those adolescent days of his ministry, Simmons had studied the Bible and attended an extension of Lee College, a Church of God Bible school based in Cleveland, Tennessee. But like most Pentecostal ministers, he considered what he called "the school of hard knocks" the best preparation for the pulpit, insisting "That's where it's at, being out there firsthand and knowing what's going on." He reviewed his own beginning years: the clumsy attempts to hold revivals before he was prepared, the juggling of out-of-town meetings with a full-time job, the financial scraping. When I asked if most revivalists start out that way, he answered yes. "It's to see if you've got what it takes." He leaned forward, earnest. "God can't use a sissy. God has *never* used a sissy."

Simmons had learned from his own impatience the importance of an "apprenticeship" under an established evangelist. Although he insisted he had his own preaching style, he acknowledged listening, even now, to the recorded sermons of men like A. A. Allen, Jack Coe, T. L. Lowery, Jimmy Swaggart, R. W. Schambach, even Baptist evangelist James Robison. "There's been so many that's touched my life," he said nostalgically, "but I guess we have to say I preach like no one. I had just a landslide meeting in Memphis back in April, and people said, Man, you preach like Swaggart. Now, Swaggart is a great preacher, but he's a greater singer, *I* think. You know, nothing would really impress me to try to copy Swaggart's preaching. But they say, Man, you're just like Jimmy Swaggart. We've heard that a blue-million times. And then in Westmoreland, at the close of the services somebody said I was just like R. W. Schambach." He shrugged. "But I don't try to copy anyone, I'm just my own person."

Nevertheless, Schambach was his mentor, with almost a fatherlike influence. Although the two had become acquainted only a few years earlier while the then Pennsylvania-based evangelist was conducting a revival in the area, Simmons remembered first seeing Schambach in the mid-fifties when he was A. A. Allen's "front man" during a revival in Knoxville. It was a childhood memory Simmons cherished; but that very revival may well have been the one that led to Allen's ouster from the Assemblies of God.

On October 21, 1955, half an hour before he was to preach, Allen was arrested for drunken driving after his late-model Buick barreled through a red light. According to newspaper accounts, several motorists had alerted state troopers of Allen's approach, warning "You'd better stop that red car with Pennsylvania license plates before he kills somebody." Three additional patrol cars had already been dispatched after complaints that the same car had almost forced several others off the road. One motorist claimed Allen's car had approached a group of school children and "just scattered them like quail." At the city jail, Allen's drunk-o-meter test reportedly indicated a 0.20 percent alcohol content, above the 0.15 reading necessary to warrant arrest. The revivalist denied he had been drinking and complained to one officer that his arrest was "a trick of the Devil," quickly adding "Don't get me wrong. I don't think you are demon-possessed." His ardent followers concurred. At that night's service, the associate who preached in his absence told the crowd: "The Devil struck again. State police found Brother Allen on the highway today—drugged." Evangelists throughout the country shuddered when the front-page headlines read: "Dispenser Of Miracles Jailed As Drunk Driver." The following day's news was no better. In a story headed "Journal Newsman Put Out, Beaten at Tent Meeting," Knoxville reporter Al Webb described how he was thrown out of the next night's meeting after Allen discovered he was a journalist. According to Webb's account, he was jostled and punched in the ribs as he was pushed from the tent. Outside, he was mobbed by fifty followers who shouted names—some of them unprintable. "Don't ever come back," Webb was warned. "If you do, we'll really fix you up." The next night, however, he returned and was immediately surrounded by a crowd that beat and kicked at his car and attempted to get at him through a partially opened window. "That's that lying reporter!" the group railed. "Why don't you get religion, you sinner!" Another newsman was said to have been similarly abused. At the request of Allen's attorney, the case was continued until November 29 and the evangelist was allowed to leave the state under a thousand-dollar bond, which he eventually forfeited rather than face the embarrassment of a trial. But that was not the end of the matter. Shortly after the arrest, Ralph M. Riggs, superintendent of the general council of the Assemblies of God, wrote to Allen suggesting he "withdraw from the public ministry until the matter at Knoxville [can] be settled." The evangelist refused. Instead, he surrendered his church credentials and announced his plans to continue independently. "A withdrawal from public ministry at this time would ruin my ministry," he wrote in *Miracle Magazine*, "for it would have the appearance of an admission of guilt."

The arrest was not the first time the question of a drinking problem had been raised. By Allen's own admission he had been a hard drinker as a youth and, before his conversion, ran a dance hall and made moonshine. Many of his detractors believed he never overcame that weakness for alcohol, and in June 1967 the Cleveland *Plain Dealer* reported that the revivalist had faced other charges of drunkenness in Las Vegas and Laguna Beach, California. The rumors of abusive drinking followed Allen until he died in 1970.

Simmons neither mentioned the incident nor seemed aware of it. Instead, he spoke of the late evangelist in glowing terms, as the one person he felt he could turn to during his troubled adolescence. He credited both Allen and Schambach with contributing to his current success. Schambach, in fact, had asked him to assist with a revival in Haiti just this past March 1981, and Simmons excitedly talked about that trip and about other invitations he had begun to receive. Since founding Praise Temple, he again had to schedule his revivals close to home. Nevertheless, he felt strongly that he would soon be able to concentrate solely on evangelism. It was just a matter of time. Shortly before I arrived for the interview, he had received an unexpected invitation to hold a service in Eufaula, Alabama.

"I could go solid through the next twelve months just on what I have now," he said. "It's unexplainable, but I just knew that this would be the year."

"Most writers want to win a Pulitzer," I noted, "do evangelists have a comparable ambition?"

"Well—" he hesitated. "I myself don't aspire to have an operation as large as Swaggart. I just desire to be a successful revivalist, to see results. By results I mean people being healed, people being saved, and you can't have large results unless you have the numbers there, you know. So *yes*, I'm after large numbers because *Christ* was after large numbers."

Vivian Simmons attempted to clarify. "He was saying he didn't care about being as big as Jimmy Swaggart. I think he means maybe like having television programs all over the world or having schools—" she interpreted.

"Oh, that would be good!" Wayne Simmons agreed.

"But you don't really have a vision of that, do you?" she asked.

"No. . . ."

He seemed uncertain.

"You wouldn't mind doing it, though?" I suggested.

"I would do it at God's time, but right now it doesn't bother me," he maintained. "I believe God is going to let us grow, even this summer. You know, I have no lies to say and I have nothing to hide. The apostle Paul said, I know how to be abased and I know how to abound—right?" I nodded. "I've been abased long enough. I've paid my dues and I've been through the school of hard knocks. I believe God is going to increase this ministry numerically and financially."

Raising a family on a revivalist's income was not easy, he conceded. But although Vivian Simmons had worked part time in a nearby school lunchroom for five years, both insisted she had done so to occupy her time, not for the money. And this would be her last year on the job, they were certain, because of the increasing demands on Wayne Simmons's time. With the growing number of invitations to preach, he would need help.

"The ministry's just begun to bloom out," Simmons said proudly, "and it's all God's doing. You can just watch it grow. See, we talked about this last January. Nothing happened the first two or three weeks, but we knew it would. And then we felt God move us from here," he said, raising his hand from waist level to above his head, "up to here."

He leaned forward, intent, his eyes focused on mine. "You may not realize it, but *you're* not here by accident yourself," he said. "It's in God's divine plan that you were *sent* here. I know it. And it's just like this is another plateau that God's taking us to."

CHAPTER II

TOMMY WALKER:
"Singing Around the Master's Throne"

The hearse was backed up to within a few feet of the tent, waiting, but the people were not ready to yield. For more than three hours they had been petitioning God to reconsider, and still they showed no signs of stopping, of relinquishing what in their hearts they knew they must. Additional chairs had been placed around the tent, and yet another ring of people crowded beyond the chairs. The casket itself, closed and barren of flowers, rested in front of the platform.

Four days earlier, on a June Saturday in 1981, the Reverend Tommy Walker and several followers had gathered at Cove Lake to baptize those saved during the early weeks of his summer-long revival in LaFollette, Tennessee. The lake was popular among fundamentalist sects in the area. On warm weekends motorists traveling north from Knoxville on Interstate 75 could frequently witness immersions reminiscent of those in the Bible. Reverend Walker often conducted the watery rites there, and on this particular day his son Joseph had been among the half dozen baptized. Following the service, the father, nineteen-year-old Tommy Jr., and another young man decided to swim fully clothed across a narrow part of the lake, to their cars. When Tommy had swum three-quarters of the way, he called for help, then disappeared beneath the water. Later that afternoon the local rescue squad recovered the body and took it to a nearby hospital where the boy was pronounced dead.

Reverend Walker and his wife, Naomi, refused to concede their child's death. Both were convinced she had died and been resurrected shortly after they were married. God, they believed, would also raise their son from the dead. When authorities refused to release the body to anyone but a mortician, the Walkers persuaded a local undertaker to let them to take it to their home where the couple and their seventeen-year-old son, Timothy, began fasting and praying. As word of the vigil spread, hundreds of people came to the house—some to pray, others to watch. Services conducted by Timothy at the tent that night and the next attracted standing-room-only crowds. The supplications continued into the third day, until four o'clock that Monday morning when Mrs. Walker realized the body had begun to decompose and awakened her husband from a nap. After discussing the situation, they drove to the tent where Timothy was sleeping and allowed him to make the final decision. The body was waked that evening at a mortuary, and the funeral scheduled for eleven-thirty the next morning.

During the heyday of the healing and charismatic revivals of the 1950s and 1960s, claims of modern-day resurrections were not uncommon. In the mid-sixties, A. A. Allen launched a "raise the dead" program, which came to an abrupt end when some of his followers reportedly tried to ship bodies to his headquarters in Arizona. And after revivalist William Branham was killed in an automobile accident on December 18, 1965, his disciples stored his embalmed body in the attic of a funeral home, convinced he would rise on Easter. In 1978 I had followed the newspaper coverage about Daniel Aaron Rogers, an Arkansas fundamentalist preacher, storing his deceased mother in a deep freeze for two months while he attempted to raise her from the dead. When those efforts failed, he considered resorting to an Indonesian faith healer—a plan Rogers abandoned only after he was unable to raise $4,300 for the healer and his interpreter.

But in spite of the accounts of modern-day resurrection attempts that cropped up in the news from time to time, I had never expected to find myself in the peculiar position of witnessing such an event— not even when I embarked on this book. I was in Knoxville attending Wayne Simmons's revival when I heard about the Walkers' efforts. Unable to reach the family by telephone, I decided to make the hour's drive. In Jacksboro, the tiny hamlet identified on television as Reverend Walker's home, I stopped to ask directions and was told the funeral was in progress just up the road, near the LaFollette city limits.

By the time I arrived, the services had been under way for more than two hours, having started an hour earlier than scheduled. Battered cars and trucks with bumper stickers proclaiming GOD IS MY PILOT lined the highway, and opposite the tent a portable sign announced, FUNERAL FOR TOMMY WALKER JR.—TUES 9—11:30 AM—HERE. Uniformed police officers milled about the tent and along the roadside, out of courtesy to the family, they told me, although their numbers seemed unusually high for a small-town burial. The tent was a smaller version of Wayne Simmons's, but unlike his, this one was pieced together with iron-on patches, its once-rich color an arid, dry-rotted tan from sweltering under too many hot, humid days like today. Drainage pipes served as center poles, and strapped about them were old sofa cushions—perhaps as a safeguard for worshipers who, in an emotional frenzy, became over-wrought. The platform was crowded with an assortment of drums and musical instruments. A loudspeaker for the organ doubled as the pulpit, and on it rested a Bible and a man's straw hat.

A curious mixture of expectancy and ill-fated hope pervaded the tent, yet the usual manifestations of grief were strangely absent. No one was crying, not even the parents, and had I not been aware of the circumstances I would never have suspected *their* son lay in the coffin, about to be buried. Both were buoyant and smiling and bore no traces of sorrow. Naomi Walker was at the organ and her husband at the pulpit, performing as they would have for a more typical service. But although the Walkers were central to the unfolding drama, when I arrived neither was the object of attention. Instead, the crowd—the believers and curious alike—was mesmerized by a woman standing near the casket. She was quite ordinary looking, heavyset, her dark hair wound into a thick, fat bun. With her eyes closed, her arms outstretched, she spoke in a sort of King James English, uttering a message more repetitious than revelational, each pronouncement prefaced by "Yea, I say." Members of the audience fastened on her every word, their attention straying only when Reverend Walker rattled his tambourine and interspersed a spirited *"Glo-ry!"* Rhythmically, virtually chanting, the woman cried out in a prophetic voice: "Yea, I say to re-joice-ce! Yea, I say to obey my spirit! Yea, I say I *will* heal the sick! Yea, I say I *will* raise the dea-ed!" In the background, Reverend Walker's melodious tongues, his gentle praises, complimented but never competed. *ooooOOOOOO God! Amen! Aha-brababah-balabahai!* "Yea, I say to seek my advice-ce! Yea, I say for there's trouble ahead-ed!" *Habra-babadah-dadi-ah!* "Yea, I say to come together in one mi-ind!" *Ha-brabaha-labradai!* "Yea, I say for I am Go-od and I love thee! Yea, I say to hold my people up!" *O, Lord!* On and on the messages mingled, the woman's voice intensifying as she prophesized and promised, finally softening, tapering to an end. As if awakened from a trance, the crowd jolted to attention, and Reverend Walker banged the tambourine and shouted, "A-men! Give the Lord a good handclap!"

The evangelist was slight, almost insignificant in appearance. His sober three-piece suit and severe haircut hinted of a regimented life-style, yet he bounced and danced and strutted like a carny. "Glory to God and shout for joy!" he encouraged, his delivery evolving into an emotional chant. "Praaaaise God! Ooooooooooh, halleluuuuuu-jah! Well, God!" The people contributed their own hosannas as Reverend Walker lapsed into tongues. *"eh-comdeka-kakakubra!* Hallelujah! Thank Ya, Jeeeesus! Glory to God! *akori-kabahama—"* Without warning, a gray-haired woman interrupted and, like the first, prophesied in a stilted English. "Yea, I say to exalt my anointed and do my prophets no harm, yea, for my people are going forth with pow-er! Yea, I say if I be with ye, tell me who can be against ye?" A man cried *"Yes!"* and the woman wound down. "Yea, for I will go before thee. Yea, I will fight your battles, thus saith the Lord." The crowd applauded, and Reverend Walker singsonged, "Yesssssss, halle-lujah! oooooOOOOOOO God! Praise the Loooooord! A-men!"

As if by signal, the clamor ceased and Reverend Walker moved to the microphone to tell about the blinding of his son John, reminding the audience of the father's past demonstrations of faith and of the possibility that God could still, at that very moment, raise Tommy from the cold, metallic-blue coffin. "My son standing right here had his eye put out, amen, it was ripped open with a curtain rod while they were playing David and Goliath. It was Tommy that did it. Tore his eye open and he went instantly blind. It *reeeally* upset Tommy, amen, and you know what John said to him? Said, Tommy, don't cry. It'll be all right. God'll give me my sight back." The audience listened, riveted, as the evangelist's pace quickened. "He went instantly blind. The white was all red. The blue was solid black. We got in church the next night, we laid our hands on him and prayed for him. Tested his blind eye. He couldn't see a thing at all. The second night the same thing. On the third night he got up and he began to sing the song we sang a-whiiiile ago that I wanta sing a little of again." Reverend Walker's voice quivered, and then, accompanied by the organ and a guitar, he began to chant. "Hallelujah, and he begin to sing about that second verse, about the blind man that cried, I can-not see, thou son of David, have mercy on me. Then Jesus spoke so sweet and low, A-riiiiise, my son, thy faith hath made thee whole." Above the organ music he whooped, "If Jesus *said* it, I *be-lieve* it! His *wooord* cannot lie. If it's writ-ten in the Bible I'll *believe* it till I die. Though the mountains be removed and cast into the sea, God's Woooord will live for-ever, through-out e-ter-ni-ty. Somebody shout amen!"

The congregation's voices swelled into one *AMEN!*

And like a rapids the story rushed on. "For three days I didn't see it happen, but I didn't give up praising God for it. I continually thanked God for restoring John's eye. I kept claiming the promise even though I didn't see it right away, hallelujah, and that's what we've done with Tommy, amen. Even though we didn't see him raised right away, we kept praising God anyhow, we kept thankin' God anyhow, and I'm *still* thanking Him! I'm *still* praising Him!" Cheers and applause rose from the crowd as the frail evangelist raised his eyes and his voice in praise. "Hallelujah, Father, I *thank* Ya for raising Tommy Walker Junior from the dead! I thank Ya, Lord, that You raised him up as a living witness. I thank Ya that You brought Tommy out of the captive to rejoice in the Holy Ghost! To praise You! And to *mag*nify You! *Habdakabraba-kudadai!*"

The preacher's pace slowed, and he offered his followers the op-portunity to reaffirm their faith. "I'd like ever'body that'll believe God with me to come lay your hands on this casket. *Hatah-rababa-kura-basah-durabai!* I want the believers to come, hallelujah, for the prom-ise of God is to them that believe. *Hata-kabra-soutakamaki!* GlooooOOOORY to God!"

Except for the merely curious, the people pressed forward, twisting, writhing, reaching toward the casket and to one another, a pulsating mass of arms and legs and bodies. The organ music, too, grew ram-bunctious in the midst of Reverend Walker's incantations. "I thank Ya, Lord, that He that believeth in Thee, *though* he were dead yet shall he live! Hallelujah, I believe Your Word. I believe on You! *Whooof!* ooooOOOOOOO GOD, I thank Ya! By faith I rejoice in the resurrec-tion of the dead!" The crowd parted to watch a young woman dance. Her eyes rolled inward, and she tossed her head and her long, auburn hair around and around until it resembled a hovering ball of fire. From the people flowed a mournful *ooooooooouuuuuuuuuuuuuuuuuuuu*, rising and falling and winding around Reverend Walker's words: "I thank You, Lord, that You're a blind-eye opener, that You're a deaf-ear unstopperer, that You're a cancer healer, that You're a tumor disappearer, and You're a *DEAD!* raiser! oooooooooooOOOOOOOOH, hallelujah! I thank Ya, Father, for raising my son from the dead!"

Baffled by the evangelist's thanksgiving, I strained to see the coffin. In the midst of the pulsating mass it remained immobile, yet no one seemed aware of the harsh reality, of the incongruity of his words. Or were they simply not ready to accept God's decision as final? Members of the audience shrieked *Oooooooooh!*—just that, the sound long and shrill like a siren. They jumped and jerked and twirled as if possessed, with no control over their bodies or themselves, their expressions curiously vacant. Frantically Reverend Walker banged and rattled the tambourine, with the organ and drums hurrying to catch up as he began to sing, "If Jesus said it, I believe it—His Wooord can-not lie. If it's written in the Bible, I'll believe it till I die . . ." Naomi Walker swayed from side to side as she played and sang the harmony, the crowd joining in. *"Though the mountains be removed and cast into the sea, God's Word will live forever, through-out e-tern-i-ty."* Over and over they repeated the verses until the organ gradually soured and ran out of energy. *". . . they removed that stone, and He arooooose from the dead."**

"Amen! Glory!" Reverend Walker cried out. "Give the Lord a leap offering!" He bounced up and down, encouraging the crowd to join him. "C'mon, ever'body, leap for joy and rejoice by faith. O Lord. Thank Ya, Jesus. A-men!" His voice momentarily calmed, and standing still he spoke in a more normal, pulpit delivery. "I'll tell you one thing: Since Tommy died, there's been a lot of people that have come to believe in raising the dead."

The audience shouted, *Yes.*

"I mean, there *has!*" Applause interrupted him. "Praise the Lord, we appreciate everything God's done. We're going to turn it over

---

to—" Reverend Walker turned nervously to his wife. "I'm not much at conducting funerals." He stalled, visibly uncomfortable. "Is there something I'm supposed to do?" His wife shrugged, and he seemed increasingly lost, as if God had abandoned him. He floundered, anxiously searching for guidance, and appeared relieved when a fragile young woman made her way to the microphone.

"Praise the Lord," she said in a nasal mountain accent. "I wanta say somethin' to the people here who don't know Jesus. The Lord was speaking to me on the back of the stage. There are many of you God has touched by His Spirit today and you've never felt the Spirit of the Lord and there are many of you can hear the P.A. system and you're in your cars or you're here because you're appointed to be here. You'll be changed."

As the young woman returned to the rear of the platform, a new burst of praise and applause bolstered Reverend Walker's confidence. "Shout for glory one more time! Praise the Lord!" he shouted above the din. "I tell you one thing, no matter how you look at it, my son is alive and well!"

Yesssssss!

"I'm proud of my son! I'm *proud* of what he did for the Lord! I'm proud that he was a preacher! *HALLELUJAH! Whoooooof!* Ooooo-OOOOH, Glory! I'm proud of every song he ever sung, of the guitar he played, of the bass he played, the piano, the organ, the drums, ever'thing else that he played, hallelujah, how he backed us up in our services, amen, how they sang in their trio and rejoiced in the Lord!" He rushed on breathlessly before his tone became foreboding. "I tell you something, brother, if you're gonna do something for God, you better get it done, amen, because you don't know how many days you've got left and you better not fool around and waste them away —somebody shout amen!"

The tent vibrated with a concerted *AMEN!*

"Amen, because God may cut *your* days short too, hallelujah! You can mess around and fool around, watching your ol' TV programs and going to ball games and wasting your time on dominoes and bingo and foolish games and ungodly literature and stupid comic books and trash and filled with the pleasures of sin for a season and waste your life away." The evangelist broke out of his rapid monotone, and his voice soared. "GLOOOOOOOOOOO-ry to God, hallelujah! I'll tell you what, brother,

I'd rather be a preacher of the Gospel and a singer and a musician for the Lord—like Tommy was—and go at nineteen than to live to seventy or eighty or ninety and fool around sucking on cancer sticks, chewing tobacco, dipping snuff, amen, and women trimming your hair and painting your face, decking out in jewelry and wearing short sleeves and short dresses and pants and shorts and halters and see-more blouses and *allllll* the mess of ungodliness and lukewarmness, amen, and maybe lose your own soul over it. Somebody shout amen! Halleluuujah!"

AMEN!

"I wanta tell this before I go. I've *got* to tell it!" he said urgently. "The Lord spoke to me a couple of years ago and told me if I didn't preach 'clothesline' at ever' revival God would take the life of my son. I didn't know He was talking about the older boy. I thought He was talking about the baby, and I made the consecration that day that I'd sing the Gourd-vine Preacher's Song and preach clothesline in ever' revival, hallelujah, and I kept my word for a while. But one time I didn't do it. And after I didn't preach clothesline, the next day my son went down a hill, Joseph went down—" In Reverend Walker's haste he stumbled over words. "A-a-and flew off his bicycle—almost killed him—and landed in the street. Amen, the second time it happened awhile later, the very next day my baby was hit by a car. When I came home and saw him in convulsions and saw him with a fever, amen, I knew the reason. I prayed the prayer of faith, and God gave me one more chance, but when I was at Mount Olive, though I sang the Gourdvine Preacher's Song, I failed to preach a good clothesline sermon, hallelujah, and God warned me He would take the life of my son if I didn't preach clothesline and tell the men and the women how to dress godly and do that which becometh holiness inside and out, amen. Hallelujah, if your outside doesn't meas-ure up to God's standard of holiness and His Word, it's because there's *sin* on the inside. Somebody shout amen!"

A thunderous *AMEN!* rumbled through the crowd.

"If you're painted up like a Jezebel, your hair trimmed like a Jezebel, it's because you're a Jezebel on the inside. You get the inside cleaned up and the outside'll get cleaned up, and if the outside's not cleaned up, it's evidence there's *wrong* on the inside, hallelujah!" The people screamed and shouted. "I want you to know that God kept His Word to me, that God took the life of my son, amen, because I didn't do what He told me to do. *Arababkuri-sati!* But I can say like Job, the

Lord gave and the Lord hath taken away, bles-sed be the name of the Lord! I'm gonna shout *anyhow!* I'm gonna dance *anyhow!* I'm gonna rejoice *anyhow!* I'm gonna leap for joy *anyhow!* And I'm gonna live holy and I'm gonna preach holiness. Hallelujah, I wanted to give that testimony so ever'body here will know why I'm a holiness preacher, I mean a *clothesline* preacher, praise God, and I'm not ashamed of it, praise the Lord, God bless ya, amen!"

The audience burst into applause, then ended abruptly, and the evangelist again chattered self-consciously. "Ever'body that's going to the cemetery just get in line, amen." He laughed a thin, nervous laugh. "Praise the Lord, hallelujah!"

Two men in black suits eased through the crowd, toward Reverend Walker. "You better get the pallbearers," the taller man told the evangelist, who in turn asked the red-haired boy next to him, "You got the pallbearers, Tim?" The boy gestured to several young men in the audience. The people watched silently as six teenagers came forward and lined up on either side of the coffin. Then, led by Reverend Walker and Timothy, they carried the casket to the waiting hearse. When the heavy black door slammed shut, the people quickly dispersed and an assortment of dusty, aging cars and trucks rumbled into place behind the sleek limousine. As it eased out onto the highway and began its slow, circuitous journey, the cars followed. Down the highway and along Jacksboro's main street, the humble cortege inched toward its destination, turning at the town's lone traffic signal onto a steep, winding road that ended at the cemetery.

A tambourine's rattling drifted down the hillside, toward me, as I made my way to the green canopy where the casket rested next to a pile of freshly turned earth. The gathering crowd focused on the Walkers and Timothy, who stood near the foot of the coffin, out from under the protective shade. Occasionally Reverend Walker mopped his face with a folded handkerchief, but for the most part he ignored the summer sun, joyously jumping up and down and shouting, over and over, "Amen, praise the Lord, thank God!" Naomi Walker stood tranquilly at her husband's side. She too seemed oblivious to the heat. Her cotton-print dress was ankle length with long sleeves and a high neckline, her blond hair extending past her waist. "I'm a proud mother," she interrupted softly. Then with hands clasped loosely in front of her, she smiled as her husband reminded the gathering of the biblical promise that on Judgment Day two trumpets would sound: the first, to raise up the dead; the second, to call forth those believers who remained on earth, alive.

"Praise God I know today, amen, Tommy would want us to rejoice!" the evangelist exclaimed, bouncing and banging the tambourine. "He'd want us to be shouting and to be leaping, hallelujah, and to be dancing! I feel like we oughta give the Lord a good handclap!" Again the timbrel clashed and the crowd's cheers and applause swelled into a pep rally for God, subsiding as Reverend Walker's mood calmed and he praised God.

"Father, You heard my son say he'd be willing to give his life for somebody to get saved," the evangelist prayed, "and I thank You, Lord, that a multitude is going to be saved, hallelujah, through his death."

Quietly, in the background, Naomi Walker concurred, "Thank You, Jesus."

Reverend Walker went on. "I thank Ya, Father, hallelujah, for the results of this day's happening shall continue on and on and on with a *chaaaaain* reaction." *Praise God!* "O, God, we're asking You to send a mighty Holy Ghost revival to Campbell County, hallelujah. Let the fire begin in me, let it spread around the community." *Thank You, Jesus!* "We pray today that the hearts of people will be stirred to fast and to pray, to seek Your faith, to have the miracle-working power of God in their life to heal the sick, to cleanse the leper, to cast out devils, and to *raaaaaise* the dead! We thank You for it, in Jesus' name, amen and amen!"

The crowd screamed and applauded, and in the midst of the uproar, Naomi Walker's thin voice rose in song, the rhythm set by her lone, firm claps. *"Rejoice in the Lord, for this is the will of God . . ."* The others joined the spirited singing accompanied by the beat-rattle-beat of Reverend Walker's tambourine, sounding like a Salvation Army street ensemble.

Timothy stepped forward. "I want you to pray with me that I'll be able to fulfill many of his goals," he said in a cracking voice.

His mother murmured, "Praise God."

"His desire was to see souls saved, to be a soul winner. That's what I'm going to do, even though he's going to get the reward for it—"

Amen.

"You know," the brother said, his tone brightening, "we ain't got nothin' to be sorrowful about."

The tambourine jangled and the people offered a united *No!*

The sun beat down on the canopy and the people, perspiration forming beads on their foreheads and darkening the backs of their clothing. The colors of the canvas, the flowers, the grass intensified. Only the people seated under the canopy escaped the glare. One of them, an older woman, stood for attention. Like Naomi Walker, she wore a long print dress, and her stringy brown hair trailed down her back. She spoke in a small voice, almost a little girl's, that seemed even frailer coming from her stout body. At times her words quivered, yet she never succumbed to grief. "I wanta say he was my oldest grandson, and I loved him with all my heart," she said, "but I'm *glad* he's with the Lord, hallelujah, I'm *glad* Jesus could take him to heaven. I'm thankful Tommy was a good preacher and a wonderful singer, and I'm so glad he's with the Lord."

As she was sitting down, Timothy again spoke. "His tombstone, on the bottom it says, Singing Around the Master's Throne. That was his favorite song," he explained, "so I'm gonna sing the chorus and I want ever'body that knows the song to sing with us." In a hoarse voice he sang, *"By the time they find me missing, I'll be liiiiiv-ing over there . . ."** The people joined in, the clattering tambourine and Naomi Walker's fragile harmony adding ruffles and trills to the humble choir.

When the song had run its course, evaporating into the heat, Reverend Walker meekly recalled how that morning God had spoken to him first in a dream and then, after he awakened, with a phrase from that song—final proof, he said, that Tommy would not be raised from the dead, that he was at home, in heaven. As he described the revelation, the father seemed at last satisfied. He had done everything he could.

The undertakers stepped forward and signaled, and as the pallbearers approached the casket, the crowd dispersed like a dandelion's tufted seeds scattering in the wind, some lingering to speak to the family, others drifting down the slope. The sky was a clear, cloudless blue, lighter than the distant foothills of the Smokies. I too headed toward my car, walking with the people yet not a part of them. From behind came the tambourine's faint tinkle and Reverend Walker's muted praises, the words and sounds gradually becoming indistinguishable from the warm rustling breeze.

---

*"By the Time They Find Me Missing" by Kenny Hinson. Copyright © 1979 Kenny Hinson, by Songs of Calvary/BMI. All rights reserved. International copyright secured. Used by permission.

* * *

When I returned to the tent, a man and woman were absorbed in conversation. Neither of them seemed to take notice of my presence or of the aimless dabbling on the drums by three teenage boys. Except for these and a young woman seated apart from the rest, the tent was virtually deserted, its emptiness laying bare the full extent of its shabbiness and disrepair. Rips and tears were clearly visible, and a plastic trash bag stuffed with fast-food wrappers rested against a center pole. There was about both the tent and the people a sense of loss and of powerlessness that folks in these parts had long since come to grips with, indeed had found solace from in a religion and a God Who would reward their adversity by and by. As the man and woman conversed I studied their faces and pondered the fruitless struggles by them and by their forebears in coal mines and on marginal land that yielded so little. Both were middle-age, plain folk with the whiny, nasal accents indigenous to these foothills. The man was so ordinary in size and appearance he could easily have become lost in a crowd. His speech was soft in contrast to that of the woman, who was large, rather tall, thick, solid—the sort of female who, out of shouldering a family's failures and disappointments, comes to dominate a man, a household, a gathering, as she did this simple searching for reasons that would absolve God of Tommy's failure to be raised from the dead.

"They'd a made a god out of him," she said, speculating as to why God couldn't permit the boy's resurrection. The man agreed, "Yeah, not given credit unto Him that—" but before he could complete his argument the woman broke in with "You know how people are. They would be people that'd start worshipin' him." She shook her head disapprovingly. "Still, I'll never be the same after this. Brother Walker *sure* has demonstrated what he's always preached. He believes, Praise the Lord in all things, an' I'm tellin' you, he sure did, didn't he?"

The man nodded, but it was the woman who answered her own question. "I never *seen* such faith. I mean, kids an' *all*. I never experienced nothin' like this, a funeral like this."

"You ain't?"

"Never seen a funeral where they rejoiced," she was positive. "I've seen 'em where they got happy an' ever'thing but not much as this."

The man drew tall. "Well, the Lord said, Rejoice over the death of the one that's done gone home." He quoted scripture. "Like He says, This joy has been fulfilled, thus saith the Lord."

Throughout the exchange the young woman had remained expressionless. But when I asked to interview her, Rachel Blakeman spoke freely of the religion she had embraced since coming to the area ten years ago to attend college and then teach elementary school. Her mother had been raised Baptist, her stepfather Methodist, and neither understood or accepted those tenets that deemed cutting or even trimming her waist-length hair a sin. She had known the Walkers for eight or ten years, not intimately but from attending their services, and had committed to memory their vital statistics in the way other less devout young people follow the lives of rock singers and movie stars. Rather than go to the cemetery she had remained at the tent as a favor to the family, to tidy up and keep an eye on the musical instruments.

When I asked if she had felt Tommy would be resurrected, she was firm in her conviction. "I figured he would, 'cause there was so much faith and so much belief." She cocked her head hesitantly, conceding "But you get this human factor, this little percentage that says, Well, he might not too—and you've gotta overcome it. Or you try to overcome it. But all in all, when I left here last night I had the faith he'd be raised."

"Even after he had been taken to the funeral home?" I pressed.

"It wouldn't have surprised me to see that casket open today, and him come out of it," she replied wistfully, "and I wish it had."

The boys busied themselves with the drums and timbrels, while the older couple continued their conversation, emphasizing their intended loyalty to the Walkers in the days and weeks to come. But Rachel Blakeman tuned them out. She preferred to examine her own impressions, her own theories as to why God had not granted what the Walkers and their followers—and *she*—had wanted so badly.

"Maybe God saw something out in front of Tommy that he couldn't've overcome," she speculated. "Or maybe Timmy couldn't step into his ministry until his older brother was moved out of the way." Her tone grew distant, filled with a mystery that perhaps would always be with her. "And Brother Walker told us as they left to go to the cemetery that it was through *his* disobedience God took Tommy, that God had told him to preach a certain sermon in every revival and he'd failed three times to do it."

According to her, the tent had been as crowded during the prayer vigil as it had for the funeral, the atmosphere as joyous and loud. "There was some crying," she said, "but it wasn't a mournful crying. It was more happiness crying. You know, a deep kind of passion—maybe love."

"Had you ever been to a funeral like this?" I asked.

"I've been to one other that was joyful, that the people shouted and it was really a joyful time. It was back in January, down here in La-Follette," she recalled. "A man had cancer, and he just went on to heaven. I mean, he told ever'body he was goin' to, so why be sad?" She shrugged. "And it was a joyful time, but not maybe as loud or as joyful as this one."

When I asked about the two women who prophesied at today's service, Rachel identified them as friends of the family. "I know Lizzie Welburn more than I know Sister Sharp," she said, admiration in her voice. "Now, *she* really believes a lot. She's been healed of cancer and of a leg problem, and she believes in raising the dead. In fact, someone's told me she has actually laid hands on a dead person and they raised up."

"On the TV newscast Mrs. Walker said she had been raised from the dead," I observed.

"Reverend Walker told about it today," she said and then, realizing I had missed that part of the service, recalled the details. "He didn't tell what happened, I don't believe—" She hesitated, to make certain of her facts. "He just said she was expecting Tommy—the boy that died? —and she had already gotten cold, her pulse had quit and her breathing had quit, and the preacher that was in the room told him to just forget it, to call the funeral home, and Brother Walker wouldn't do it. He kept on praying with her and ever'thing and he said when the preacher left, then her soul came back in her. And let's see—" Again she paused. "I have to think what he said," she apologized, laughing self-consciously. "He said she looked up at him and told him she couldn't hear, and so he prayed for her hearing and she told him the best thing he could do was to get her to church if he wanted to see her completely healed. And so he did." Now the story moved smoothly, without interruption, the young teacher's voice reflecting her unquestioning belief in its validity. "He took her to church and asked her where she wanted to be and she said, Sitting at the organ, where she always sat. And so they set her at the organ and she played and then she asked him to take her to the pulpit and he didn't know it but she was blind. They helped her to the pulpit and she called a lady out that was sick and when she laid hands on that lady to pray for her, then the lady received her healing and Sister Walker received her sight. And, course, if she was dead and cold, then obviously the baby in her probably was dead and cold also, and so both of 'em have been raised from the dead."

"Had you known about this before?"

"I didn't until I heard it told today," she replied, "but I've heard things similar to that."

"You *have* heard of other people being raised from the dead?"

She nodded. "There's a young girl that lives on Steeple Creek that when she was a child she died and she was raised from the dead. Right offhand I can't think of any but I *do* know some more, I'm sure."

"What do you think would have happened if Tommy had been raised?"

Rachel Blakeman considered the possibilities. "People would have been happy, but I honestly think a lot of people would have fainted. I really do. But there would have been so much joy, and what a great testimony Tommy could have given and Brother Walker and the whole family could have given, for him to be able to raise from the dead. I've changed my mind about Brother Walker," she admitted. "I thought he was a little overdoing it with the shouting, and he dances constantly, but after last night I've changed my mind about him, because anybody that knows their son's laying at the funeral home and can still shout and praise the Lord like he did, he's gotta have something."

From the highway there was a constant whizzing by of cars. Otherwise the tent was quiet, the boys having disappeared and the couple tired of talking.

"How do you think people would have reacted to Tommy?" I asked.

Rachel Blakeman glanced across the tent, at the woman. "You heard what she said," she replied thoughtfully. "But I don't think they would have worshiped him, as such. Not the true Christians. To me, if God had let him come back, I'd've just felt like Brother Walker had prayed and so many people had prayed that they changed God's mind."

The next day when I returned to the tent shortly after noon, several teenage boys were chunking rocks and wrestling, laughing boisterously as they dodged one another's blows. A blond raced a beat-up car across the parking lot, skidding to a halt and gunning the motor, ignoring the demands of a harried-looking woman that he stop, *now!* As she turned her attention to me, her aggravation gave way to curiosity. Earlier when I telephoned the Walkers' house, Timothy had told me his parents were out looking for a place to relocate the tent. The owner of this lot, after receiving complaints about the noisy funeral, had insisted they move the tent by tomorrow. The woman gestured toward a ramshackle Oldsmobile. One side was bashed in, and a bumper sticker read: IF YOU FEEL FAR FROM GOD GUESS WHO MOVED.

"That's Tommy Junior's car there," she informed me. "I 'spect they'll be back right soon."

While we were talking, a station wagon pulled onto the lot and idled next to the Oldsmobile. It too was battered and bruised, with rumpled clothing crammed in the back. Reverend Walker sat behind the steering wheel; his wife, in the passenger's seat. As I approached, he rolled down the window. They had noticed me at the cemetery, Naomi Walker said, leaning toward the driver's side for a better look. After I explained about my book, they invited me to their home. The evangelist hurried over to the Oldsmobile, and with his wife in the station wagon leading the way, we followed the same route the funeral procession had taken, turning just before the cemetery onto a winding road that led to a subdivision of working-class homes.

The Walkers' one-story house was perched on a steep incline, looking out over the rolling countryside at a church nestled in the distant hills. The interior was modestly furnished and disheveled, and Reverend Walker apologized for the clutter. As we passed through a room with two unmade beds, one of them covered with a quilt naming books of the Bible, I wondered where Tommy had lain during the prayer vigil. In what appeared to be the living room, Reverend Walker and I shared a sofa and his wife sat across from us in a platform rocker, with Bessie Utley, the grandmother, looking on as they reconstructed the drowning.

At close range Reverend Walker bore none of the flashy qualities he had exhibited the day before. He seemed, in fact, somewhat shy and insecure, frequently turning to his wife or to their son Timothy for support, or for prompting when he had trouble recalling a scripture, a hymn, a detail. Both the evangelist and his wife were in their mid-forties, and although his dark-brown hair was beginning to gray, his face was lean and boyish. He was not a tall man although, because of his thinness, he gave that impression. By contrast, Naomi Walker was clearly the stronger of the two, in size and personality. Her thick, long hair, the color of fresh sawdust, was wound into a twist at the back of her head. She wore no jewelry—not even a wedding band—and her face was freckled and free of makeup. Like her husband and mother, she wore the same clothing from the day before, the ankle-length print dress and simple white sandals. Her attire was part of the Holiness doctrine referred to by Reverend Walker at the funeral. She and the more ardent female followers wore only floor-length dresses with high necklines and long sleeves. They considered even trimming their hair a sin and wore their long tresses loose or wound into a bun. The men also shunned short sleeves and kept their hair close-cropped, their faces clean-shaven. The strict dress codes were reminiscent of the Puritan ethic, as was their notion of a God Who was intimately involved in each person's life and Who communicated directly through prayer, visions, and the Bible.

The Walkers and many of their followers believed in raising the dead as avidly as they accepted the virgin birth, and at times spoke so nonchalantly one would have thought modern-day resurrections were a common occurrence. Their decision to ask God to raise Tommy had been made as routinely as other families select a cemetery plot. As we gathered in the living room, the couple appeared tired, but otherwise showed no visible effects from their son's death, nor did they seem disturbed by talking about it or their unsuccessful attempt to resurrect him.

"I'd be *more* ready to do it now than I was two days ago," Reverend Walker said firmly. "We've seen God raise the dead four times—including my own wife—so naturally anybody that was around us or was a member of the church, we would attempt to raise them from the dead."

Naomi Walker was supportive. "That experience gave me faith to believe God could do this for my son," she said of her own "resurrection." Although she preferred not to relate her own experience in detail because Timothy wanted one day to write about it, she recalled the dilemma of trying to let her husband know she was alive. "I kept trying to speak," she said, "but there was nothing coming out, and I thought, Now, if I could just *move*—I remembered my mother saying that when somebody else in our family died—" She turned to Bessie Utley. "And you saw them move?"

"It was our good friend that I stayed with and helped take care of her children," the old woman corrected her. "She died and they had her in the mortuary covered with a sheet. She had her hand out and when someone came in the room, he saw her little finger move and he right away told 'em and they went over and looked at her, and sure enough, she was alive. She got up, and she lived several years after that."

"I remembered my mother telling me that when I was just a young girl," Naomi Walker continued, "and the thought went through my mind, Well, if I could just *move* so he'd know I was all right, and I kept trying to move but I couldn't. After that, I don't remember anything. But my son believed in this and preached it, and I backed him in everything he preached," she said firmly. "That's why when he died I had to give God that opportunity, because not only of *my* faith but because of *his* faith. If it had been *me* in that bed laying there dead, he would have done the same thing."

"Tommy would have?" I asked.

"Yes, he would have," she was confident. "One time I said, If ever I die I don't want anybody crying at my funeral, and Tommy said, There'll be nobody crying because we'll all be shouting because we're gonna raise you from the dead!"

The Walkers' five surviving sons had gathered in the room, some leaning against the door frame, others sitting on the floor. They shared their father's cleft chin, his clear blue eyes, and except for Timothy, the eldest now, had tousled blond hair. Sometimes the boys contributed to their parents' accounts of miracles, visions, and conversations with God, but mostly they listened to what, for them, held more fascination and excitement than the wildest westerns and science fiction—tales that, at school, no doubt earned them both ridicule and esteem. They gave no hint of the latter now, especially as their parents described the crowds, the long-distance telephone calls, the interviews that had brought fleeting fame to the family.

Within their own circle of believers and in their immediate community, the Walkers had attracted a certain amount of notoriety due to their mode of dress and undue emphasis on shouting and rejoicing. The evangelist himself was known as the "Dancing Preacher," or sometimes simply "Dancing Tommy Walker." On his flyers he billed his services as DANCING DELIVERANCE REVIVALS, citing Psalm 150:4, "Praise him with the timbrel and dance." Nevertheless, the Walkers emphasized, their attempt to resurrect Tommy had not been to gain attention.

"It was just a personal thing between us and our son and our belief in God and His ability to raise the dead," Naomi Walker maintained. "I thought maybe a handful might come—twenty, thirty, maybe forty people, the people we've been ministering to, but the *vast* amount of people—" She sighed. "This really stunned me!"

"Me too!" her husband agreed. "I was *amazed!* There were *hun*dreds of people that came through the house. Forty and fifty at a time."

"Other people came in the house to pray for him?" I asked.

Although I was certain many would be drawn out of curiosity to the bizarre drama, I thought they would watch from the street, as bystanders, out of both respect and squeamishness. Nevertheless, Reverend Walker assured me, "Right, to pray." When Timothy suggested, "Some just came to watch," his father insisted, "Very few. They may have watched, but a lot of people prayed too." He shook his head in awe. "I was *a-mazed* how they found out so quick and how so many came!"

"That's the thing I can't figure out," Timothy puzzled, excitement building within him. "The word was put out so fast you wouldn't believe it! We had people calling from Indiana and Michigan and—"

"People you knew?"

"See, we're known *all* over the country," the boy explained. "We've been in forty-eight states doin' revivals."

"Must have been people from ten or fifteen states," Reverend Walker vouched.

"He was just so well liked," Timothy said. "And we've only lived here—how long? Five years?"

The evangelist confirmed the figure. "Almost five, and the casket wasn't opened either. That keeps a lot of people from coming if the casket's closed."

"I just laid a picture on the casket, his football picture," Timothy said. In a sports shirt and jeans, a baseball cap on his curly red hair, he looked like a typical seventeen-year-old, yet the topics that excited him were not those the average teenager cared about. Unlike most, his heroes were not Michael Jackson or Madonna but rather Jesus Christ, the late A. A. Allen, and his older brother, Tommy. As he and the Walkers related events surrounding the drowning, there seemed a need that transcended normal family pride to make Tommy larger than life, to impress the world with his preaching, his popularity, his musical talent, his athletic prowess. I wondered if this eulogy was a catharsis, to replace the tears they had not cried, or if they indeed believed he was more than an ordinary teenager.

When I asked how long Tommy had been a minister, his father answered "Oh," in the sense of a long, long time, adding "He was out preaching when he was in diapers and the guy across the street yelled at him, told him to shut up and quit that preaching, and he said, Mister, you didn't call me to preach and you're not going to tell me when to quit. And the fella cursed at him and told him to go to, uh, hell." Reverend Walker laughed, self-conscious about repeating the word. "He said, Mister, you may meet God and go there sooner than you think, and that night they carried the man out feet first. He was dead."

"Died of a heart attack," Timothy explained.

Reverend Walker himself had been in the ministry full time for twenty-seven years. Although christened an Episcopalian, he had joined the Pentecostal faith when he was seventeen. A year later he began preaching. After studying at the Assemblies of God's Central Bible Institute in Springfield, Missouri, he evangelized and pastored small, independent churches, and eventually embraced the Holiness tradition. He and Naomi met when she played the piano for a revival he conducted at her home church. They migrated east in 1969, finally settling in Campbell County, Tennessee, in the late 1970s. For the most part, Reverend Walker was away from home a month or more at a time. Each year when school was out she and their six sons would join him, with Naomi assisting in the music as she had as a youth in the Assemblies of God, the Salvation Army, and various independent Pentecostal churches. The two no longer identified with a denomination, classifying themselves as "independent Holiness." For now, they planned to conduct a summer-long revival in the tent, borrowed for a sum of ten percent of whatever offerings they collected. By fall they hoped to have raised the down payment for a church of their own.

As the interview unfolded, I realized the Walkers and their followers lived in a world that transcended the everyday and provided meaning for their lives. The people I had observed at the funeral seemed out of step with the rest of society. Most had little education, were poorly dressed, and drove dilapidated cars and trucks. Although Reverend and Mrs. Walker said they themselves had attended high school, their lot appeared no better than that of their followers: their own car was falling apart and their house was poorly furnished. Yet their religion transformed what might otherwise have been a drab, lonely existence into an exciting world filled with miracles and with heroes and villains. It was a world in which they "belonged" and in which only God controlled their destinies. Their lives were not compartmentalized, with church a twice-on-Sunday, once-during-the-week affair that remained separate from their work and recreation. Rather, everything had religious meaning. Even the worldly goods they could not afford became sinful in their moral code. Not indulging in jewelry, makeup, flashy clothes, beauty parlors, and movies set them apart—in their view—as God's special children.

At times Naomi Walker seemed to assume the role of a Virgin Mary in the eyes of their followers, for unlike most revivalists I encountered, Reverend Walker did not fill the usual role as God's "mouthpiece," or "right-hand" man. Even while conducting the funeral, he seemed a lesser figure, perhaps a Joseph. The drowning and the attempt to raise Tommy from the dead eerily paralleled the death and resurrection of Christ, with Timothy cast as the risen Messiah. Just as the schoolteacher had speculated that God may have taken Tommy's life to make way for Timothy's ministry, the Walkers also seemed to recognize their son's new role. During our interview the parents frequently sought his guidance as to what I should be allowed to quote, just as they had placed Tommy's fate in the younger son's hands, allowing him to decide whether the resurrection attempt should continue or the body be turned over to the mortician.

A train's whistle howled long and lonely somewhere off in the distance, its cries becoming more urgent as it approached, until the train itself finally rattled and roared past, maybe a block or so away from the house. Reverend Walker and Timothy seemed not to hear, intent instead on cataloging the phone calls from people and congregations—many the family didn't know—claiming to also have experienced resurrections and assuring the family they too were conducting prayer services for Tommy.

"A lot of churches filled up just to pray for him," Reverend Walker said with satisfaction.

"Our own crowds went from about seventy to two hundred," Timothy noted.

"Yeah," the father agreed. "Many people have come to me and said, Brother Walker, we *know* now that you practice what you preach."

In another part of the house a telephone rang, and Naomi Walker left the room to answer it. Reverend Walker paused, following her with his eyes. When he again looked at me I thought I detected in him a sense of resignation, an emptiness. "Looking back," he said, "I realize now God *did* finally reveal to me when I woke up the morning of the funeral, the Lord spoke to me through song. The Lord speaks to me a lot when I wake up," he digressed. "It'll be maybe a phrase of a song, like just one line'll be going over and over in my mind, maybe for *hours*, and I'll know that God is speaking to me through that. It's happened *innumerable* times," he said, "and that morning that song was going over in my mind about singing around the Master's throne. By the time—" Unable to recall the lyrics, he turned to Timothy. "How's it go?"

The son prompted, "By the time they find me missing, I'll be living over there."

"That song was going over in my mind," Reverend Walker said, "the same one."

"The funny thing about that song," Timothy said, "that was his favorite song but he'd never sing it. He always wanted *me* to. And that's what we had put on his tombstone—singing around the Master's throne."

As the father and son reconstructed those final days and hours before Tommy's death, Timothy was eager that I know his brother's last words and the most minute details of his final comings and goings and his plans for the future. The two brothers had shared a room, jointly conducted revivals, and performed with John as a trio, yet Timothy's recollections seemed more than simply those of a boy who idolized his older brother. His tone was proud, boastful, but equally filled with awe, especially when he told of Tommy appearing to him in a vision shortly before the body was taken to the funeral home.

"I had been praying for about forty-five minutes," he recalled, "and I just felt, I looked and he was just—just like my brother sitting right here." He gestured toward one of the younger boys. "He was standing right beside me, put his hand on my shoulder, and he said, I love you, he said, but you're gonna have to do my work because I can't do it. I told him, I said, *No*, I can't, I don't want it, no, *please*. And he said, You have to, and that was all he said." The urgency vanished from Timothy's voice. "I didn't see him anymore, but it just seemed like I could feel him with me in the tent for a couple of hours. Then I went on down to the mortuary and helped pick out the casket."

Absolving God seemed crucial to the evangelist and his followers so that their belief in Him and the truth of the Bible would not be undermined. "I can only explain why God permitted this to happen to me," Reverend Walker said. "There were personal reasons, no doubt, in Tommy's life that was the reason why God took him. The Lord knowing all things, even from the beginning, it's very possible

Tommy reached the peak of his consecration so God took him for him to reap the greatest reward. He was getting ready to go preach, and he really made a good consecration," he said with fatherly pride. "Preached a *tremendous* sermon—His last sermon was at Mount Olive, a black Baptist church. The preacher got the Holy Ghost in that revival. He'd been saved for *forty-eight* years, and he got filled with the Spirit and started speaking in tongues. And you know, Tommy's last sermon was faith to raise the dead."

From another room came the one-sided questions and observations of a telephone conversation. As Reverend Walker stopped to listen to his wife's muffled words, the air grew heavy with remembrances of events that seemed removed by more than a day. We sat silent for a moment, until like a cloud the heaviness lifted.

"The funeral was a joyful service," I observed. "Being from New Orleans, I have been to jazz funerals, but even there you see crying and I saw none yesterday. Were most people's faith so strong they were joyful and hopeful throughout?"

"Most of the people that came to pray were not joyful," the evangelist said soberly. "I don't guess any of them were joyful."

Suddenly Timothy exploded with boyish exuberance. "The thing was, boy, when it came time for that funeral, ever'body—I guess ever'body had been praying that day, and there was such an atmosphere in that service you wouldn't believe it! When we took the casket in, buddy, you couldn't hear a word!" In his excitement, Timothy stumbled over his words like any awkward adolescent. "I mean, that church went wild, that tent. They started shouting, like, I mean ever'body was on their feet. *Ever'body!* I looked to see, and there wasn't a soul in that tent sitting down!"

As Naomi Walker returned to the room, Timothy looked to her with admiration. "You didn't cry one time at that funeral, did you?" he said.

"No," she answered softly. "No, in fact—and I don't say this boastfully. I say it because it was fact. I could understand why other people were so grieved and heartbroken, but the way I had of expressing my love to my son was to stand for what he believed. This is what he wanted, and this is what I gave him." She drew tall as she recalled entering the tent the morning of the funeral. "I went to the organ and I sat down. It was a *straaange* experience," she said dramatically, light laughter creeping into her voice, "but I began playing 'Power in the

Blood,' and the expression that came over the congregation was absolute *shock.* Ab-so-lute shock!"

Bessie Utley's soft little voice interrupted. "It was you, then, that was playing the organ?"

"Oh, *yes!*" Naomi Walker said proudly. "I was playing the organ and I jumped up and went to dancing and then Bobby took the organ and I told them, I said, Dance that thing in here!"

"Well, I was leaping while we were bringing the casket in," Reverend Walker emphasized. "A lot of people were sure we had to be on tranquilizers, to be able to have the spirit we had."

"Praise God," Bessie Utley exclaimed, "we don't need 'em, do we?"

"No," Reverend Walker allowed, "we don't even believe in taking aspirins." He chuckled, and then, struck by a new realization, remarked, "You know, I've never seen a funeral like this!"

"The only one I know that even come close was Brother Pryor's," Bessie Utley offered. "They had speaking in tongues and messages."

"Did they shout and dance?" Reverend Walker asked.

"Now, I wasn't at the funeral," the old woman admitted, "but I know they had messages come through."

Timothy emphasized, "There were prophesies given *yesterday,*" and his father, nodding agreeably, added, "You can have messages and prophesies and still not have much joy."

Joy. The mere word triggered a new outburst from Timothy. "Boy, there was enough joy *yesterday* in that tent! *Shooo!*"

"I mean, I've never heard of a funeral like that," Reverend Walker repeated. "Never have."

Bessie Utley tiptoed from the room, returning shortly to report, "On that other funeral, they did dance and shout and praise the Lord and they had messages come through."

"Oh, *goooood,*" Reverend Walker said. "Where was that?"

"In California," the grandmother replied. "It was at the funeral home, however, but they danced and shouted and got messages and interpreted them."

"Oh, *gooooood,*" he echoed, "just like ours."

"Well," she hesitated, her eyes sparkling, "they probably didn't dance and shout as much as we did," she said, as if to preserve the uniqueness of her grandson's funeral, "but they did dance and shout."

Timothy spoke up bravely. "Many people ask me myself, they say,

I don't understand this, they say, we're supposed to be comforting you, but here you are comforting us."

His father nodded knowingly. "That's the way it was with all of us," he said. "I've been preaching this all my life, but I've never had a chance to demonstrate it, to *actually* experience the death of a loved one and still rejoice, even when I was putting the dirt on the casket, you know, shouting and speaking in tongues." His voice shimmered like the delicate tinkling of a tambourine. "Hallelujah, I knew when I could do that I had the victory."

Both Reverend Walker and his wife saw only good resulting from their son's death. They spoke optimistically of the souls that were already being saved and of the growth they had observed in Timothy. They remained equally convinced that God did indeed raise the dead.

"I wouldn't hesitate a minute to pray for somebody else in this same situation," Naomi Walker said firmly. "This is the ultimate: to raise the dead, to cast out devils, to heal the sick. This is what revival is, to revive the saints."

"By their faith and joy and love," her husband contributed.

"Revival is when God's people take hold of faith and put it in action," she said. "And the more you believe God, the more you *can* believe Him. You don't always *see* everything you believe that He'll do," she conceded. "I have a brother that had some of his fingers cut off. Now, I believe God can put those fingers back on his hand just as easy as I can believe God for anything. And just because He *doesn't* do it, doesn't mean I don't believe He can. It wouldn't surprise me in the least if God would do this."

"So you *would* do it again," I concluded.

"I'd be *more* ready to do it now than then," Reverend Walker replied. "There's *hundreds* of people around here that didn't *really* believe in raising the dead before this incident. And even though Tommy did not rise from the dead, just bringing the scripture to their attention and just the idea that somebody would *dare* to have, as some would say, the audacity to *attempt* it—it just *really* stirred people till they really, actually believe that it's possible."

Softly, yet firmly, came Bessie Utley's little voice, "It is possible."

CHAPTER III

R. W. SCHAMBACH:
God's Super Salesman

The big voice bounded above the barrage of shrieks and hallelujahs: "This is *not* the World Series." *Noooooooooo!* "This is not the *Super Bowl.*" *Noooooooooo!* "This is a Holy Ghost revival!" *Yeaaaaaaaaaa!* "This is your radio host R. W. Schambach greeting you from under the big gospel tent in Baker, Louisiana." *Hallelujah!* "Thousands of people are assembled, and we are seeing God move mightily." *Thankyajeezusssss!* "Souls are being borne into the kingdom of God. Miracles of healing are taking place. And people are being filled with the Holy Ghost." *Praise the Lord!* "So this is Brother Schambach urging you to stay tuned for the next fourteen minutes."

The scoreboard clock was being overhauled at a factory back East, yet the broadcast portion of the revival moved with snap-the-finger precision through a foot-stomping gospel duo, several well-rehearsed testimonies, and teasers for the upcoming services, with the main message to be lifted from the sermon and spliced in before air time the next morning. There were no cue cards. Only the revivalist's prodding and prompting, to stand, cheer, applaud, to shout hallelujah, and the people—three thousand or more—eagerly complied. Like God's super salesman the evangelist promised to "preach the arthritis right out of your joints," lay hands by proxy, and pray an eightfold blessing on children to keep them from sin, disease, drug addiction, alcohol, accidents, and homosexuality. "So come on out," he urged, "and let God do something for you!"

With a grand, sweeping gesture he signaled the tent audience to its feet, beamed his voice toward heaven, and, on behalf of those car-radio listeners who "may be running from God," prevailed upon the Holy Ghost to "stop them in their tracks!" His tone switched from soft to savage. "Satan," he warned, "you're trespassing on God's property. I command you to *loo-oose* your hold!" Then, turning to the audience, he boomed, "Be thou healed and receive a *miracle*!" Above the collective amen he coached the crowd, "Keep both hands raised, will ya? Just go ahead and pray, everybody. Shout a little while I bring this broadcast to a close." Like a radio sportscaster, he began his fast-paced wind-up. "This is Brother Schambach inviting all our friends to the big gospel tent in Baker, Louisiana—now through Sunday—on the grounds of Bethany Baptist Church. Three services *every* day. Ten o'clock—two-thirty—and seven-thirty. This is your radio minister R. W. Schambach reminding you—*You* don't have any trouble. All—you—need—is—faith—in—God! And eve-ry-body shouted—"

A-A-AMEN!

Under the sharp noonday sun, the tractor-trailer trucks had lost their shadows, the four of them neatly, evenly parallel to one another and perpendicular to the tent with the word POWER across the front of each in bold, block letters and on the sides, JESUS SAVES—HEALS—DELIVERS. Hovering above, a miniature plastic zeppelin heralded SCHAMBACH REVIVALS INC. One of the rigs had hauled the vinyl; another, the poles; still another, the sound equipment and bookstand merchandise; and the fourth—the one that thrummed and whirred—two generators, the life-line for the revival and for five house trailers that lined a nearby fence. A fifth rig was en route from headquarters in Tyler, Texas, carrying an additional two thousand chairs to accommodate the growing crowds.

The tent was the largest I could recall seeing, the size of those colossal big tops that rise up in childhood memories of circuses and then loom larger with the intervening years until they bear little resemblance to reality: almost $90,000 worth of vinyl, poles, and cables. The robin's-egg-blue top could easily have spanned a city block with yardage to spare. And the prayer tent, a small replica that stood nearby, would have excited many a fledgling evangelist.

Sounds of the morning service drifted from the larger tent: the smooth, soothing baritone of the Reverend Arvell Garrett pleading, virtually singing, *"Let Him do it! Let Him fix it! Let Him give it to you now-ow!"* It was more like summer than early November, and the outside brightness silhouetted the small group of people clustered around the platform. *"The Lord move in yo' circumstances . . . as nobody else can do. Hallelu-jah . . . halleloo-OO-JAH!"* A stand of drums stood idle with only the organ and the people's murmurs and moans accompanying his chanting, yet there was no need for other instruments. The black evangelist was in and of himself an orchestra of strings, woodwinds, timpani, a human harp as his full, rich voice gracefully glided and whirled in a melodious symphony that levitated the soul.

The rest of Baker's population—a township that had grown toward and become a part of Baton Rouge—was tending the state's business and the refineries, chemical plants, and wharves that line the Mississippi, their shift work making it possible to draw crowds to three services a day instead of the usual nightly one conducted in most areas. The morning service—"Breakfast with Jesus," as Brother Garrett preferred to call it—had been attracting 100 to 150 people. And in the afternoons about 25 showed up to hear associate evangelist Dave Bryant.

For off-duty members of Schambach's team, the lyrical praise was a spiritual Muzak for their daily chores. As I neared the mobile homes, a young man approached with a stack of mail, handing out an envelope here and there to the men and women who surrounded him, reaching, eagerly reading over his shoulder. Billy McCullough watched until the last letter had been distributed, then ambled off toward the huge tractor-trailers, disappearing between two of the rigs. I found him next to the truck that housed the generators, measuring a length of pipe for storage racks he and his tent crew were constructing under one of the rigs. He had the build of a scrubbed-up roustabout, his body short and solid, his arms muscular and hard, his hands calloused and scarred. One thumbnail was blackened, and he wore a turquoise-and-silver wedding band. He spoke the eclectic language of the road, the collected accents and colloquialisms of a childhood spent following his father from factory to factory. Even now he was a restive man, the kind with no ties who is always ready to pick up and go, as he had in 1962 when he drove a car from California to Arizona for A. A. Allen's tent manager and stayed on with the evangelist for two years. He had joined Schambach's team under similar circumstances. Except for a brief leave he had worked for the revivalist since 1973, and neither he nor his wife of fifteen years had any desire to settle down. Last year he had been elevated to tent manager, a position that placed him in charge of the mammoth tent, the trucks and mobile homes, the equipment, and ten people—including wives. At the revivals I had attended, tent managers were the unsung heroes who put up the tent and took it down, and nursed it through high winds and thunderstorms. They took a backseat to the evangelistic team, the revival stars. Nevertheless, at thirty-eight Billy McCullough had not outgrown the childlike excitement that comes with first responsibilities and power, and he spoke of his work with a quiet pride. The six men on his crew worked split shifts: half of them were on duty from eight in the morning until one o'clock, the others from one to six, with the entire force returning for the evening service. A watchman patrolled the grounds until the morning shift returned. When Schambach and the platform team conducted auditorium meetings, Billy McCullough and his crew traveled ahead to the next location to erect the tent and, if time permitted, patch and mend the vinyl and service the equipment.

"We never get caught up," he said as he stretched an expandable ruler over the pipe, pausing to mentally record the length. "Like yesterday I had *ever' one* of the guys servicing the trucks. We changed the oil, the filters, done ever'thang to the trucks." He studied the sky. "And now this afternoon we're gonna try an' wash 'em all."

"What does a member of the tent crew have to know how to do?" I asked.

"Almost ever'thang," he replied with an air of importance. "I try to hire a man that does a little of ever'thang an's not a master of any of 'em. Usually if I hire a man that's a professional, I find he's not good for nothin' except for what he's a professional at. If you hire a truck driver, that's all you get is a truck driver, an' if you hire an organist —like we've got one of the finest organists there is but that's all that man is good for."

Although the wives didn't help erect the tent, they too shared in the work, setting up chairs, arranging the platform, and handling bookstand sales. On the road, McCullough's own wife kept books. "If we have to get permits on the trucks, she usually takes care of that," he said. "Ever' state we go in we have to have a fuel permit, a temporary permit for all the trucks. It's a road-tax permit, you might say. A highway-use tax."

"How much does it cost to go through a state with five trucks?"

"It can vary from three dollars to twenty dollars, usually not no more than that," he estimated. "Once in a while we'll have to get a trip permit, like a license plate, to go across a state. They usually cost twenty dollars, but they can go fifty, sixty dollars, some of 'em."

Arrangements for the grounds and for putting up the tent were made by an advance man who traveled year-round scouting for land, obtaining the necessary insurance and legal papers, meeting with local pastors, and setting up publicity—tasks that could keep him in an area as long as two months. Copies of his transactions—the names and telephone numbers of property owners and officials, and a list of local codes—were passed on to Schambach, his son Bobby, and Billy McCullough.

"That paper'll tell us ever'thang we need to know," McCullough explained. "It'll tell us if we need permits an' it'll give us all the phone numbers for the Port-o-Johns or anythang we need to do."

He glanced toward a young man pumping oil into the generators, Schambach Miracle Revival Inc.'s most recent acquisition at an expenditure of $25,000. "One runs in the main service," he told me, "an' the other one, a smaller generator, in the daytime." It was too soon to determine the operating costs, but to keep both going around the clock would run roughly fifty dollars a day, including maintenance—cheaper than the electricity bills in many locations and certainly more convenient. "Sometimes when we'd go into a city it was hard to get hooked up an' hard to get *unhooked*," he complained. "Now we can pull onto a lot an' three days later start havin' church."

Again Billy McCullough surveyed the tent, the trucks—his domain. "We have a pretty sophisticated electrical system," he boasted. "We have lighted exit signs. We have emergency lights, an' our tent, I believe, could pass any code in America. It's fireproof. It won't burn. Our poles is aluminum an' they won't burn." He smiled proudly. "We try to keep ever'thang up to date."

It was one o'clock and Billy McCullough, off duty now, invited me to meet his wife, Gabby. She was a soft-spoken woman, as plain and unpretentious as the couple's trailer. From a broken home, she too had had a transient childhood, moving with her mother from Oregon to Colorado at age three and later to Arizona where she met Billy. Like her husband, she seemed shy and insecure. She sat quietly while he talked about the problems of a tent manager: the threat of wind and rain, the stringent fire and electrical codes, sometimes discovering the advance man hadn't obtained the proper permits. The biggest difficulty, Billy McCullough conceded, was keeping good help. "Ever'body thinks it's real glamorous travelin' out here on the road," he said. "They like to go to church an' they like the tent meetin's, but when they get out here an' realize it's not jist go to church. You gotta drive to the meetin's. You gotta put the tent up, tear the tent down. You gotta maintain the trucks. An' the women, lotta times they come out here an' they get lonely an' homesick an' after a while they wanta go home, an' they do."

In the course of my research I had wondered about the loneliness of confronting a new town, new faces every week or so, month after month, year after year, with no predictable end in sight; the isolation of the little trailers huddled in the midst of the crowds; the chance to see family only at Christmas or when the revival passed through or near their hometowns. On the highway the seclusion was even greater, for the men drove the eighteen wheelers and the wives, in pickups, pulled the trailers—each driving alone.

"That must be lonely traveling," I said now. "You don't even have company, do you?"

"Well, we all got two-way radios in our vehicles," Billy McCullough said, "so we can keep in communications."

"And we play a lotta tapes," Gabby added softly.

Earlier when the young man was distributing the mail, joy had spread through the living quarters. I had watched the expressions of antici-pation, excitement, and disappointment for those who, like Billy McCullough, walked away empty-handed.

"Is that a special moment when you arrive in a city and have a letter waiting?" I asked.

Billy shook his head. "Not really, 'cause nobody really writes us much," he said. "Most of the time when people starts travelin' like we do and as long as we have, you lose all the friends you've left behind. Eventually you're not in contact with 'em. They move, you know, an' they don't write for six months or a year, an' it's got to a point now where we really don't have anybody *to* write to us."

"Do you regret that?"

"I don't regret it at all because we pick up new friends out here," he assured me. "We go in a city an' we meet people an' stuff. Now we won't hear from them people, but If we go back to that city they're always at our meetin's."

Several nights earlier I had arrived at the grounds to find most of the crew away having dinner at the home of a local revivalgoer. Now when I asked if their host had been someone they previously had known, Billy McCullough cocked his head, puzzled.

"That night when you all went out to dinner," I reminded him, "was that at the home of somebody you already knew?"

Recognition crossed his face. "No, them was new friends that we'd jist made. *Now* them people'll probably be our friends ever'time we're in this area."

I remembered a conversation with another revival worker about the reluctance of most outsiders to befriend the evangelistic team. "People are a little standoffish," she had commented. "I don't know if they're afraid we don't want to be bothered or what. They're nice and they speak, but as far as coming and knocking on your door and saying, Hi, how about coming to my house for coffee—people don't do that very often."

Nevertheless, Billy McCullough insisted, "We make friends an' meet 'em all over the country an' a lotta times we'll go back into a city an' they'll invite us over to their home for dinner." Sometimes he and Gabby had people to their trailer, mostly for lunch, since at night it doubled as an office and a place for Schambach to relax. The fact they couldn't truly call the trailer *their* home did not bother them. They were willing, even eager, to make any sacrifice to be counted among God's servants—whatever the capacity.

"Do you think you will ever be an evangelist?" I asked.

He shook his head. "All of us can't be preachers," he reasoned. "Somebody has to put these tents up an' move the trucks an' help in other areas. I witness to people an' I talk to them about the Lord an' I enjoy it, but far as will I be an evangelist or a preacher, no, I feel like this is the call of God on my life, to be a tent manager or a—" He turned to his wife. "What is it?"

Softly she prompted, "A minister of helps."

Later, when I stopped by Gaye Bryant's mobile home, she was preparing a grocery list. At twenty-eight she was wholesomely pretty, with thick, dark hair worn long and loose on the platform and pinned up now for relief against the heat and humidity. Her eyes and her voice hinted of private enthusiasms: with becoming a star of big-time revivalism, and with receiving standing ovations and seeing her photograph on record albums—the ultimate dream, I imagined, of a Pentecostal young person with musical ambitions. She had been raised in one of the almost 2,500 Foursquare Gospel churches started by Aimee Semple McPherson, who—at Gaye's age—tasted her first success as a traveling faith healer. The Bryants themselves had been on the evangelistic circuit since they graduated from Mount Vernon Nazarene College in Ohio in 1973, traveling first on their own and then with Schambach as his featured singers. Dave Bryant also preached the afternoon services and for six months had been the elder revivalist's "platform man."

Once a year the couple made a missionary trip abroad, and mementos from those ecclesiastical excursions decorated the trailer: a carved giraffe from Africa, wooden shoes from Holland, a brass vase from India. In the course of their work, they had owned three mobile homes of varying shapes and sizes. This one consisted of a living room, bedroom, kitchen, and bath.

"Life on the road is just about like in a house, except you're always in a different place," Gaye Bryant said as she showed me through the trailer. "You do basically the same things. Clean, vacuum, make the bed, make breakfast, do the dishes, go here, go there, go to the grocery, do the laundry."

In the cotton dirndl skirt and terry-cloth top, she looked like a college coed, even as she rehearsed her daily routine and told how she scoured the supermarkets for sales. "You have to be a good steward out here so if I find lots of bargains I'll stock up." Like many women, she enjoyed checking out the shopping malls and especially looked forward to Schambach's annual month-long camp meeting when she could settle in and get to know a community. While their belief in faith healing eliminated the need for doctors, scheduling other appointments posed a problem—one she and her husband solved by going to walk-in dental clinics and postponing eye examinations until the longer revivals.

Although the tent and evangelistic teams—including Schambach and his son Bobby—received regular paychecks, Dave and Gaye Bryant preferred to "live by faith," she said, explaining "That's just trusting the Lord to bring in the finances and not having a set income. We don't draw a salary from Brother Schambach, but he does give us an offering, usually every meeting or every other meeting—however the Lord leads him. Plus we sell our records in the meetings, which helps us financially, and he does give us gas expense."

Their other expenses seemed minimal: insurance premiums, payments on the trailer and an extra car, clothing, and food, which I had seen revivalgoers bring in by the boxfuls. I was certain "living by faith" was not easy, but the Bryants appeared to have fared well. Their mobile home was new and tastefully furnished, and while their clothes were not expensive, neither were they secondhand bargains other, less prosperous workers made do with. Once a year they went to Africa, India, or Europe—trips many young married couples could ill afford. Nevertheless, Gaye Bryant viewed their bills as "just like everybody else" observing, "The Lord always meets the needs. Like when we feel it's time to go overseas, the Lord always brings the money in."

Across the trailer a parakeet screeched and chirped, and Gaye Bryant laughed. "Pepper's helping me out." She and Dave had bought the bird a month ago to replace another one that, she boasted, could say its name and "Praise the Lord." Although none of the five couples associated with Schambach had children, most owned pets. On the road year round except for a Christmas break, the couples, and the Schambachs and four single men who stayed in motels were like a family. They shared the good times and the bad; they were loving and at times quarrelsome.

"Any time you have different personalities you're gonna have clashes," Gaye Bryant was candid. "There's days when you rub each other wrong. You wanta say Get out of my hair! But you just have to let the love of Jesus overrule those things and try to get'em out of your heart." She treasured those few nights when she and Dave accompanied Schambach to his auditorium engagements and the couple could check into a camp ground, alone. "Sometimes you enjoy being by yourself and doing what you want to do and not have to answer to anybody or have anybody knock on your door. Nobody knows you. Nobody bothers you. But then you get to thinking, I'll be glad when we get back to the tent, and you start missing everybody."

Sounds of the afternoon service drifted from the tent. In four days this revival would end and the team would fold up tent and drive 150 miles to Beaumont, Texas, and the cycle would begin again: erecting the tent and setting chairs, running cords and water lines to the trailers, unpacking the odds and ends that turned their trailers into "home." The revivals were like links in an unending chain. While attending a fifteen-day revival in Knoxville, I had found it increasingly difficult to muster the energy and motivation to shower and dress for another night's service. I longed just to remain in my room and relax, and I wondered if the evangelistic team shared my waning enthusiasm as the days wore on. But when I asked Gaye Bryant if she ever wanted to take the night off, she answered no. "It's always pretty exciting," she insisted. "Brother Schambach's services are all different. They're not dull by any means." Even when she did feel tired in the body, her reluctance was short-lived. She was, after all, expected to be on the platform every night, and the Lord did bless faithfulness.

The last strains of the altar call had died away, and I could hear people rustling past. The door to the trailer opened, and Dave Bryant entered. Perspiration darkened his long-sleeved shirt and beaded his brow, and Gaye hurried to prepare him a glass of iced tea. He was a personable young man, almost thirty, of medium height, with neat blond hair, gold-rimmed aviator glasses, and a North Carolina drawl. Unlike his wife, he had not been raised Pentecostal and, in fact, as a child attended church only once, for a Christmas pageant. He played in a rock 'n' roll band until he was saved during a revival when he was sixteen. After that, he burned a two-thousand-dollar record collection and, for a time, put away his guitar, convinced his music was "a work of darkness." When he picked it up again, it was to play a new song for the Lord, a song with a similar rhythm but decidedly different lyrics.

Although this afternoon's audience had amounted to thirty people at most, Dave Bryant was undaunted. "It's hit or miss," he said philosophically. "In different cities people have different life-styles, and it just so happens that here people can get out in the morning. In Puyallup, Washington, I was running about a hundred fifty, two hundred people, sometimes three hundred."

Overall, he reckoned, it was easier for an unknown evangelist to draw crowds in the North. "The South, in a way, has been spoiled by having an abundance of this type of ministry," he said. "We've had tents for years and years and years. Little tents, big tents, and people, they're almost at a place to where you've almost gotta top the guy that was there before."

"Do you ever feel that a service goes badly?" I asked.

"There's times the Devil tries to hinder services," Dave Bryant acknowledged. "We've had *all* kinds of things happen. People come in and try to attack us or try to steal the offering or—"

I cut in. "You really have had that happen?"

"Oh, yeah," he was emphatic. "Sometimes you'll be preaching and somebody'll stand up in the middle of the congregation and start yelling at the top of their lungs."

"How do you handle somebody like that?" I asked.

"You just have to take authority over 'em," he said coolly, "and if they don't calm down then you have to remove 'em. We don't have bouncers or anything like that, but we have ushers take them to the back and try to calm 'em down. Obviously you've never seen anything like that."

"I have," I responded, "I was just wondering what you did."

"Well, I'll just say you take authority over them," Dave Bryant said flatly, "because when you're preaching you're the one that God's using to bring the message. It's out of order for anybody to stand up and try to interject when the Spirit's flowing through you and using you to minister to the whole congregation."

His reasoning surprised me. Many Pentecostal preachers considered themselves God's mouthpiece and prepared neither a written sermon nor an outline, relying solely on His direct inspiration. In some less sophisticated services, that anointing might just as easily fall upon a member of the congregation so that one was never certain who would preach on a given night. Even so, Dave Bryant firmly believed such behavior was out of order and had to be dealt with.

"I've seen people stand up and say *all* kinds of things," he said, "just crazy, off-the-wall stuff."

"Those must be difficult moments," I remarked.

He agreed. "Big cities, especially. Maybe they come in drunk or they're high, been smoking marijuana and they'll come in, they're mad and sometimes they'll take a swing at you. In fact, there was a preacher in New Orleans just two weeks ago from High Point, North Carolina, my hometown, a man walked in the tent and shot him on the platform."

As it turned out, Bryant was mistaken about location. The murder had occurred in Topsy, a small community in southwest Louisiana. On the fourth night of a ten-day revival, the Reverend Willie Odell Bowman was standing behind the platform with open Bible in hand waiting to be introduced, when a young man shot him through the heart with a double-barreled derringer. While few disturbances were of this magnitude, revivals over the years had attracted their share of problems. The Klan had been known to threaten more liberal evangelists and break up integrated meetings. Billy McCullough also had told of attempts to steal the offering and warned me to keep a close eye on my pocketbook. His own wife's purse had been stolen during a recent revival in Philadelphia. In my travels I had witnessed several minor incidents—one in which a woman loudly objected to something the evangelist said and then left in a huff.

In spite of the hazards, Dave Bryant had aspirations to again have his own ministry and considered working with Schambach valuable preparation. "I'm sitting under one of the best," he said. "We feel God's teaching us a lot of things while we're here. Maybe when we go out we'll do it different, 'cause God doesn't want everybody to be the same. But I believe what we've learned can be incorporated in a very powerful way into our ministry and while we're raising up people to preach the gospel, of course we know how to lay hands on the sick and pray for 'em and to see all their needs met also."

"When you say you know how to lay on hands and pray for the sick, do you study that in Bible college, or is that something that comes from praying?" I asked.

"It's like Paul said in the Word. He said, I haven't come in enticing words of man's wisdom, but, he said, I've come in power and demonstration. That's what I mean when I say we're learning. Brother Schambach has been preaching and laying hands on people for *years*, and I can kind of draw from him some things he's went through and he's been wise in and he knows about that I don't know about."

Dave Bryant viewed his relationship to Schambach as that of a son and described the elder evangelist as a very loving man. "He's probably the hardest-working preacher in America," he said with obvious admiration. "I've never seen anybody that lays hands on as many people as he does and preaches like a house afire, for an hour, hour and a half, two hours sometimes. It's easier to put the tent up and take it down than it is to get under it and preach."

Schambach assumed the roles of all twelve apostles, the Devil, and a Jesus who sounded remarkably like the workaday folks in the audience as he reenacted the familiar biblical account of Christ walking on water. Swinging the microphone behind him, the evangelist drew back with exaggerated surprise. "*It's Jesus*," he comically mimicked the startled disciples upon discovering their leader strolling toward them on the choppy sea. Then in another accent and still another: "That *ain't* Him, man. That's just somebody that *looks* like Him. He's *walkin'* on water! He never done *that* before! Awwwwwwww, that can't be Him! That's His ghost!"

The service had been in progress for almost two hours, but except for the fretful cries of babies fighting sleep there were no symptoms of restlessness, of minds meandering. It was as if the evangelist had cast a giant net over the crowd, captivating it with a topic normally considered anything but amusing. As the story unfolded, the people sat on edge, rapt, responding with laughter and applause that would have gladdened the most seasoned trouper. And indeed the performance was akin to a vaudeville act, the revivalist playing the entire cast of characters in a one-man Bible extravaganza.

As Schambach paced the platform delivering his lines, he reminded me of Charles Laughton. Like the late actor, he was a man of sizable proportions. But there was more than his physical appearance, more than the pink shirt, baby-blue suit, and graying blond curls that commanded, indeed demanded attention. Schambach's presence equaled his girth. At fifty-five he was a pro. He had learned at the side of the late A. A. Allen—described by one writer in the 1960s as "the nation's topmost tent-toting, old-fashioned evangelical roarer"—and for another twenty-odd years he refined that craft in rented halls and under his own canvas. Like his mentor, he had perfected the biblical vignette made popular by Billy Sunday. And he knew how to play to an audience: his tone, his timing, his expressions were flawless. He spoke the language of his laboring-class followers, putting *aint*'s and double negatives into the mouths of everyone from God on down to Satan—not condescendingly, but to appeal to the people, to put them at ease, and because as one of twelve children raised on a railroader's pay he too had been versed in that same vocabulary.

Unlike most evangelists I had observed, Schambach was virtually his own "front" or platform man. After allowing young Dave Bryant to lead a few songs, the elder revivalist, with jacket removed, vest unbuttoned, got down to the business of warming up the crowd, selling, singing, shuffling, sometimes striding back and forth across the platform, the microphone cord draped around his neck as he banged a tambourine from hip to hand. The talents that had gained him name recognition during those early days with Allen were apparent as his smooth voice soared above the crowd's singing, leading, musically massaging their souls, as much entertainer as preacher and faith healer. The dual roles were not unusual. Pentecostal ministers have long recognized the importance of music in their preparation so that many young aspirants to the pulpit take up singing and musical instruments—most often the guitar. In his autobiography, Allen wrote of the role rhythm and music played in his youth, acknowledging his "first ambitions were to be an entertainer, a musician, or a singer, perhaps an actor." His successor Don Stewart once said of the late evangelist: "When he walked into the tent, every eye was on him." The same observation could be made about Schambach, for his presence filled the big tent. Several people I interviewed compared him to his mentor, with one veteran revivalist describing his style as "absolutely Allen personified." But while many had questioned Triple A's conduct, Schambach, most agreed, was above reproach.

Due in part to his own humble beginnings in Harrisburg, Pennsylvania, Schambach had chosen not to follow the hell-and-damnation route of most revivalists but, like a modern-day Moses, to lead an already beleaguered people out of despair. Even when he chastised, he did so in a light-hearted vein that evoked more laughter than remorse, giving the audience a few hours' relief from bill collectors and unemployment lines. He also recognized the value of audience participation, of allowing a people who stood outside the social and economic mainstream to feel a part of something with their hallelujahs and amens and their scraped-together contributions. In their growing competition with the radio, the automobile, and the silent film, his turn-of-the-century predecessors had learned that "a laughing audience was a responsive audience." It was a lesson future revivalists would not ignore. Thus Schambach's services became good-natured give-and-takes, with the evangelist and his team constantly urging "Can somebody shout *amen!*" or "Give the Lord a good hand offering" or, while instructing the crowd on how to fill out magazine subscription cards, "Let me hear you say *print*." After the word vibrated through the tent, his associate would persist, "One more time—"

Schambach liberally seasoned his sermons, even his admonitions, with humor. In lecturing a Baltimore audience on the growing tendency among some to avoid calling themselves "Pentecostals," he ridiculed "charismatic" as "sounding like a transmission." To make the point that being born into a church-going home didn't automatically make someone a

Christian, he ribbed, "If a cat gave birth to kittens in an oven they ain't gonna be biscuits." After altar calls he sometimes advised the newly saved to "think chili peppers when you're looking for a church—find one that's red hot." His showmanship and encouragement of audience participation had paid off. Schambach was to the Pentecostal circuit what Billy Graham was to more main-line Protestants. He no longer felt compelled to boast that his tent was "a hundred yards longer than a football field." Today he was the undisputed record holder.

Yet for all the seeming informality and fun, Schambach's revivals—like those of Dwight L. Moody—were drilled and well rehearsed, beginning precisely on time and virtually marching from Dave Bryant's opening songs through the final amen as if conforming to a script, with each performer's role committed to memory. There was little room for ad-libbing. No rambling testimonies, only effectively worded "commercials" for God. While the crowds shrieked and twirled and jigged and shouted, their verbal responses were like a brushfire that occasionally flares but never gets out of control. The evangelist was seldom thrown off track. Once when a woman broke into piercing screams after a particularly dramatic healing session, Schambach gently encouraged her to "go right ahead, honey," then raised his own voice until her cries eventually faded away. When an airliner flew over during an altar call, he told the people, "Keep your heads down while we get that man saved flying over in that plane." With eyes lifted, his right hand raised, he broke into a hexlike tone: "Every member of that crew . . . everybody on that plane . . . be *saved!* and filled with the *Holy Ghost!*" and then, without missing a beat, continued his "countdown to eternity." Even the offerings were like grade-school fire drills with Schambach marshaling the audiences forward by sections past a line of associates holding plastic trashcans.

Tonight, most of the three thousand chairs were taken, although few in the audience—other than those confined to wheelchairs—remained seated very long, constantly jumping to their feet to applaud, whirl, dance, sometimes singly to an inner music in a private moment with God; at other times as a group, their hands raised, swaying. At least a third of the people were black, a racial melange I found surprising in an area where many whites still took pride in the Rebel flag and a redneck heritage, an area where five years earlier I had interviewed Ku Klux Klansmen and attended rallies where they too invoked the name of God and sang "The Old Rugged Cross" with a fervor that equaled tonight's singing of "Power in the Blood." In the midst of the interracial hugging and touching and outpouring of love, I studied faces of folks whose station in life was no different from that of the people I had met at those Klan rallies. Many, I felt certain, were related by blood as well as by social and economic circumstances. Why, I wondered, in their feelings of isolation and alienation from mainstream society, had some turned to the Klan, others to religion?

The intertwining of races was not uncommon in the history of Pentecostal revivals. At the ones I already had attended blacks were usually present, though never to this extent, their numbers seldom more than half a dozen. As far back as the 1880s, Mrs. M. B. Woodworth-Etter, a popular faith healer of the day, raised Southern eyebrows with her integrated revivals, and some Pentecostal historians trace the movement's beginning in this country to a mixed gathering spearheaded in 1906 by a black elder named W. J. Seymour at the Azusa Street mission in Los Angeles. Almost from the outset of the healing revivals launched in the 1940s, there was "a racial openness," with the evangelists preaching to mixed audiences, even in the South where a rope usually separated the races in order to satisfy local ordinances. Both Oral Roberts and William Branham conducted integrated revivals in the late 1940s, with a black minister among those healed at Branham's first meeting. Although Jack Coe was the first to draw large numbers of blacks, A. A. Allen led the way in making a conscious commitment to biracial revivals and in publicly condemning segregation. During the racial unrest of the fifties and sixties, he staged mixed services in Little Rock and Atlanta, added a black singer to his team, and pledged himself to an interracial platform, which, according to historian David Edwin Harrell, "many others followed but none equaled"—at least not until his protégé Schambach launched his own ministry, in the early years attracting predominately black audiences. Today blacks still outnumbered whites at his meetings in some cities, accounting for approximately ninety percent of the audiences in New York and Baltimore, and, like Allen's, his evangelistic team had long included blacks. Before passage of the Civil Rights Act, Schambach and his fellow revivalists had to separate the races, label the Port-o-Johns "colored" and "white," and be on the alert for the Klan. But those problems seemed remote in the midst of a chain-reaction of hugs and greetings among people of mismatched skins.

* * *

Schambach's face was flushed as he progressed with his account of Christ walking on water, drawing the audience into what had become a comic thriller punctuated with a moral here and there and related in terms the people could understand and identify with. "Peter said, I know a sure-fire way to find out whether that's Him or not. Stood up in the boat and—" The revivalist cupped his hands to his mouth and hollered, *"Hey, Jesus! Is that youuuuuuu?"* The crowd chuckled as Schambach hung his head and groaned theatrically, "Ooooooooo, Peter—give him some faith. And then Jesus said, *Come!* He didn't give no sermon. He just said one word: *Coooooome!"* The laughter was loud and constant as the evangelist reenacted the scene. "Peter put those number twelves over the side of the boat," he said, hoisting his own right foot with exaggerated effort as he called to the crowd, "Did he do it?"

The audience roared, *Yessssssssss!*

A smile crossed Schambach's lips. "I can just hear the rest of 'em saying, Look-Look-Look, look who's walking on water!" The tent sounded like Tiger Stadium, across town, in the midst of a Saturday football skirmish, cheering Peter on. "When I get to heaven, I'm gonna ask him how it felt," he sighed. *Thank Ya, Jesussss!* Suddenly his face and his voice darkened. "But the waves begin to come, and Peter took his eyes off Jesus and he saw the waves and he said, *Eeeeeeeeeee!* and while he was sinking, he was crying, *Looooooord, save me!"* The audience chortled, but Schambach cut the laughter short as the message moved closer to home. "See, the moment you start employing faith and doing something supernatural, something miraculous, ol' sluefoot don't like it." The congregation grew quiet as the evangelist lectured them on faith, theirs and his own, the stillness shattered when he bellowed, *"Unbelief!"* his voice full, forceful, indignant. "Every time I give an altar call, the Devil's standing right over my shoulder, saying, Don't give one tonight, they're all saved." Schambach scowled. "I say, You lying Devil, stand up here and *watch* 'em come." The crowd applauded. "The Devil will cause us preachers to pray for the sick in the back room. What if they ain't healed?" he whined. Then, his voice firm, he proclaimed, "If God's gonna do it let's put it out in the open where ever'body can see it, can somebody shout amen!"

A-men!

"The Devil said to me, What would you do if you prayed for somebody and they died? I said, I'd just pray for the next one." *Hallelujah!* "And if they died I'd pray for the next one. I ain't no healer nohow! I couldn't heal a flea with a headache!" he exclaimed, borrowing a favorite Allen line, one of the many disclaimers faith healers resorted to after the late Jack Coe was arrested in 1956 for practicing medicine without a license.

Praises and applause rose from the audience, and then as the message moved closer to home, Schambach's voice regained its composure. "You don't see unbelief at the racetrack," he said sanctimoniously. "If they don't win the first race, they'll go back and get another ticket. They go back for the third race. The fourth race. And when they don't come in they tear up them tickets and say, I'm gonna try again." The crowd chuckled knowingly. "But not you church folks," Schambach lectured, his tone still tinged with laughter. "You get in the prayer line and don't get nothing and you say, Wellllll, the Lord don't want me to have it," he whined, "I ain't goin' back ag'in." He rared back, offended. "Not *me!*" he shouted. "I'm gonna keep comin' back because GOD—IS—THE—HEALER!"

His face glistening with perspiration, Schambach outwaited the shrieks and screams that burst forth from the audience. An impish smile curling his lips, he urged the people, "Turn around and tell somebody, say, The Devil's a liar. Tonight's *my* night for a miracle!" The words reverberated through the tent like an interminable echo in the caverns of the soul: *Tonight's my night for a miracle tonight's my night for a miracle tonight's my night . . .*

The people made their way from the tent, their hallelujahs and amens subdued but steady, like the contented hum of crickets, as they moved through the dark. Gradually the grounds grew quiet, and the tent's glare softened to a night-light with the crew efficiently lowering the sidewalls and covering the amplifiers and drums. In Billy McCullough's trailer, Schambach settled into the built-in sofa. Although he and his wife, Winifred, were checked in at a nearby motel, its whereabouts more closely guarded by his staff than the evangelist himself, he seemed to consider the cramped trailer his "second" home, a place to unwind and find a measure of solitude from the spiritually, physically, financially desperate who pursued him for a word of assurance, a prayer, a touch—all of which he gave willingly, as I had witnessed earlier in the evening when an anguished young woman pleaded with a staff member to have Brother Schambach come to her car to lay hands on her dying mother.

Schambach was obviously tired, and I remembered Dave Bryant's admiring description of him as "the hardest-working platform preacher in America." Many outside observers agreed that his brand of evangelism was arduous. Particularly grueling healing sessions frequently left William Branham staggering, and on more than one occasion he had to be carried from the platform. Far heartier men than Branham also felt the strain. Jack Coe died when he was thirty-nine, and throughout his career A. A. Allen was said to have "tottered constantly on the brink of psychological collapse."

Schambach's exhaustion, however, seemed more akin to the exhilarating fatigue runners experience after winning a long-distance race. Except for the thickening gray in his sideburns, he looked very much like the 1955 newspaper photograph I had seen of him seated next to Allen at the time of the late revivalist's arrest in Knoxville. His face was fuller perhaps, but he appeared robust from regular workouts and three-mile walks, even while on the revival circuit.

I had not expected to like Schambach. My initial impression stemmed from a raucous revival in Baltimore's Civic Center the spring of 1980, when for four hours the word "money" was invoked as often as the name of the Lord. That service had been liberally peppered with pitches to buy a book, a Bible, a tape, a promise of financial prosperity—indeed wealth—that thus far had eluded most members of the audience. I cringed while janitors and domestic workers dug into their pockets and purses, chuckling along with the evangelist as he playfully chided, "Don't ask me for no change! If you can't trust God with a twenty-dollar bill, forget it!" Strutting across the stage, banging a tambourine, he had come across as brassy and brash, a traveling medicine man peddling heavenly elixirs. But as we arranged an interview, I found him warm, jovial, and seemingly genuine. The eyes that had been alternately funny and foreboding during tonight's service were no longer performing; the voice that boomed and bantered was surprisingly soft. Even his humor was unrehearsed as he joked with Billy McCullough about making certain some promised Louisiana gumbo came directly to *him*.

The next day Schambach met me at the trailer punctually at noon, fresh and exuberant, in a serious-gray suit and tie and hand-tooled cowboy boots, easing onto the couch as if slipping into a warm pool. After almost thirty years of living out of suitcases and in mobile homes and Holiday Inns, he had learned to make himself comfortable on the platform and off. There was no mention of the full schedule ahead: the meetings with sponsoring pastors, the transmission of his daily radio broadcast, a guest appearance on evangelist Jimmy Swaggart's television show. I got the distinct impression he would have been equally relaxed had we been sitting in the midst of his crowded tent. Perhaps that was the secret of his survival, of how he remained on the road night after night, singing the same lyrics, preaching the same sermons, delivering the same one-liners with first-time spontaneity. Throughout our conversation he was polite, attentive, apologetic for interruptions, yet unlike anyone I could remember interviewing since my beginning days as a reporter, he never lost control of the interview. Repeatedly he steered me back to a point, to stories *he* wanted to emphasize, many of them lifted verbatim from his sermons and bimonthly magazine and told, even now, with scaled-down theatrics. When I asked about his religious upbringing, he responded with an account of his sidewalk conversion that scarcely departed from the version I had heard in Baltimore.

Like so many offsprings of Catholic-Protestant marriages, Schambach had a churchless childhood. "I always like to tell this story about my conversion," he said, recalling his encounter with a street preacher near the farmers' market where he worked as a teenager. "What caught my attention was the words he proclaimed over the loudspeaker. He hollered, *Haaaaaay, sin-NER!*" Schambach belted the words, then snapped his fingers, his tone and his timing shifting from conversational to dramatic. "I stopped in my tracks. I wondered, Who knows me around here?—because I knew I was a sinner. I *knew* it. I stopped, leaned against the telephone pole, and the next words that came from his lips is what changed my life." He paused for effect. "He said, You don't have to sin any more. Good news. That's what gospel means, and that was the best news I ever heard in my life, as a young man."

The circumstances of Schambach's spiritual rebirth paled in comparison to the experiences of other evangelists I had met or read about: visitations by two-hundred-pound angels, nocturnal flights into the heavens aloft a bed, confrontations with a nine-hundred-foot-tall Jesus. In his autobiography, A. A. Allen wrote that before his own conversion at age twenty-three he had "both feet planted foursquare in hell." To amuse his parents, he and his six siblings had been encouraged to swill from a jug until they were drunk. By his own admission, Allen had smoked two packs of Camels a day by the time he was seven, lost his virginity when he was twelve, lived common-law at eighteen with a woman ten years his senior, and was arrested two years later for stealing corn. Shortly before he was saved, he and his mother made moonshine and operated a dance hall. "If there was a sin I missed, it was only by accident, not design," he wrote. Allen's tale of a wayward youth were not unique. It was what one Southern writer called "the Prodigal Son motif." In my own travels I listened to endless confessions of youthful carousing. While some admissions were accurate assessments, the tendency to exaggerate was not unlike the tent rivalry of an earlier day: The bigger sins a man could credit to his past, the larger he seemed to loom in his followers' eyes.

Now as I studied the amiable Schambach, I wondered what deeds darkened his past. "What were you doing at age sixteen that was so bad?" I asked.

"Wellll," he hedged, "it's not so bad. It's not the degree of sin. Sin is sin. And when you recognize the fact that you're a sinner—I believe everybody realizes that. The things that you do, the gangs that you belong to, and the things that are related to gangs—"

I stopped him. "You were a member of a gang?"

"Oh, all of us had gangs we belonged to," he said casually.

"Are you using 'gang' to mean—"

"Not in the sense that gangs are now," he clarified. "I'm just talking about neighborhood crowds. It was our gang that we played with, and we were always getting into trouble."

"Serious trouble?" I pressed. "Were you arrested?"

"No, nothing like that," he quickly exonerated himself. "Never arrested or anything. I mean just doing things you had no business doing, far as gangs are concerned."

Schambach, along with his entire family, soon became active in the street preacher's church, an Assembly of God. A year later, in 1943, when he enlisted in the navy, he preached aboard ship in the south Pacific, sometimes in the midst of combat. "My pulpit was a five-inch gun mount," he reminisced. "I cherish those times. That was where I got a lot of my training. Thrust out into the world with a bunch of sailors—sailors synonymous with the word drunken. Drunken sailors. But God kept me from that, and I had a fruitful time on the ship. That's when the call of God came on my life."

After the armistice, he passed up a scholarship to play college football and basketball, put aside a boyhood ambition to be an FBI agent, and enrolled in the Assembly of God's Central Bible Institute in Springfield, Missouri. His first pastorate was in south Philadelphia at a church too poor to pay a salary and so, in addition to his clerical duties, he worked as a boilermaker at the Atlantic-Richfield Refinery. Within a couple of years he became the full-time minister of a church near Pittsburgh, where he remained only briefly before joining A. A. Allen in 1955. For five years he worked with the flamboyant revivalist, first as his afternoon speaker and then as his pianist and "platform man," quickly earning name recognition and a reputation as being "enormously gifted."

"I consider that like a boot camp," he said of those years with Allen. "Some of the greatest training and the most precious moments I hold dear was when I worked with him because I was by his right hand, and I saw how God used him. It made me hungry." The nostalgia that had crept into his voice vanished abruptly. "But there came a time in my life when God had to separate me from that and push me on my own. That was in nineteen-sixty, and I've been traveling the world ever since."

Adrenaline seemed to surge through his veins as he reviewed those embryonic days of immediately buying time for a daily radio show and heading to Newark, New Jersey, for his first revival. "I sort of went in on my own like a maverick," he said, chuckling at his youthful boldness at going into a new town without local sponsoring pastors. "I had handbills printed, and I stood out on the street passing 'em out myself. Couldn't afford no people to work with me. I preached twice a day, and you see this is the part people don't look at," he complained. "All they see is the big tent and the car you drive. They don't realize there's a starting point when you did all the work. And we had *such* a meeting. I stayed there for about two months."

"You had your own tent?" I asked.

"Couldn't afford a tent," he said. "We rented a theater building, and we got so many people saved and converted we *had* to establish a church. It was *forced* on us. Pastors weren't sponsoring the meeting so I didn't know where to send the new converts so I bought the building that we rented."

"And this was your *first* revival?"

"First revival," he confirmed, "and I seemed like to be forced into it. It was an old Jewish Y, a Young Women's Hebrew Association," he recalled, then expanded on its features: an auditorium that seated fifteen hundred, three hundred guest rooms, a swimming pool, bowling alley, indoor gymnasium. "Moss Hart, the great producer? He did the famous movie *Act One*, filmed it from *my* church. And great names like Jerry Lewis, the comedian that worked with Dean Martin—his name is still there backstage where they got their start on that stage. *My* church! And we bought that building back in nineteen-sixty. That's when I left Allen, see, and we bought it *that* year. I didn't have a dime in the bank and God blessed me with that building. For seventy-five thousand dollars I bought it."

"That was a lot of money in nineteen-sixty," I remarked.

"Absolutely," he agreed. "Ah, it brings back a lot of memories."

Reluctant to again settle in one location, Schambach arranged to return to Newark each Sunday before he moved on to New York, where he again handed out flyers and did all the preaching.

"I started out with thirty-five people," he said.

"That was your attendance?"

"*On* Broadway, if you please!" he said with a mixture of pride and amusement. "Rented this theater that seated thirty-five hundred people, and I had thirty-five people the first night!" He laughed heartily. "But we stayed there and plodded through, and to tell you how successful it was I stayed four months. Went from thirty-five to thirty-five hundred. Jammed it. Packed it. I baptized fifteen hundred people in one night, and it was in that meeting the people gave me enough money to buy my tent, to get my first truck on the road."

"So you always knew you wanted a tent," I commented.

"*Absolutely.* This is what I wanted."

By the end of the first year on his own Schambach was ready to hit the sawdust trail with a tent only slightly smaller than his current one. "I started big," he said, chuckling at a youthful ambition he had never outgrown. "Even though I couldn't fill it, I wanted something *big!*" Again he chortled and then in a businesslike tone confided, "You know, when you see something big—Even though we only had a thousand chairs, I can spread 'em out. *I* can fill a tent. But now we got 'em close together." He nodded toward the expanse of aqua vinyl. "We got three thousand in there now."

Over the next five years Schambach acquired old theaters in Brooklyn, Philadelphia, and Chicago and converted them into churches, or what he called Miracle Temples, hiring full-time pastors to oversee them in between his own periodic visits. His properties had since expanded to include his headquarters, which was being transferred from Ellwood City, Pennsylvania, to Tyler, Texas; a Bible college, also in Tyler; a publishing house; a bimonthly magazine; an orphanage in Indonesia; and an inventory of six semis, four tents, and all the drums, organs, audio equipment, and sales items that accompany a tent ministry. His evangelistic team and the staff that operated his other holdings fluctuated between forty and fifty full- and part-time employees with an annual payroll of about $500,000. By 1981 his headquarters each month received 14,000 letters and 35,000 calls on the twenty-four-hour "Powerphone" prayer line. His beginnings had been a far cry from what Wayne Simmons had called "the school of hard knocks." God had been good to Schambach, and he was the first to acknowledge it.

"I had been traveling with Brother Allen, and my name was known," he said. "I was fortunate. I not only had my Bible training, my formal education, but I had the privilege of being with a great man of God. What I've learned about tents and the ministry I learned right by his side."

"Weren't you particularly close to him?" I asked.

"Like a son," he said. "That's the way he treated all the people that worked with him. After he died and I was in my own organization I hired his wife. She was the editor of my magazine."

He mentioned neither Allen's divorce nor his death from sclerosis of the liver in 1970 in a San Francisco hotel, and when I brought up the late evangelist's arrest in Knoxville, Schambach loyally defended him. "I slept with him in the same room, ate with him, lived with him, and never, *never*, have I had any doubts about that man's integrity," he was adamant. "The very day these charges—and I call them trumped-up charges—came out against him, I was with him. If they say they found liquor in his car, then they planted it. I was with him right on the grounds, after the arrest, and I know that it was not so."

When the Assemblies of God censured Allen after his arrest, young Schambach withdrew from the church to show his support. But unlike his mentor, he left in good standing and today remained on cordial terms with the church, frequently preaching before its congregations and conferences. Looking back, he harbored no regrets about severing ties. Independence suited him as it had Allen. "I'd possibly still be an Assembly of God preacher, and my ministry would be limited to one organization," he reasoned, adding "My ministry has covered the scope of all denominations. I don't like the word 'independent.' I consider myself an interdenominational preacher. We embrace *all* denominations."

Nor had Schambach confined his pulpit to one continent. Like many tent evangelists, he traveled overseas at least once a year: to Europe, Indonesia, Africa, the Philippines, islands in the Caribbean, airing his daily radio broadcast there as well as in Mexico, Canada, and Guyana.

In the early days, his wife had remained at home in Bryn Mawr while their three children attended school, with the family joining him during the summer. Now that their youngest, Bruce, was a senior at Evangel College with an invitation to try out for the Dallas Cowboys, Winifred Schambach was again with him on the road.

"A lot of wives teach their own children, but we didn't want that," he said of the family decision to remain at home during those years. "But now that the children are grown we're going to sell it. We're never home. If we're not in the tent, we're in an auditorium meeting, so the Holiday Inn's our home." His smile widened. "I'm refurbishing an old trailer I used when I was with Allen. Had somebody go in and redo the whole thing, and pretty soon my wife and I will be living like a honeymoon couple in that little eight-foot-wide trailer." He chuckled good-naturedly. "Won't that be nice?"

"That will be nice," I agreed.

"That's better than the Holiday Inn."

What might have seemed like boasting in some individuals struck me as an unflagging enthusiasm for his work. In the course of his ministry, he had owned five gospel-sized tents, this latest one being the largest at 160 by 360 feet. It came in sixteen sections and had a maximum seating capacity of ten thousand. By design, its dimensions—like those of an expandable dining table—could be altered by adding or subtracting sections and center poles. But since a storm severely damaged the tent the first time it was erected, in April 1981, it had been confined to its present twelve sections and four center poles with space to seat six thousand. It was the second time in less than a year the evangelist had a tent fall victim to high winds, the third in his career. For even with his expert team and first-class equipment, he was not immune to the crippling blow of losing a tent, especially before the advent of the more patchable vinyl. And the expense of putting up a tent and taking it down, of paying a crew and maintaining a fleet of eighteen wheelers, far

exceeded the rent for most auditoriums and civic centers. Nevertheless, when Schambach spoke of tents he was reduced to a small boy who
still believed in Santa Claus and tooth fairies.

"There's something about a tent . . ." he said, choosing his words
carefully as he attempted to pinpoint precisely what attracted him and
the audiences, as brush arbors had drawn the Methodists of an earlier
day. "In an auditorium you have the plush seats, the air-conditioned
building, and sometimes when people come to a place like that, they're
coming with their good clothes on and they're just sitting there. They
want to be entertained." Again he hesitated, and then suddenly his
feelings somersaulted into words. "But when you get people under
the tent they're in their shirtsleeves, women got on their housedresses.
Some of 'em got their hair up. And when the services start, they let
their hair down. They get with it. Instead of being spectators, they're
participants. A lot of times we draw people that figure it's a circus.
They hear the organ grinding and they come running over to see." He
leaned forward, smiling. "I got 'em hooked once they're there," he
said craftily. "It's a drawing card, really—a tent is."

"Is that some of the thought in having the zeppelin?" I asked.

"Yeaaaah." He grinned. "I like that. That's new. We use it as an
advertisement, just to let people know where we are. Goodyear got a
blimp . . ."

"So you might as well have one," I laughed along with him.

"Yeah," he chuckled, "got my own blimp!"

It was a man of Schambach's proportions and personality, one Dwight
L. Moody, who ushered in the grand-scale use of advertising and publicity to attract crowds. Or, in the words of one historian, "merchan-
dised" the revival. A shoe salesman when he moved from Boston to
Chicago in 1856 at age nineteen, Moody had a natural bent for business.
By the time he was twenty-four he was earning $5,000 a year—a very
large sum in its day—through a combination of jobbing, wholesaling,
and speculating in land. Another $5,000 was drawing interest in the
bank. He promised to become another Rockefeller or Armour with an
empire like those in oil, steel, meat, and rails that rose around him.
Instead, in 1861 the young entrepreneur abandoned the marketplace to
devote his life to saving souls, bringing to the task all the shrewdness and
skills he had acquired in the business world—not the least of them being

a feel for the newly found powers of mass communication. "He had a feel for the gigantic," historian Bernard Weisberger wrote of Moody. "He could organize and consolidate like a supermanager. He could present his message in the brisk and simple terms of a salesman who trusted his product and knew his customers." As a result, his revivals were superbly organized, lavishly financed ($30,000 for an eight-week crusade in Philadelphia in 1875), and widely advertised, even on amusement pages and "worldly" bulletin boards. The publicity and organizational machinery set in motion by Moody was perfected by William A. ("Billy") Sunday after he hit the sawdust trail in 1911. At a time when "old-time" religion could no longer count on a captive audience, the former baseball player successfully vied for attention—and headlines—with film stars and heads of state. Turning revivalism into a combination of big business and showmanship, he hobnobbed with the financially and politically powerful and once tossed the first ball at the World Series. Never again would evangelists rely solely on God to attract crowds. With increasing frequency, clowns, apes, child evangelists, even pickled demons shared the platform. Over the years the use of celebrities as a drawing card was not to be confined to "big names" like Billy Graham and Oral Roberts. On the smaller circuit, evangelists with the financial wherewithal to pay an honorarium also featured movie stars, Miss Americas, professional athletes, and bearers of such colorful titles as the "World's Strongest Man" who combined his particular testimony with a weight-lifting demonstration. With the advent of radio and television, the possibilities for promotion were limited only by the genius, bank account, and boldness of the revivalist. In the mid-fifties A. A. Allen attempted to entice viewers with this TV advertisement:

SEE! HEAR! ACTUAL MIRACLES HAPPENING BEFORE YOUR EYES. CANCER, TUMORS, GOITERS DISAPPEAR. CRUTCHES, BRACES, WHEELCHAIRS, STRETCHERS DISCARDED. CROSSED EYES STRAIGHTENED. CAUGHT BY THE CAMERA AS THEY OCCURRED IN THE HEALING LINES BEFORE THOUSANDS OF WITNESSES.

Over the years, miracles became the prime drawing card, prompting one pioneer revivalist to observe: "Healing was 'like ringing the dinner bell' to lure sinners to salvation." The most modestly financed evangelist learned early that publicity was as basic as knowing the scriptures, even if it was only a hand-lettered roadside placard promising SIGNS—WONDERS—MIRACLES. The all-time master of promotion was Aimee Semple McPherson, the eccentric founder of the International Church of the Foursquare Gospel who sometimes used skywriting to advertise her meetings. Flamboyant and not just a little unorthodox, Sister Aimee thrived on controversy and rivaled the most glamorous silent-screen stars for attention. In 1926 after a much-publicized kidnapping that officials suspected was engineered by the former Canadian farm girl and her alleged lover, more than 100,000 people lined the streets of Los Angeles to greet her rose-draped car. At Angelus Temple, built after her meteoric rise as a traveling faith healer, she organized her own spiritual army, replete with uniforms, and was given to interrupting hymns to cry out "Clear the one-way street for Jesus!" At the height of her popularity she made the front pages of the Los Angeles papers an average of three times a week and is credited with originating the saying "I don't care what they say about me, so long as they spell my name right!"

But promotion was only one ingredient that went into the making of a successful revival. More than anything, it took a special breed. The independent evangelistic associations that cropped up after World War II lived or died, according to historian David Edwin Harrell, "with the charisma of the evangelist." Harrell described those leaders of the early revival as bold and ambitious with "a powerful control over their audiences and an unwavering confidence in their own charisma." Still another chronicler referred to them as "rugged individuals." Now when I asked Schambach what it took to be a good tent revivalist, he immediately answered, "The call of God," then after a moment of private assessment expanded. "Not everybody can stick with a tent," he said bluntly. "You have to have intestinal fortitude, a lot of guts. There's a lot of work, a lot of preparation. You don't just set up like a carnival."

As a beginning evangelist Schambach had pitched his own tent, distributed his own handbills, but with time he had learned to delegate responsibility, especially the manual labor. "I can be more beneficial to people if I'm fresh and alert mentally," he explained. "You don't learn this right away. As a young person you want to do it all. You're so full of fire and a lot of smoke and not too much steam," he chuckled.

"But the preacher's life, he has to be entirely devoted to the ministry, to the word of God and the preaching."

Although he referred to his eldest son Bobby as "my radio man," the twenty-eight year old seemed, in all but name, to be the manager or orchestrator of Schambach Miracle Revivals. A tall, soft-spoken young man with a wife and three children, he had joined his father on the road immediately after graduating from high school in 1971. And while he did indeed engineer the daily broadcasts, he also handled bookstand receipts, wrote nightly crusade reports, maintained a mental inventory of staff, equipment, and expenditures, and kept himself and his father abreast of the evangelist's schedule. When time permitted, he, like the sons of many revivalists, served as drummer. At the Bible college he taught both the technical and broadcast aspects of radio.

The teaching sessions were part of his father's attempt to provide aspiring revivalists with practical training along with the more traditional classwork. Between semesters, students were encouraged to take the college's two tents on the road. "They've got to learn to put their own tent up, maintain it, and conduct their own services," the elder Schambach told me. "Lead their own singing, do their own preaching, pray for the people, raise their own offerings. I tell 'em, Don't you ask me for help for money. *Pray* it in. And we teach them how to do it."

Outside, the generators' hum was strong and steady, and Schambach glanced through the curtains, toward the rig that housed the units. "Those are brand-new," he said. "Cost me twenty-five thousand dollars, and that's nil. You can run them diesels just about forever." Up until this revival he had had to pay each local power company a thousand dollars to hang a transformer and another thousand—roughly a hundred dollars a day—in electric bills for the tent area and mobile homes. It was too soon to determine the operating costs for the two units, but he was confident there would be a savings. Billy McCullough had estimated fifty dollars a day, including maintenance; Bobby Schambach figured no more than five dollars an hour. Whatever the amount, I was certain it represented only a fraction of the total outlay for a meeting of these proportions. Wayne Simmons's two-week revival in Knoxville was nowhere in the league with Schambach's operation, and it had cost six thousand dollars.

"How much does a revival like this cost?" I asked.

Schambach shrugged. "It fluctuates. Here it's not costing that much because the pastor of this church donated his grounds. Now, the place we just came from—Atlanta—cost ten thousand dollars just to rent the lot."

"For how long?"

"Six days."

I gasped.

"See what I mean?"

At Schambach's revivals, especially in Baltimore, I had found his unrelenting requests for money, his dangling of financial prosperity distasteful. Yet off the platform he did not appear to be in it for personal gain. His car was neither flashy nor late-model; his clothes not obviously expensive. He stayed in moderate motels when he could have gone first class. During a telephone interview, David Edwin Harrell told me, "All of them need money. It's an expensive business." On seeing Schambach's operation, I was beginning to grasp the full extent of that statement.

In an earlier conversation, Bobby Schambach had estimated the absolute minimum for a ten-day meeting at $15,000, including salaries, travel expenses, advertising, and, before acquisition of the generators, electric bills. That figure did not take into consideration expenditures for chairs, emergency lighting, musical instruments, sound equipment, and the tent itself. The vinyl alone cost $60,000. The poles had been purchased secondhand—some in 1960; the rest, in 1972—for a total of $22,500, and Bobby Schambach had no idea what they would cost today, new. To replace the six semis, he figured, would run roughly $200,000.

And the tent expenses were only starters. While individual salaries —including Schambach's—were confidential, the business manager had rounded off the annual payroll at $500,000. The printing bill for each issue of *Power*, the evangelist's slick bimonthly magazine, was $30,000; postage was another $8,000. To air the daily "Voice of Power" on 250 radio stations added up to $160,000 a month. There were also the operating expenses for the central headquarters, the Bible college, the Miracle Temples, and the orphanage in Indonesia. The production costs and air time for his occasional television specials, I felt certain, had to be staggering. As Schambach and I talked, the figures boggled my mind.

"Do you ever worry about money?" I asked.

For a moment Schambach was thoughtful. "If you worried about money, you'd be worrying about praying for people," he said. "It's the same thing. If you worry, you're not practicing what you preach. You get concerned," he admitted, "but faith—it always comes through in the end."

CHAPTER IV

THE SNAKE-HANDLERS:
With Signs Following

The church was a scant two miles from Newport; forty-five, at most, from Knoxville; and even less from the ski lifts and water slides in Gatlinburg. But as I left Interstate 40 and passed beyond the dead trucks and workaday bungalows, I felt as if I were going back in time, to a world removed from anything I had ever experienced. As a journalist I had allowed myself to be locked into rooms with Black Panthers and armed Klansmen; now I wanted to turn the car around and run. A part of me hoped I would not find the church or that its members would refuse to let me enter. For all the precarious situations I had put myself in, I had never seen anyone die. And I didn't want to now.

There was precedent for my apprehension. On an April evening in 1973 two men had died after drinking strychnine during a service in the same East Tennessee church I was headed for. Since the practice —along with handling deadly snakes—was central to the congregation's beliefs, no one had become alarmed that night when Jimmy Williams emptied a vial of lethal powder into a glass of water. "This is the Word," the young preacher said before drinking almost half of the poison. At first he showed no ill effects and in fact had resumed handling an assortment of rattlesnakes and copperheads when Buford Pack felt moved by God to finish all but an inch of the liquid. In less than three hours both men were dead. The tiny congregation was shocked, yet its faith had remained unshaken. The men were laid out with Bibles opened to the sixteenth chapter of Mark, and as their coffins were lowered into the ground, fellow believers passed serpents over the open graves. In the wake of the deaths, Cocke County's attorney general had asked that the church be padlocked and its members enjoined from drinking strychnine and taking up serpents. He also called for the indictment of Liston Pack, the pastor and a brother to Buford, on charges of involuntary manslaughter. A circuit judge granted a temporary injunction against snake-handling but refused to close the church. Both he and a grand jury exonerated Pack, taking the position that the deaths had been suicides and that the law could do little to prevent the drinking of poisons.

The injunction had been ignored by authorities and believers alike, although church members seemed a little less zealous about partaking of such deadly substances as strychnine and battery acid. The practice had surfaced sometime after a preacher named George Went Hensley introduced serpent-handling to the hills and hollows of southeastern Tennessee during the summer of 1909. While most Pentecostals rejected both modes of worship, Hensley had modest success in spreading the rituals, most notably snake-handling, to isolated mountain communities from Florida to Ohio. Between 1936 and 1973, at least thirty-five people—including Hensley—died from snakebites during religious services. Another five deaths resulted from drinking poisonous substances. The deaths prompted most states—including Tennessee—to pass laws making the display and handling of serpents during religious services a misdemeanor, punishable by imprisonment and/or a fine. Over the years the sect was to find itself at odds with the law over still other matters. After a 1945 snake-handling revival caused traffic jams in Chattanooga, Hensley and protégé Tom Harden were arrested for disorderly conduct and ended up working several days on a road gang when they refused to pay the fine. And in 1975 seven men were given prison sentences for "assault with a deadly weapon" after flinging copperheads at members of a non–snake-handling congregation during a free-for-all between two rival churches in Georgia.

But in spite of the deaths, arrests, and derision by a disapproving society, the believers held to the conviction that they were "doing the work of the Lord." The practice persisted, as it does today, in Tennessee, Kentucky, Georgia, Alabama, Virginia, West Virginia, the Carolinas, Ohio, Indiana, and Michigan, with believers in the last three states comprised mostly of former residents of southern Appalachia who migrated to industrial centers such as Akron, Fort Wayne, and Detroit. Adherents base their belief in snake-handling and drinking strychnine on a literal reading of Mark 16:17–18:

And these signs shall follow them that believe: In my name shall they cast out devils; they shall speak with new tongues; they shall take up serpents; and if they drink any deadly thing, it shall not hurt them; they shall lay hands on the sick, and they shall recover.

Although the churches are independent of one another, many members are acquainted and frequently attend three or four services a week, sometimes driving fifty and sixty miles each way to visit other snake-handling congregations. This one in Carson Springs, Tennessee, had grown out of a church in Big Stone Gap, Virginia, which abandoned serpent-handling in 1968 after its pastor was fatally bitten. The deaths here in 1973 did not have such a chilling effect, and on that evening in July 1981 I felt a heavy foreboding as the blacktop gave way to red dirt and gravel, with the road hugging the hill and winding and rising through a canopy of trees to a point where it forked. One branch descended to the right over a flat wooden bridge and disappeared into some trees; the other rose and followed the slope. For a moment I hesitated, letting the motor idle, then seeing nothing that suggested a church was near I pressed the accelerator to continue up the steep incline. Instead, the tires spun in the loose gravel, and the engine struggled and finally stalled. Again and again I tried to start the engine, but each time I moved my foot from the brake to the gas pedal the car rolled backward down the hill until it became hopelessly lodged in a shallow ditch.

Reluctantly I got out of the car and studied the dwindling light. There was no way of knowing how far I would have to walk to find help or when—or if—another vehicle would pass. I could not even be certain this was the right road. The last dwelling had been just after the turn-off from the main road, and I looked about me trying to decide whether to walk back to that or head in another direction. Below, through the trees, I caught a glimpse of a white frame structure and set out across the bridge, following the dirt road a short way until I came to a simple house. The shades were pulled, but out back clothes were drying on the line and as I neared, through one of the windows, I could see a light. I was about to knock when I looked down and, next to my feet, saw a wooden box. It was the same type box I had seen in photographs accompanying articles on snake-handling: thin, narrow, maybe two feet long with screen across one end and a hinged lid secured with a padlock. I bent down, for a closer look. Finding it empty, I looked past the yard, through the trees, and for the first time noticed a high-pitched roof. Walking briskly, I returned to the road and followed its curve past the trees until I came to another clearing, edged by the meandering little stream. A half-dozen cars and trucks were parked to either side, and beyond them, at the far end, stood a tiny frame building with neither steeple nor stained-glass windows— only this sign over the door: HOLINESS CHURCH OF GOD IN JESUS NAME.

Two women were seated in one of the cars talking quietly to a teenage girl leaning against the passenger's side. All three watched as I approached, not speaking until I asked if the services had begun. "Nome," the woman in the driver's seat replied, "but it's fixin' to." They studied me with a gaze that was direct yet not intimidating while I explained that my car was stuck and asked if anyone could help. Without answering, the driver got out of the car and hurried toward the church, her crimped brown hair bouncing against her back, the skirt of her long green dress rustling about her legs. It was impossible to know her age, though at the time I might have guessed late thirties, possibly forty. Her skin was tanned and what few teeth she had were in near ruin. At the doorway she called out, to no one in particular, "This lady needs help with her car."

On a bench up front against the wall, two teenage boys stopped strumming guitars and along with the dozen or so others inside looked first to the woman, then at me. Several men who had been gathered about the pulpit started toward me. The one with close-cut gray hair asked for my keys and said I needn't accompany them. They would drive the car around. He and a younger man addressed as Brother Bud disappeared through the trees, and for a moment the rest of us considered one another with awkwardness and mutual curiosity, the people suspicious of my intentions and I not certain what to expect of folks who knowingly picked up snakes and drank poison.

To relieve my own uneasiness and to hopefully put their minds to rest, I attempted to explain my presence to those around me, to assure them that Preacher Grooms, home this night on account of nerves and a bad back, had said I was welcome to attend the homecoming revival. They in return listened politely yet resisted being drawn into conversation, and after a time I sat on a back pew, relieved when Rayford Dunn introduced himself as one of two evangelists who would be conducting this revival.

He was a tall, gangly man in his forties with hair the same color as his leathery skin. His hands were noticeably large for his size, strong and rough from the construction work that supported a wife, three children, and a ministry that provided little more than gas money— if that—for trips from Chattanooga to wherever he was preaching. For this meeting, the round-trip was three hundred miles, a commute he and a man named Perry Beetis would make throughout the week-long revival, arriving in time for each night's service, heading home after the benediction in his rackety black car. What most folks might have regarded as drudgery was for Dunn enjoyable, an intermission, I speculated, in an otherwise bland existence. Overall, he struck me as an unlikely individual for the role of evangelist. He was shy, seemingly lacking in the self-confidence and charisma—even ego—that so many called to the pulpit come to possess, and he spoke with the unlearned speech of a man whose education had lost out to bootlegging and the bottle. Only as the nights progressed would I understand that here, unlike any revival I had attended, the evangelist was not placed on a pedestal, nor would he necessarily end up giving the sermon. While a man called to preach was accorded added stature, he was, in the end, a member of the congregation.

Rayford Dunn was one of eleven children born to a poor Alabama farmer. Until his mid-thirties he had been far from religious, and he talked freely about his years of going to nightclubs and the two-sided conversation with God that led to his conversion.

"I was goin' up Main Street one night," he reminisced as we headed outdoors to wait for my car, "an' they had a li'l ol' mission, a little hole in the wall, and God spoke to me an' tol' me, said, Go in there. I said, I don't have time, an' I went on. About a week later I was goin' by an' I was early for the nightclub an' God spoke to me and said, Go in there. I said, Okay, I'll go in there tonight. I said I'm a little early tonight for the nightclub. So I went in there and they begin to preach an' have service an' first thang I knew I was in the altar." He ended softly, with an embarrassed chuckle. "I didn't make it to the nightclub."

It was six months before Dunn took up his first serpent, a twelve-inch copperhead. Although he felt "called" three years later, he waited awhile longer before actually becoming a minister. "I didn't feel I was educated enough in order to preach the wisdom of the Word like it oughta be preached," he said to explain the delay. "So I read in the Bible where that man's wisdom wadn't God's wisdom an' I jist begin to obey what He would give me. He'd give me a little an' I'd take a little, an' He'd jist keep addin' to me an' finally I jist overcame all the fear."

"Do you pastor a church?" I asked.

"I jist evangelize—" He stopped and backed up. "Well, I got an appointment in Marshall, North Carolina, ever' second Saturday in ever' month an' I come up here pretty often." Mostly, however, he held weekend meetings in Georgia, Alabama, and West Virginia. "We jist go wherever God leads us," he said. "Me an' Brother Perry, most a the time we run together."

In the distance I could hear a motor struggling, and Rayford Dunn, reading my concern, assured me Brother Fish knew how to drive MGs, that I needn't worry. But I did, unable to tune out the spinning tires. Finally, through the trees, I saw an orange blur and then my car bounded into the clearing, coming to a stop next to the other vehicles. Brother Fish got out and gave me the keys and a curt "You were in the ditch," as he and Brother Bud hurried past, scarcely slowing to say even that.

It wasn't until my car was safely parked that everyone filed back into the one-room church, less than two dozen people altogether, the men seated in front, women and children behind them, in eight short pews to either side of a center aisle. Rayford Dunn took a seat on the first pew, with Perry Beetis joining Brother Bud on a bench pushed against the righthand wall, opposite the two teenage boys who had remained inside with their guitars.

In the excitement of coming face to face so abruptly with the entire congregation, my attention had been diverted from any thought of snakes and strychnine. But now my apprehension returned. I looked past the people in front of me, trying to locate a wooden box like the one next door. Nervously I eyed the platform—first the pew where

Perry Beetis was sitting, then the mourners' bench, finally the pulpit.
I stopped. My muscles tensed. Next to a large, unopened Bible, next
to a bottle of Progresso olive oil, rested a mayonnaise jar half filled
with clear liquid. The label had been removed, yet I knew what even
it would not have told me: These contents were deadly.

I attempted to focus my attention elsewhere, to put my fears aside,
if only for a moment, forcing myself to concentrate on every detail of
the tiny sanctuary: three bare bulbs across the front, the noisy air-
conditioners in the room's only two windows, a pair of unstained doors
along the back wall, a marquee-type plaque that recorded last Sunday's
attendance as fifty-two and the offering, $4.84. A calendar advertising
Mane's Funeral Home brought me abruptly back to the bottle and the
nagging fear that someone might feel compelled to drink from it, if not
tonight, another night, before the revival ended—while I was there.
And although I did not see a serpent box, I worried that it was simply
behind the pulpit, out of sight, and would appear as soon as the Spirit
moved.

There was neither a piano nor an organ, only the guitars attached
to a pair of amplifiers. Their strings were seldom still as the teenagers
plucked and played regardless of whether the congregation was singing
or praying. Even while Perry Beetis was opening the service, they
tightened and tuned and the strings whined until three women, led
by the one in green, came forward, and they were free to break into
a spirited rendition of "This Little Light of Mine." For more than half
an hour, with prodding from Perry Beetis, womenfolk came to the
platform, singly and in groups, to sing of the better life God had waiting
for them. Out of shyness, they stood with backs to the congregation,
their voices nevertheless lusty and strong with conviction. The songs
were simple, the verses endless and easy to remember—for there were
no hymnals. The most timorous joined in with confidence and abandon,
a wiry little man next to Rayford Dunn jangling a tambourine and at
times wailing, still others contributing rhythmic clapping and verbal
encouragements. Even John Fish, less given to displays of emotion,
added a regimented "Lord in Your Name!"

All the while I kept my eye on the half-filled jar, and waited. The
songs continued like endless turnings of a wheel, the people responding
with increasing freedom. As the service moved from testimonies to
Brother Rayford's sermon, I realized that everybody but me seemed

oblivious to the bottle and to the fact there were no snakes. Without
exception they were immersed, with their whole beings, in that moment of worship.

When at the end of two hours the congregation was dismissed, I
silently thanked God for getting me through one night and tried not
to think about the five services looming ahead. Perry Beetis walked
alongside me down the aisle, toward the door. He was a round, jolly
man, fresh and glowing as though just awakened from a good night's
sleep. "You know what I'd like to see?" he said, grinning. "I'd like to
see you git filled with the Holy Ghost an' go shoutin' all over these
mountains!" The prospect of that and all it implied gave me pause;
nevertheless, I felt comforted by his gesture of friendship and returned
his smile.

By the time I was in my MG, the church was dark and only car
lights shown in the clearing. One after the other, the tired old cars
departed, and I too followed, their tail lights like giant lightning bugs
leading the way down and around the curves, away from the hollow,
toward the outside world.

George Hensley was in his thirties, living in time and place on the
outskirts of the Pentecostal movement's gathering moment and less
than ten miles and eleven years from the Scopes "monkey trial" when
he felt compelled to test those verses in Mark 16. During a service at
Sale Creek, Tennessee, he challenged worshipers to take up a rattlesnake found on a nearby mountain. Soon scores were following his
lead. Gatherings in brush arbors and in members' houses continued
for almost ten years, until the first of the faithful was bitten. Although
the victim recovered and more ardent believers settled the theological
dilemma by denouncing him as a backslider, the practice was abandoned in East Tennessee, and Hensley moved on to Harlan, Kentucky,
to spread his doctrine to a new body of followers. Serpent-handling
did not return to its place of origin until 1943 when Raymond Hayes,
a Kentucky convert, traveled to Grasshopper Valley to conduct a revival. Many in attendance remembered the services of an earlier day,
and to commemorate the revival, they decided to build the Dolly Pond
Church of God with Signs Following, drawing on the verse in Mark
for the name.

It was in that very church that Perry Beetis, as a young man of seventeen, first encountered snake-handling—a fact he related with some pride as the two of us sat in the hollow the next evening waiting for the service to begin. Although raised in the Dolly Pond area, thirty miles north of Chattanooga and across the Tennessee River from where Hensley took up his first serpent, Brother Perry conceded he knew about that moment only through hearsay and was not certain of the details: It had occurred twenty years before he was born, plus he and his six siblings had never been exposed to religion in any form.

"My daddy was a bootlegger," he explained. "He bootlegged there fer years an' years. He was the first man ever made any white liquor, fer as bein' knowed, in that end of Tennessee. Course, I was raised in a whiskey still, an' after he got shot an' killed, why, I jist took up where he left off an' started makin' whiskey an' sellin' it, bootleggin' it, haulin' it—anythang to make a dollar, that was what I done. Now when I repented I quit it," he was quick to emphasize, "quit drinkin' it an' quit foolin' with it an' God delivered me."

"Did your family have much money when you were growing up?" I asked.

Brother Perry shook his head. "Not any atall, hardly. Daddy he was a whiskey man, like I said, an' maybe he'd have five hunderd dollars today an' tomorrow he wouldn't have a dime. He'd go on a drunk an' spend it on some woman or a roadhouse, an' come back broke flat as a flitter. I had two pair a britches. One of 'em I wore to school an' one of 'em I wore at the house. The one I wore at the house had holes in the knees an' the seat an' was ripped in the straddle. An' me an' my brother wore the same pair a shoes all winter long."

"You each had a pair?"

"No," he corrected me, "we *shared* a pair of shoes between us. He'd go out in the snow an' play a while an' I'd go out an' play a while. We couldn't git out together. We'd slip out once in a while, you know what I mean, but we was poor." He laughed good-naturedly, the way folks do when reminiscing about childhood adversities that have been overcome, though his lot today seemed little better. Both nights he had worn bib overalls, and he owned no car, having to rely on a son-in-law to bring him to tonight's service after Rayford Dunn was unable to come. Nevertheless, Beetis was a cheerful, outgoing man who seemed to take it in stride. During one sermon he thanked God that money didn't mean much to him. "I'd like to have a good car, somethin' that

I could go in that won't give me no trouble," he told the congregation, adding "but you know, I jist ain't got that an' I'll make out with what God's give me, and I'll be contented with it too. He said for me to."

Sitting now on the ground contentedly chewing on a blade of grass, a denim engineer's cap covering his bald spot and what remained of his salt-and-pepper hair, he described his schooling as equally meager. "I ain't got no education. I never did learn nothin'," he said, embarrassed that he could neither read nor write anything more than his name. "First grade's fer as I ever got."

"You can learn without going to school," I attempted to reassure him.

"Well," he said brightly, "they wasn't no man learnt me how to preach. That's a gift from God."

When I asked if, as a boy, he had ever attended church, Brother Perry replied, "I was raised *around* the church an' I went to the Grasshopper Church of God jist fer trouble, not—" He hesitated, then came straight out with it. "I didn't go fer the benefit of the meetin', in other words. I was jist a boy an' I wanted somewheres to go an' that's the only place there was in the country where I lived, back in the hills."

"Did you go every week?"

"Nearly ever' week, an' then Raymond Hayes come down from Kentucky an' Hutton an' all those folks come down an' started preachin' there at Dolly Pond an' handlin' serpents an' I got to goin' down there. Course I hated 'em an' I was wild. I'd do anything to git to 'em. I even took a mare down thar an' rode her in the church house, an ol' mare I had."

"You were mean, huh?" I said jokingly.

"Oh, I was, yeah," he agreed. "I got a snake that killed the only man that was ever killed at Dolly Pond. Course I was a sinner an' it didn't do anythang to me. I figured that was his business if he wanted to handle it an' git killed, an' it *did*. It killed him. It bit him eighteen times 'fore he turned it aloose. He set down on the floor an' held it. It'd bite him on this arm an' he'd change hands an' it jist bit him on his legs an' arms both." He demonstrated how the man had changed hands back and forth and the snake would swing its head over to bite his hands and arms. "Bit him eighteen times. An' he died jist in a few minutes."

It was on one of these outings to church that Perry Beetis met his wife, Flora, who was already a serpent-handler. "The night before I asked to walk her home she got snakebit by a copperhead on the arm," he recalled, "an' why of course we walked—we didn't have no cars— but anyhow we walked an' she was snakebit an' I had to hold her by the other hand."

He laughed nostalgically, glancing across the clearing at the woman he had married the day he turned eighteen. At fifty-six, three years older than her husband, Flora Beetis was the epitome of a sturdy mountain woman, tall, lean, with hook nose, weathered skin, and hair drawn into a bun that resembled a ripe boll of cotton. Unlike Perry Beetis, she had been raised in a Holiness, God-fearing family, though for a time she fell into his ways.

"When we married she was livin' right," he said, "but I was so stinkin' mean an' full of that whiskey an' ever'thang, she couldn't live right so she quit an' backslid an' we lived thataway fer a year or so, an' then she went back to church, her an' my mother went an' they repented an' then, course, they started on me an' directly I made it right."

"When did you repent?" I asked.

Perry Beetis stopped to figure out the year, remembering they had two children. "I believe I was twenty-two, twenty-three years old," he said. "Some fellas was preachin' a revival—it was at the Church of God down on Fifty-eight Highway, Oak Grove Church of God, an' I repented an' went to the altar an' that's the night I quit the whiskey an' ever'thang else that wasn't right. I wanted to live right an' that's what I done. I joined the Church of God an' stayed with 'em fer five years an' I got baptized in Jesus Name an' they turned me out."

"What do you mean, they turned you out?"

"Turned me out of church because I was baptized in Jesus Name," he said simply. When that failed to end my confusion, he attempted to explain the complicated Jesus Only–Trinity debate that still divides Pentecostals. "See, I believe in baptizing in the name of Jesus Christ for the remission of sin. Church of God baptize according to the way it's in Matthew twenty-eight:nineteen, you know, Father, Son, an' the Holy Ghost. I baptize according to Acts two and thirty-eight."

"What do those scriptures say?" I asked.

"Acts two and thirty-eight it was Peter apreachin' to 'em on the day of Pentecost. He said, Let the whole house of Israel know that God has made this same Jesus who you crucified, both Lord an' Christ. An' the Bible says, An' they was pricked in the hearts an' said unto them, Men, what shall we do? Peter told 'em, he said, Let ever'one of you repent an' be baptized in the name of Jesus Christ fer the remissions of sin, an' you shall receive the gift of the Holy Ghost. For it is promised unto you an' unto your children an' to them that is afar off, as many as the Lord thy God shall call." Without pausing Beetis moved on to the verse in Matthew. "He told them to go an' be baptized in the name of the Father an' of the Son an' of the Holy Ghost, teachin' them to observe all whatsoever I have teached you. He said, Lo, I am with you until the end of the world," he ended confidently, adding his own theological interpretation, "An' when they come off of that mountain wherever it was at an' when His disciples came off from there, I believe they knowed how to baptize, I believe they knew what the name was."

Perry Beetis had recited the verses almost verbatim, scarcely missing or omitting a word. "You told me you didn't read or write," I said. "How did you learn the Bible?"

"The Lord give it to me. It's a talent. I have it read to me. I've jist got a mind to memorize it."

"How much of the Bible have you memorized?"

"Oh, there ain't no tellin'," he said, pleased, "an' I don't even know my ABCs. Can't learn 'em. My wife tried to learn me. My kids tried to learn me, an' I jist can't learn 'em."

"But you can learn the Bible," I observed.

"Oh, yeah," he said, "it's jist natural for me. My wife reads it to me ever'day. She reads it an' I study it. Course she's got a kinda void on understandin'. She ain't plumb dumb, but she jist don't understand it like I do."

"Well, she hasn't been called to be a preacher like you have," I suggested, as a possible reason.

"Oh, no, we don't believe in women preachers," he hastened to explain.

"But couldn't that possibly be why she doesn't understand it as well as you do?"

Perry Beetis pondered that momentarily. "That probably is, it could be," he said. "She's a member of the body, of course, but ain't been called into the ministry work. If God calls a minister, then He qualifies

him an' ordains him an' gives him power to do the job, you know, but
I jist can't find where He ever ordained a woman."

It was Tom Harden, a second generation snake-handler, who brought
Beetis into the Church of Jesus Name. Like Brother Perry, he was
born in Grasshopper Valley and claimed he could neither read nor
write until he was filled with the Holy Ghost in 1938. Throughout
much of the 1940s, he and Raymond Hayes had led the snake-handling
movement in East Tennessee. Even though Beetis began working with
Harden after being turned away by the Church of God, he himself did
not immediately embrace taking up serpents.

"I was baptized but I still didn't believe in serpent-handlin'," Beetis
conceded, amused now by his initial squeamishness. "I didn't perform
it, that's fer sure, an' I wouldn't git around 'em."

"But you went to services where it was done?"

"Eventually I did. I went to Straight Creek, Alabama, an' the first
one I ever handled, Brother Walters gimme one an' I handled it an'
they took it away from me an' course they figured I had it long enough
an' probably I had, you know," he chuckled. "I was twenty-four or
-five, somewheres in thar, maybe twenty-six."

"What do you remember about that first time?"

A touch of nostalgia came to Brother Perry's voice. "I was standin'
on the pulpit where the people set—they had a rope stretched across
the front an' they said anybody don't wanta handle these snakes or
don't wanta be around 'em, said, don't cross under that rope. So they
got to havin' the meetin' an' I got to singin' with 'em an' the first thang
I knowed, why, I was under the rope an' the next thang I knowed the
ol' brother give me his serpent." His light chuckle gave way to awe.
"But they was a flame of far an' I could shut my eyes an' see it or I
could open 'em an' see it, an' it wasn't but about four inches long."
He held up his fingers, to illustrate. "An' as that flame got shorter they
was somethin' come down over me jist like you was apourin' ice water
on me or somethin'. It was runnin' down my body, an' it jist got shorter
an' shorter, like a match if you hold it an' the flame goes out, jist goes
on down, an' directly when that thang went out, well, that feelin' went
out the bottom of my feet, an' I wasn't a bit more scared of that snake
than I am of you."

Since then, Perry Beetis estimated, he had handled thousands of snakes and never been bitten. "The Lord's been good to me," he said, remembering the satisfaction of each experience. "It's a good feelin' an' it's a confidence that builds your faith an' builds you up in the Lord, an' you jist can't explain it. Or I can't. But they's anointin', they's a spirit that will take care of you, jist like the one that took care a Daniel in the lions' den an' took care a the Hebrew children when they was throwed in the fire."

Brother Perry adhered to the church's strict moral edicts, which frowned on dancing, drinking, smoking, and movies as well as cosmetics, the cutting of women's hair, immodest and extravagant dress, and jewelry, even wedding rings. While believers of an earlier day abstained from tea, coffee, soft drinks, chewing gum, and even pork, Perry Beetis didn't hold to that.

"I'm a firm believer in the divine healin',' speakin' in tongues as the Spirit gives utterance, an' castin' out devils," he said, "an' if they wanta drink strychnine, then I'll leave that up to them."

The bottle on the pulpit flashed across my mind. "Was that strychnine up there last night?" I asked.

"Yes, ma'am, an' you better not drink it," he warned me.

"Have you ever drunk any?"

"No, I never have, never tasted of it, got no desire to," he was firm. "If God ever moves on me, I'll drink it. It don't matter what it is, but I'm gonna wait on God jist like I have about the serpents an' if I wait on Him I won't git hurt, but if I don't wait on Him I'm liable to git killed the first go-'round."

After he repented and gave up bootlegging, Beetis had been employed at a saw mill, then at a foundry, and finally at a furniture factory before an on-the-job injury forced him to retire. Since then, his life had revolved even more around religion. Although he considered himself primarily an evangelist, he had pastored churches in Cleveland, Tennessee, and Kingston, Georgia, and now had one near Dolly Pond that he looked after in addition to his work with Rayford Dunn. When I asked how long he himself had been a preacher, he had to stop to think. "I'd say somewhere around seventeen, eighteen years, somewhere in the neighborhood of that. I don't know exactly. I remember what happened."

"Would you tell me about that?"

"Well, yeah, if you wanta hear," he said, uncertain. Once I assured him I did, he proceeded in an awe-filled voice. "One night I went to bed an' course I was in the bed by my wife and that's when that twenty-two-year-old boy was jist a baby. An' we went to bed an' sometime in the morning, around two or three o'clock in the mornin,' they was a man come an' got me outta my body. He come right through the roof of the house an' come right down there with me, come an' got me outta my body an' I crawled outta my body an' left it layin' in the bed an' he carried me right through the roof of the house an' when we got away from there I looked back an' I was alayin' in the bed, my body was, with my wife an' baby. I could see it jist as good as I'm alookin' at you right now. An' he carried me away into another world, back in this northern direction." Beetis gestured over his shoulder, through the trees. "We looked back on the earth an' I could see the saints begin to rise through the ground burst. An' this man spoke to me, he said, How did they all git up there at oncet? I said, They all left at oncet. An' that's the only two times he spoke to me. An' he said, How many are they? I said, Man, you know I don't know." Perry Beetis's face and his voice filled with wonderment. "But I seen the resurrection. An' he brought me back an' I come an' crawled in the bed, crawled in my body jist like I come out of it, jist like you'd crawl in a grass sack. An' I seen *allll* this an' seen the saints risin', seen the lights from 'em an' I seen them sailin' toward heaven an' I could see the glow from another world up yonder that we was sailin' toward. But, anyhow, whenever the light from them would shine through this earth an' out on the other side jist like—you've seen the sun, what they call the sun drawin' water from the earth, you know, an' the clouds be ashinin' through? That's what it looked like, the light from them. They would shine plumb through the earth an' out the other side. If a man coulda, you coulda got up on that an' walked. It wouldn't a been any trouble. It woulda helt you up, the light would.

"An' when I come to, when I revived, I was scared to death. I jumped outta that bed an' I headed to the livin' room an' I got in there and prayed. An' I couldn't keep from cryin'. Jist abawlin' an' cryin' like I'd been whupped. I feared I was gonna die ag'in. So I went in thar an' I woke my wife up. I said, You're gonna have to git up with me. I believe I'm gonna die ag'in. An' we got the Bible, she did, an' read out of the book of Revelations an' when she did, I hadn't never had no understandin' of the scriptures to amount to anythang, but when she read that to me it jist come to me like—" He snapped his fingers. "Aw, jist as clear. I had an understandin' of it. An' God spoke to me an' said, Son, I've called you to preach my Gospel, and said, I'm gonna give you a sign for a witness. Said, Rise an' prophesy and tell the people that three days from now, one of your loved ones will be dead, dressed, an' ready to bury. I arised an' prophesied, jist like God tol' me to. But He said, This is a sign that I've called you to preach my Gospel. An' three days from that day—my brother lived right across the road from me—an' three days from that day his baby was dead, dressed an' done in a casket an' ready to bury," Brother Perry ended, humbleness in his voice. "There's no mistakes in God."

The strychnine remained on the pulpit, near the Bible, but there were no snakes that night or the next. In conversation several people assured me someone would bring a rattler or maybe a copperhead to Sunday's homecoming, yet no one seemed to regret the absence of snakes, nor did it inhibit their energetic worship. Throughout each service, members of the congregation were seldom still, striding back and forth, shuffling, shouting, sometimes shaking their fists in the course of testifying or when they felt God "moving." Even in the midst of the sermon, folks would run up and down the aisle screaming, while whoever was preaching simply paused until the anointed individual signaled him to go on.

In *Migrants, Sharecroppers and Mountaineers*, Robert Coles wrote of church 'being an "event" for the rural poor and of their unself-conscious talk about *doing, going, being*. He quoted a North Carolina tenant farmer as boasting: "I come out of there and I'm taller. I'm feeling bigger." And so it was with the snake-handlers in Carson Springs. The first night Rayford Dunn told the congregation: "Whenever we come to the truth an' knowledge of God, we can have this same an-ointin'. Hallelujah to God, you can drink your strychnine, you can take up your snakes, you can do whatever your hearts desire tonight if we'll jist wait upon the anointin' of God. I believe if God tol' me to go out there on the freeway tonight an' this big tractor-trailer come down the road doin' a hunderd miles an hour, an' if God tol' me to wait till that truck got within a hunderd feet of me an' walk out in front of it, I believe, glory to God, I believe I could walk out there an' God would stop that truck."

Although the nightly singing lasted thirty or forty minutes, these services, unlike other revivals I attended, were not aimed at entertaining a people who put little stock in recreation and, in fact, considered diversions frivolous, even sinful. There were none of the usual jokes nor was there laughter, and instead of the often-humorous biblical monologues popular with many evangelists, the sermons here were simple, serious messages, sometimes stern rebukes about such everyday matters as godly dress and disciplining children. On one occasion Perry Beetis lectured parents: "Just whup him, don't threaten to knock his brains out. Don't be a devil while you do it. God give us them children to raise." While the lively, repetitious singing about heaven and a sweeter life soothed tired spirits and bruised hearts, the services were at times emotionally wrenching. For a people trapped in a hard, bitter life, they served as a sort of spiritual bloodletting, a means of releasing pent-up frustrations and hurts—even anger—most would have been hesitant to express outside the confines of church.

The services were always free-form, dependent solely on the leading of the Holy Ghost; nevertheless, each had a certain sameness: testimonies, a lengthy song session, a noisy "concert" prayer or two, a sermon of sorts, and a laying-on of hands. Occasionally a clattery old car would pull up bearing visitors from Canton, North Carolina, or maybe Jolo, West Virginia, but most nights the congregation consisted of the same faithful few—thirty or forty, at most fifty. During the services they worshiped with abandon unintimidated by my presence, at least as far as I could tell. But at other times they continued to hold back around me. At first, in my notes, I jotted down descriptions to identify members of the congregation: the small man with the crewcut, the curly-headed drummer, the woman in green, the young couple with the baby. Only gradually, as the nights passed, as they relaxed toward me and a form of trust began to develop, was I able to put names with faces and, more slowly still, facts of lives with the names and the faces.

Clyde Ricker had arrived during the song service carrying a worn black Bible, the word JESUS printed along the edge with a ballpoint in large block letters. I had recognized him immediately from photographs in periodicals reaching from the *Newport Plain Call* to *The New York Times*. Later when I mentioned this and that I hadn't expected to come across him in my travels, Ricker nodded understand-ingly. "There's been so much quoted," he allowed, "there's no telling where you'll meet me."

He said this as if he were somewhat pleased, though his tone certainly was not boasting but rather more of desperately wanting to please, and to attain some measure of acceptance among outsiders, for although a man of thirty, he had the round, soft innocence of a boy and the eagerness still for praise. His close-cropped hair was like freshly har-vested wheat and of that same color. In denim overalls, a wristwatch his only visible luxury, he seemed a simple mountain boy, born twenty-six miles away in Hot Springs, North Carolina, where he lived, even now, with his wife of ten months, tending Ricker's Odds 'n Ends. His few excursions from the area had been to snake-handling churches in other states, seeking them out in much the way more worldly youths do rock artists and rodeos. He did so out of the same longing for adventure and also because there he could feel accepted by people who shared his convictions and his lot in life and thus could bestow recognition for his courage in taking up serpents, drinking strychnine, and, above all, going to prison for his beliefs.

When I approached Clyde Ricker after the service, he had eagerly agreed to an interview and, with Pam and Jimmy Morrow in his pickup truck, led the way to an all-night restaurant off Interstate 40. There, with an air of importance, he took it upon himself to have the waitress find a quiet back room. "This gospel what we're talkin' about needs to be told," he said as the four of us took chairs, "an' that's what I'm here for. We're telling the story of Jesus an' what we believe." He backed up. "It's not exactly what we believe, it's what the Bible says."

As Pam and Jimmy Morrow looked on quietly, Brother Clyde re-called how he had first learned about snake-handling ten years ago from a preacher named Alfred Ball. "I met him an' started talkin' to him an' I wanted to learn more," he said. "I couldn't stay away, an' so I come down to the church an' repented an' whatever—joined the church—an' been with 'em ever since."

"Were you brought up in a church?" I asked.

"Freewill Baptist," he said, indicating that his parents and three brothers remained active in that faith. "They're completely against us, from all this. I'm the only one in our family that's a minister an' that believes in Holiness."

Jimmy Morrow nodded in agreement. Six years ago, when he was twenty, he had given up chicken fighting and gambling to join the Jesus Name faith. "God kept callin' me an' callin' me," Morrow remembered, "but I wouldn't take heed, an' I was out thar an' we was fightin' chickens an' it sound like a voice from heaven. It tol' me right thar, it said, It's me or the chickens, an' I knowed it was the Lord right then. I said, Lord, give me till tomorrow, an' I'll get shed of my chickens. I got shed of 'em an' I was under a conviction about eighteen months before I ever made it right."

Before that, Morrow had gone for a time to a Missionary Baptist church, which most of his family still attended. "I got three brothers an' three sisters, an' Grandma—my mama's mother—she had sixteen children. We got about two hunderd an' seventy cousins, but I'm the only one come into the Holiness faith." He leaned across the table, a certain gravity in his voice. "See, ever'one of 'em's ag'inst me today. Ever'one. They'll jist tell you that you gone crazy, you gone bad, but you know, they go around speakin' evil about thangs they don't know nothin' about."

Although until now we had not spoken, I had noticed Jimmy Morrow, a stringy young man with dark-blond hair and a mustache—the only one among the clean-shaven believers. By nature he seemed shy, yet I had seen him suddenly become loud, bold, boisterous when he fell under the "anointing"—the term used to refer to those moments when the Holy Ghost took possession of the believers, and their words and actions were considered to be those of the Spirit. During tonight's service, in the midst of Perry Beetis's sermon, Morrow had suddenly jumped to his feet and strode back and forth across the front of the sanctuary, waving his fist, talking in tongues, sometimes stomping up and down until, physically and emotionally spent, he sank into the pew and motioned for Brother Perry to go on.

His wife, Pam, was not given to such animated demonstrations of her faith. A Missionary Baptist before their marriage three years ago, she had yet to handle snakes. Nevertheless, she shared her husband's conviction that God had power over them and insisted if He ever told her to, she would take up a serpent. At twenty she was delicate and fair with rich red hair. And although that beauty seemed doomed to be eroded far before its time, she did not complain about the hard, spare life she shared with her husband in a village twenty miles to the north, where he made traps, farmed—did whatever a man with less than a fifth-grade education could.

This church had offered the Morrows and Clyde Ricker something neither the Baptists nor the outside world could: a taste of heaven. "The Holy Ghost, they said, is joy unspeakable an' full of glory," Brother Clyde said. "It's somethin' that's hard to explain. You jist have to feel it." He grappled for words to express perhaps the most prized thing in his life. "It's what heaven will be like," he sighed. "We are goin' to a place that God has prepared an' that Holy Ghost that we feel is jist a taste of what heaven is going to be like. Jist a little taste." His faced glowed as he imagined a time when his world would change. "If we really git to the point that we can stay in the Holy Ghost, stay in the spirit of God, it'll be like heaven right here on earth, but it gits so strong that you can't stand it," he said firmly. "I have had serpents in my hand an' the anointin' of God gits so strong that it'll kill 'em."

"Kill the snakes?" I interrupted.

Brother Clyde nodded. "Kill the serpents. Kill 'em completely. One time we had 'em in our hands an' it killed it and I lay it in the box an' it come back alive. But it's still the anointin'. If I had hanged onto it, it woulda never come back alive."

"Did you squeeze it?"

"No, jist helt it in my hand, jist like that."

One such case made *The New York Times* of July 23, 1945. That brief story reported that a rattlesnake which bit a man during a revival in Grasshopper, Tennessee, died the next day, while the victim "put in a full day working unconcernedly in the hot sun on his farm." Duke University anthropologist Weston LaBarre wrote of similar occurrences related to him by the snake-handlers he interviewed for his 1962 book *They Shall Take Up Serpents: Psychology of the Southern Snake-Handling Cult.* "The cultists explain that some of their members are filled with a strong power 'like electricity,' " LaBarre wrote, "and that snakes are shocked to death by this power." According to him, members of the Dolly Pond church claimed that when the mother of Tom Harden took up a snake it immediately ceased to struggle and became "limp as a necktie." LaBarre explored various explanations—including the possibility the serpents died of fright or injuries—but, in the end, came up with none that scientifically satisfied him.

But for Clyde Ricker, the answer was simple: It was the power of the Holy Ghost. He said he felt that same "taste of heaven" when he prayed for the sick and cast out devils, but the sensation was strongest when he handled snakes. "It covers me up completely. Sometimes it feels like my hair is standin' on end an' my hands are not even there. My legs, my face gits so numb, I git to a place where I don't care who's settin' beside me, who's settin' behind me, I don't care who's thar, I jist go ahead an' obey the Lord."

Indeed, during the two services I had attended, Clyde Ricker had participated freely, testifying, offering prayer requests on behalf of others, assisting with the laying-on of hands. When he came forward to sing, he was more animated than most, gesturing and sometimes placing his hands together and pointing his index fingers toward the congregation like six-shooters. There was in him, I speculated, a need to be seen, to be on the frontline. In June of 1975 when the church —with the help of the American Civil Liberties Union—unsuccessfully challenged Tennessee's law prohibiting snake-handling on the grounds that it violated First Amendment rights, Clyde Ricker was among those who took up a two-foot copperhead in a rare public demonstration in front of the Cocke County courthouse. And when the *Knoxville Journal* showed up for the church's 1980 homecoming, he willingly posed for the photographer with a giant timber rattlesnake.

Earlier Perry Beetis had told me Clyde Ricker was among those arrested during the 1975 melee in Kingston, Georgia, and, in fact, had served the longest time in prison. When I asked about this, Brother Clyde acknowledged that he had—not with any shame but rather boldness and perhaps a bit of pride. In the eyes of the faithful, his sentence—like the strychnine deaths of Jimmy Williams and Buford Pack—marked Ricker as a modern-day Christian martyr.

The incident occurred on August 17, 1975, when Clyde Ricker, then pastor of the Kingston church, and six of his members showed up with serpents at a nonsnake-handling church and attempted to witness, creating what both sides agreed was "a commotion." At the trial, the Reverend Doyle Hatfield, minister for the Calvary Holiness Church, said he was struck in the face with one of the snakes and his sister was bitten on the arm by another when she tried to come to his aid. According to news accounts, the ruckus started when the Calvary congregation drowned out Ricker's testimony with singing and he went to his car and returned with a serpent box. The defendants swore the box contained only two copperheads; a member of Calvary Holiness insisted that besides the copperheads there were at least two or three rattlesnakes. Whatever the total, witnesses said they saw both Ricker and Carl Porter, Jr., handling the serpents. Some accused the visitors of flinging copperheads at Calvary Holiness folks, and the Reverend Hatfield told the jury Porter "hit me in the face with the snakes." The latter acknowledged that when Hatfield "got to pushing on me," trying to get him to leave, he reached and got the snakes. "I might have hit him," Porter conceded, "I won't say I didn't." However, Porter's father, also a defendent, vowed, "I didn't see nobody hit nobody with no serpents." In the end, Clyde Ricker and Carl Porter, Jr., were sentenced to six years in prison for disturbing a public worship service and for assault with a deadly weapon—snakes. The other defendants were charged only with disturbing a worship service and ordered to serve twelve months each on a county work-release program.

Now Ricker told his side of the story in halting, measured detail, insisting he had been falsely accused. He had not hit anyone with a snake nor had he turned any loose. The pastor's sister, he said with gentle accusation, had lied about being bitten. Although sentenced to six years (three to be served in prison, three on the outside, under supervision in a work-release program), he ended up actually serving fourteen months in the county jail at Cartersville, Georgia.

"How did you feel when you were sent to prison?" I asked.

"I cried," he said quietly. "I felt let down, but while I was there in prison I got to talk to people that had two and three hunderd years, five or six life sentences, people that had committed murder, people that had done all these crimes, but the Holy Ghost jist covered me and I could testify an' tell them about the Word of God."

"Did being in prison change your life?"

"No," he insisted, "it made me want to be closer. It made me want to go on an' do what I can for the Lord." As a trusty he was allowed to attend church every Saturday night, he said. One weekend, after some deputies found a copperhead near the church, they came to get Ricker, watching as he carried it from the road into the sanctuary— an incident Brother Clyde interpreted as God's way of allowing him to witness to the officers. "Through the anointin' of God," he told me, "anythang can happen."

In several stories I had read that at the time of the interview Clyde

Ricker was recuperating from a snakebite. Now he said he had been struck twenty-five times.

"Were any of them bad?" I asked.

"I swelled up a few times," he said, quickly adding "but I never at one time been to the doctor. At any time I've been bitten I went to Doctor Jesus, that's all I went to, an' jist prayer." He held up his middle finger. "See, now here's a cottonmouth. This nail come off. From this joint up is completely numb, an' when it gits cold, *it's* cold. That happened back when I was in Georgia, before I went to jail."

In the beginning days of serpent-handling, the practice was abandoned for more than twenty years in its East Tennessee birthplace after the first of the faithful was bitten. Eventually, however, a snakebite came to have no negative theological ramifications unless the victim died, and in time many leaders began to somewhat proudly let it be known that they too had been victorious over snakebites. Hensley himself once boasted that he had been bitten four hundred times "till I'm speckled all over like a guinea hen." And when he died on July 24, 1955, at age seventy after a diamondback rattler bit him on the wrist during a prayer meeting near Altha, Florida, hundreds turned out for the funeral to pay their respects.

Still, opinions as to why people are bitten vary widely. While some, like Brother Perry, believe that "if we git bit an' hurt we ain't jist exactly where we oughta be or it wouldn't a happened," most do not see snakebites as punishment or a sign of sin. As one West Virginia woman who had been bitten six times told a journalist: "That's just the way God wants it. This is a suffering life, and you have to suffer if you want to reign with Him." According to Mary Lee Daugherty, a religious scholar raised around the Holiness beliefs of Appalachia, the survival and even the deformities of victims sometimes demonstrates to believers that "Jesus still has power over life and death." When a person dies, Daugherty has written, some believe "God allowed it to happen to remind the living that the risk they take is totally real."

Clyde Ricker's own belief was that God sometimes allowed the faithful to be bitten for a reason, sometimes to spread His Word. "One time I was in Columbus, Ohio—I went up there for a revival, an' there was a sister prophesied that someone would git bit but it wouldn't hurt the Word," he illustrated. "This was on a Tuesday night. I got bit in the chest by a copperhead. On Friday night the revival started an' we run a revival for a week or more, an' the house was packed ever' night. See, that was for a reason. It had to come to pass to confirm the Word. She said that I would git bit but it wouldn't hurt the Word." He patted his worn old Bible. "The flesh it would hurt, but the Word that dwells in me it wouldn't hurt."

Clyde Ricker's life, like that of Pam and Jimmy Morrow, went strictly by that big, black book, most especially the verses in Mark 16 and the signs promised them, as believers. They had been anointed to do all of them, even partake of poison and handle fire. The latter was actually practiced—sometimes with a blow torch—on the strength of three Old Testament passages, including the one in Daniel relating the deliverance of Shadrach, Meshach, and Abednego from the fiery furnace.

Now Ricker demonstrated how it was done. "You take a bottle, a Coca-Cola bottle or a can, put kerosene in it with a wick come up about so high," he said, holding his hands apart roughly the height of a soft-drink bottle. "You put it under your chin, hold it there. Or I seen a brother take a sister's hair and hold it there. He'd go right through her hair an' wouldn't even singe it or burn it."

"Is it done very much?"

"Sometimes quite a bit."

With Jimmy Morrow's help, Brother Clyde enumerated some of the church's other doctrines. "We don't believe in a sister cuttin' her hair," he said. "We don't believe in a woman or a sister that goes to church an' wears her dress up way high. It don't have to be floor-length but long enough to be becomin' to Holiness."

"We believe in ever'thang bein' decent," Jimmy Morrow explained.

Opening his King James to Deuteronomy, Brother Clyde proceeded to read from the twenty-second chapter. "A woman shall not wear that which pertains to a man, neither shall a man put on a woman's garment for all that do so are an abomination before the Lord thy God." He looked up from the scripture. "See, we don't believe in a woman wearin' britches. We don't believe in women takin' an' goin' swimmin' unless the sisters go together or the brothers go together because the Bible says ever'thang we do we need to do in the name of the Lord decently an' in order. We don't believe in free love. We don't believe in the sisters kissin' the brothers or the brothers kissin' the sisters. We believe in a sister greetin' a sister an' a brother greetin' a brother."

"Greet the brethren with a holy kiss," Jimmy Morrow quoted scripture. "Hit don't say greet your sister with a holy kiss."

Earlier Morrow had said he would be at the next evening's service if he caught some snakes. Now I asked where he would go to find them. "Anywhar a man can git out an' git 'em," he said, "back through thar in them mountains an' stuff."

"Do you usually have serpents?"

"Sometimes we do," Brother Clyde volunteered. "A lotta times at a homecomin'." He smiled. "I think there'll be quite a few there this weekend. The brothers that come from West Virginia, they'll have aplenty of 'em."

"But at a regular Sunday-night service you don't always have them?"

"Serpents in this part of the country never do crawl till up in July an' August," Jimmy Morrow said.

"So the rest of the year you don't find them?"

"Ever' once in a while we run across some, but it's not all that many in this part," he said, explaining the brothers often tried to keep the snakes through the winter. "I caught one in October an' I kep' him up to January—that's as long as I kep' him. I fed him an' stuff, but he froze out when hit got real col', an' then I had three one time I kep' nine months. Clyde handled 'em several times—you remember I brought 'em out thar in the holler?" Ricker nodded. "Clyde handled 'em an' we all had good vict'ry over 'em."

When the conversation turned to strychnine, Clyde Ricker said the only way you could buy it was to tell the pharmacist it was to kill rats. "We don't do that," he said. "See, some people bring it to us, some other people from West Virginia. They can git it legal."

"Were you a member of this church when Jimmy Williams and Buford Pack died?" I asked.

"I was there when it happened," he said, recalling that night. "Jimmy Williams took a little small jar of strychnine, took a glass about this high—a little skinny one—he filled it full of water, to about right there. He took a teaspoonful of strychnine, put it in the glass, stirred it up." Ricker took a spoon from the table and swirled it in a small water glass. "He come up, he drunk half of it an' set it down. Jimmy Williams, he first drunk it. Buford come along, he drunk the rest of it, 'cept jist a little of it in the bottom. And then I went up there an'

started to drink it an' the Lord said, *Not yet.*" Brother Clyde's voice
deepened dramatically as he spoke on behalf of God, and it remained
grave as he continued. "I set it back down, an' Buford died in twenty
minutes after he drunk it. Brother Jimmy lived until the next mornin'.
He died in his truck."

Those were the only strychnine deaths Clyde Ricker knew about,
and the memory of them was vividly imprinted on his mind. The church
had been jam-packed for Jimmy Williams's funeral, and serpents had
been handled over the grave where he was buried in a cemetery up
on the hill. Buford Pack had been laid to rest in Marshall, North
Carolina, where he lived.

"How did you feel when that happened?" I asked.

"I felt sorrow," Ricker said, the sadness in his voice soon lifting,
"but I felt joy because I knowed where they was goin'. I knowed that
they was goin' to a better place. It was a lotta people said, Well, they
killed theirself. Let me put it this way: It was jist their time to go."

The night their father died Allen and Jimmy Williams, Jr., were
sitting in the tiny one-room church. Yet neither could recall much
about the incident that had brought a sort of fleeting fame to a simple
man whose death, along with that of Buford Pack, became national
news, written about in *The New York Times* and slick magazines,
mentioned, even, in books and on prime-time television. Although
Allen was only eight at the time and Jimmy ten, I felt the details must
have been imprinted on their young minds, as early childhood memories often are, from having heard them repeated over the years by
relatives and friends. Surely both had to sometimes think about the
deaths, especially when they watched other believers drink from containers of strychnine in that same sanctuary. But on the Thursday
afternoon we met, neither was willing to talk about that night except
as a point of reference, a means of dating other events, other observations, like the fact their stepfather Liston Pack had been pastor when
"our father left out." Liston, brother to Buford, now husband to Mary
Kate Williams, stepfather to Allen and Jimmy Jr. and their older sister.

From the first service I had noticed the young men, unaware of who
they were, impressed only with their all-American wholesomeness:
Allen, tall, slender, and tanned, in a football jersey, his smooth blond
hair precisely combed; Jimmy, of average build, in a freshly starched

shirt, his curly dark hair cut just below the ears. Either could have been the high-school basketball star, the student body president, the boy most likely to succeed. And indeed I had assumed, by their appearance, that they were of a new, more progressive generation who came to the revival not because of shared beliefs but out of duty and perhaps affection for their elders, and like so many rural young people would soon be seeking greener futures. But as we spoke, that impression was soon dispelled. Their lives, like their father's, revolved around church and the same narrow hollow. That was what they had known since birth, and they had no more desire to change than he had. Both had quit school in the ninth grade. At eighteen, Jimmy, employed at a furniture mill, was married and the father of a year-old girl. Allen trimmed trees with his brother-in-law, the same Alfred Ball who had helped found this church and who now pastored another a few miles away, on Cosby Highway.

When I asked if either had any special ambitions, Allen shrugged. "Not really," he said. "Jist keep on goin' to church. That's the main thang. Stay in church."

"Do you think you would ever become a pastor?"

Again he shrugged. "If the Lord called me to, I would be. If He don't never call, I jist soon stay like I am."

When I turned to Jimmy, he was equally indifferent. "I might one of these days," he said. "Don't know."

He and his wife, Teresa, lived in the house next to the church. Inside was disheveled and furnished with bric-a-brac, yet the couple didn't seem to mind the clutter or living without a telephone and a bath and having to share the church's outdoor privy. After all, Jimmy and Allen Williams were used to a rigid life-style. Their late father had been a strict disciplinarian, never permitting his family to have a television or a phone. The latter was not wrong, Jimmy Jr. remembered him admonishing, it was just best not to have one because all you'd do was talk about other people. And Allen agreed, that's most of the time true. Both young men now watched TV and went to movies, and Jimmy's somewhat rebellious wife trimmed her hair and on this day wore slacks. Otherwise, they adhered to the elder Williams's teachings and centered their lives around the church.

As small boys they had not thought it unusual that people handled snakes. "I wasn't really afraid," said Allen, the more talkative of the

two. "I'd seen it done all my life. It was jist somethin' you believed."
He himself had taken up his first serpent this past winter; Jimmy said
he had handled quite a few, whenever he could get hold of one. He
and his brother agreed the anointing was a marvelous feeling, something they couldn't describe beyond that.

Neither had ever drunk strychnine, and when I asked how they felt
about their father's death, only Jimmy responded. "That's none of my
business, really," he said in his characteristically low-key manner. " 's
between him an' the Lord, I guess."

"Did that affect your wanting to drink strychnine?"

"No," he insisted, "it don't bother me. If God told me to, I guess I
would, but if He don't tell me to, I'm not goin' to."

What both did remember was the reaction toward them in school,
as they were growing up. Allen, active in sports and more outgoing,
had fared better, with some of his friends taking up for him. But the
quieter Jimmy had not been so fortunate.

"They always made fun an' stuff," Jimmy said. "It was pretty hard.
Even the teachers done that. They'd call you strychnine drinker, stuff
like that. Snake-handler. Crazy."

"The teachers did that too?"

"Some of the teachers made fun," he reiterated, "but they didn't
come out an' tell you."

"What was the reaction when your father died?"

The room was quiet, but Jimmy Jr. answered so quickly that I did
not catch his words and had to ask him to repeat what he had said. "I
ain't," he said in a low, firm voice, "gonna say nothin' about that."

From the first night, John Fish had seemed as out of place among
the snake-handlers as I did. He had the look and manner of a small-
town businessman and was better educated, more prosperous too, than
the others—he and his wife, Mary, each drove a car, one of them a
Fiat sedan that stood out among the decrepit cars and trucks. It seemed
incredible that he should have much, if anything, in common with the
rest of the congregation; more incredible still that he was among the
most vocal. Although less prone to show his emotions, he actively
participated in the services, reading scripture, offering prayer requests,
seeing that the offering plate was passed for Rayford Dunn's gas money,
even punctuating the sermon, the testimonies, the singing with con-

trolled yet forceful responses. While I could imagine him as a deacon in a Baptist church or a worldlier Assembly of God, I found his presence here puzzling.

My curiosity was equaled by his distrust of me. The first night he had confronted me, wanting to know who I was writing for. Even after I gave him the name of my New York publisher he eyed me with suspicion. "You ain't with *Hustler*, are you?" he pressed. I assured him I wasn't. Still he hadn't seemed satisfied. "They did an article and published it without telling us," he said, "and we didn't appreciate it."

Fish was cool toward my request for an interview, indicating we might be able to talk Saturday, before service. When I asked Mary Fish, she said she would have to check with her husband. She herself was a pleasant woman, warm and friendly in spite of her shy nature. Like her husband, she was actively involved in the services, coming forward each night to sing with Peggy Brown or Brother Bud's mother-in-law or one of the younger women who showed up from time to time. She was slightly taller than average, with long, dark hair wound into a bun and secured on top or at the back of her head. Often she wore long dresses in colorful cotton prints, and although at thirty-eight she was missing some teeth and her skin was pitted, I could imagine the once-unspoiled beauty that must have attracted John Fish, ten years her senior. And I wondered if his slight worldliness might not have appealed to her.

As the nights passed, she—like many in the congregation—had grown relaxed toward me, thoughtfully asking if I was enjoying my stay and if I needed anything. But John Fish continued to hold back, reluctant to exchange pleasantries or to give me so much as a smile. What few words we did exchange were brief and to the point, for he was not given to idle conversation any more than he was to outwardly showing his feelings.

That Saturday as we sat in the Fishes' Fiat talking, he remained almost aloof, glancing sidelong out the window, his tone flat and disinterested and punctuated by long, bored sighs. Yet there was an honesty about him, a frank openness that caused him to carefully consider each question and to respond as accurately as he knew how, for unlike the others he had tried to base his beliefs on reason rather than emotion. Just as he had made Mary Fish show him where the Bible said a man should take up serpents, he seemed to make a conscious effort to present me with proof. Whether that was merely to preserve his own image or out of a genuine concern for those who worshiped with him, I could not tell. But he seemed to have assumed the role of protector and guardian and was anxious that what I wrote not reflect badly on him, on any of them. When I mistakenly assumed that he had lived in Cocke County all his life, he was quick to let me know he had been a career military man and had spent time in various parts of the world before returning to Newport in the early 1970s. And I had not been wrong about his appearance: He was, he said, "an air-conditioning-refrigeration-heat pump specialist."

Although Mary Fish's father had preached Holiness off and on, because of her parents' early divorce she did not have a churchgoing childhood. And John Fish had quit attending the nearby Open Door Church as a youngster after his Sunday school teacher was forced to leave the county for embezzling money from the bank. Neither he nor his wife had again become active until the early seventies when they occasionally attended a Pentecostal church in Norfolk, Virginia, where he was stationed. Then, after they moved back to Newport with John Fish commuting on weekends between there and Norfolk before his retirement, Mary, unbeknownst to her husband, began coming to the Carson Springs church.

"I'd get home about eight o'clock Friday night, then leave Sunday afternoon," John Fish recalled, "and they was having a homecoming and ever'thang over here. Mary was in a hurry for me to go back so she could come, and I didn't want her to come here where them people was handling them snakes."

"He was sure against it," Mary Fish agreed. "He wanted me to promise him I wouldn't come over here, and there wasn't no way I was going to promise him that. So he left and I come over here. Then he saw, I guess, in the paper where somebody had been bit or something or another—for some reason he knew I had been there."

I turned to John Fish. "Were you angry when you found out?"

"I don't know," he said flatly. "Don't remember."

"So what did you do?"

"Well, Mary, she told me it was in the Bible and I told her no, it wadn't in the Bible, and she showed me it was. And I got straightened out down in Morristown, got baptized at that church they got over there. Robert Grooms, the one that's pastor here, was pastor over there then." He gave another of his long sighs. "And since seventy-four we've been in it either here or at Alfred Ball's church, or over at Morristown or Marshall or somewhere."

"When did you first go to one of the services?"

"I come with Mary one weekend, over here I think it was—" he started, with Mary Fish interrupting to explain, "This was before he repented, he came here with me."

"Do you remember what you thought?" I asked.

"Well, now, they had the spirit of the Lord, these people did," he said thoughtfully, "something you could feel." He sighed and with his usual restlessness got on with the story, not bothering with in-between details. "And then after I got straightened out, I come over here and I was standing in the congregation there and it come to me—the Lord said, Why do you believe I don't have power over these serpents? It wadn't too long after that I was handling 'em, but I had no desire to handle 'em, I don't reckon."

His anointing had probably been stronger in those days than it was now, John Fish conceded. He didn't handle snakes as much as he used to, but then neither did anybody else. When I asked why, he shrugged. "Probably ain't living as close to the Lord as they should be." He hesitated, then went on. "Well, I'm a strange one. I don't get 'em because somebody else has got 'em. I get 'em if the Lord moves on me to get 'em and if He don't move on me, they can handle 'em all night long and I'll not fool with 'em."

Earlier, during one of our rare exchanges, we had talked about the church's run-ins with authorities. John Fish agreed that the period just after Buford Pack and Jimmy Williams died had been one of the more intense campaigns to enforce the Tennessee law prohibiting snake-handling.

"The law was out here one night that me and Mary come," he said. "I had a tie on and a sports coat, and they told 'em if they handled any serpents they were going to put them in the jail house. If I remember correctly, Alfred Ball said, If the Lord moves on you, go ahead and handle it. And two Tennessee Bureau of Investigation men was sitting in the congregation. Well, Liston Pack come in and got the serpents out, and he wanted the TBI men to stand up and be recognized and two of 'em did, and he said he wanted that other un to stand up too—he was talking about me."

"I guess that was the first night he came," Mary Fish said.

"I wadn't a TBI man," her husband continued, as if never interrupted, "but he thought I was. Anyway, they locked Alfred Ball and Liston Pack up. And the Civil Liberties Union took it to the Supreme Court, and they refused to hear the case and left the lower court ruling stand, that it was a misdemeanor to handle serpents or to display them in any manner or to drink strychnine or to carry it around."

The arrests of Liston Pack and Alfred Ball came after a Chattanooga man was bitten during the 1973 homecoming services. They were charged with contempt of court for ignoring the temporary injunction handed down in the wake of the strychnine deaths. Pack was fined $150, and Ball, $100. After failing to pay the fines, they were given jail sentences of thirty and twenty days, respectively, four of which they served before relatives and friends paid the fines. The ACLU then took on the case, arguing the Tennessee law violated First Amendment rights to freedom of religion. Although the State Appeals Court decided in the defendants' favor, the Tennessee Supreme Court reversed that ruling in September 1975, upholding the law on the grounds that "Tennessee has the right to guard against the unnecessary creation of widows and orphans . . . The right to believe is absolute; the right to act is subject to reasonable regulation designed to protect a compelling state interest." Six months later the U.S. Supreme Court let the state ruling stand.

Since that time local authorities had ignored the law and the 1973 injunction. "They'll not bother us as long as nobody don't get snakebit and die," John Fish said, "and if somebody gets snakebit and dies here in this church, the press gets ahold of it and then the district attorney's going to have to do something about it. And that's when it'll happen. Or if somebody drinks strychnine and dies."

Neither John nor Mary Fish had ever drunk strychnine, and when I asked if people did so very much, she replied, "Not that often," letting her husband elaborate. "Andrew Click drinks some sometimes," John Fish said. "That's what's in that li'l ol' jar sitting on the pulpit." He nodded toward the church. "And Clyde Ricker drunk some and he got scared, but the Lord moved on me to tell him he'd be all right. But he got scared anyway and they got him out here and got to walking him and he went down to the next house down there and got him some milk. He was living in Cumberland Gap, so he went back over there and he called back on Wednesday wanting to know if it'd be all right if he drunk any water, after he didn't drink nothing but milk till Wednesday. But he was going to be all right." There was a touch of exasperation in John Fish's voice that Clyde Ricker had ever doubted he would. "It's the Devil hit him, that's what it was, told him he was going to die."

"If you felt God was telling you to drink it, would you?"

Without hesitating, John Fish answered, "Why, yeah." He took a long look out the car window before continuing. "I'm kinda foolish, but I believe if you've got power over the Devil and over the serpent and if he bites you it shouldn't hurt you," he was confident. "I know an old brother, he's been bit twenty-three times. He ain't swelled up but one time and he was supposed to have the serpent put up at that time and he took somebody else's bite and suffered for it, but he had been bit twenty-two times in services and never swelled up at all. Now victory was his. You see what I'm saying?" I nodded uncertainly. "Anybody can grab up a serpent and get snakebit and swell up and die, but if you get snakebit and don't swell up, then you got the victory."

John Fish could not recall anyone dying from a bite at this particular church, though he did know of some bad cases and one fatal bite in Kingston, Georgia. I asked what reaction an "unanointed" person would have if he was bitten by a rattlesnake or a copperhead somewhere other than church, like the nearby Great Smoky Mountains National Park, and Fish said he wasn't certain. "It's according to what condition the snake was in," he said. "A snake don't have to put all his poison in at one time. He can put in a little bit or he can put a whole lot. If it's just to ward you off or something, he might not put much and you might not swell more than a wasp sting. But if he's trying to lay it to you, now you may swell up real bad. But all I ever seen that got snakebit swelled up some, except one feller and he got snakebit and it had no effect on him atall."

His answer was pretty much in agreement with that of herpetologists who say the gravity of a poisonous snakebite depends on the age, weight, and general physical condition of the victim as well as the condition of the snake's fangs and venom glands and the quantity and toxicity of its venom. Where the snake strikes and how deep it sinks its fangs are contributing factors. Experts also contend the rattlesnake's tendency is to withhold its venom and inject large amounts only when it is hurt or violently excited.

Thus far, many of the gifts of the Spirit that played such a central part in other revivals had been far less prevalent among the believers here. Little emphasis was placed on divine healing, and some members believed in seeking medical care for problems other than snakebites or the ill effects caused by drinking poisonous substances. I had seen no one slain in the Spirit and heard little speaking in tongues. The latter, in fact, did not seem necessary to be termed a Pentecostal, and both John and Mary Fish said they didn't speak in tongues, though he interpreted some. "They speak in tongues and then I know what it means," he explained.

"All the time?"

"No, just some of the time when it's meant for me to get up and say, then I know. If it's not meant for me to say then I may not know. And sometime when it's meant for me to say and I don't get up and say it, somebody else says it and it lines up with what I already know." He paused and momentarily studied the noisy arrival of cars for the evening service. "Now they's some of these women come here and prophesy and if they told me I was gonna die tomorrow," he said with conviction, "I'd be getting my burial clothes laid out."

For the most part, the Fishes' lives revolved around church. They attended three services a week, with Mary Fish sometimes going alone a night or two beyond that. Usually they went to Morristown twice a week and to Carson Springs once, visiting John Brown's church in Marshall once a month.

"That's about all we do is work and come to church," said Mary Fish, who was employed in nearby Gatlinburg. "Far as going out or anything, we don't ever do that. We might go over and visit Preacher Brown and them, but not very often. We come home from work and that's about it."

"Well, we go out to eat," her husband offered.

"But we're not the visiting type. We have a TV, but as far as going to a drive-in and stuff like that, to me it's wrong," she said, conceding "Maybe TV's wrong, but I wouldn't say that, but to me going to the drive-in, if you're a Christian you shouldn't do it. Now there's a lotta things I think's wrong that other people might not think so."

When I observed that these choices seemed like personal decisions, John Fish was blunt. "It's 'cause the letdown of the leadership of the church," he said firmly. "Now they's a lotta people you been talking to that don't even go to this church, see. The leadership of this church used to be strict and down the middle and preached hard against smoking, televisions, and various other things, being married twicet, and they preached against a wife working and I don't know what all they have preached against that they are now doing. If it was wrong five years ago, it's *still* wrong, from the way I see it."

"Do you see that as similar to what's happening to other religions, other denominations?"

"I don't know what they're doing in other denominations," he said flatly, "but I do know a Baptist man that raised tobacco and he had a fine crop. It was ready to harvest. And he took his mowing machine out there and mowed it down and ain't raised no tobacco since because he was condemned in this tobacco and got rid of it, at a financial loss to him—I don't know how much, but quite a bit. But he mowed it down and hasn't raised any since. It's what you're condemned in," he concluded. "Now they's some that smoke and they're not condemned in it, they say. And others are condemned in it. The Lord delivered Mary from smoking, and they cast that smoking devil out of her and she ain't wanted another cigarette."

"Have you ever smoked or drank?" I asked.

"I used to smoke three packs a day. I quit in nineteen sixty-seven. Used to smoke three packs a day, and I quit."

"That's a lot of cigarettes," I noted.

"Well, I used to drink a fifth of liquor a day too," he acknowledged. "I quit all that. I don't drink no more and don't cuss and don't chase women—none of that. I live pretty close to the Bible. I don't fast as much as I should and I don't pray as much as I should," he conceded, "but it seems like I'm always asking the Lord for something or 'nother."

When I asked how people reacted to him being a snake-handler, John Fish was not sure how much of his family knew. The one sister who did was opposed to it. As for acquaintances, he shrugged, "Well, most of 'em don't believe I go here, and if they do, they wanta know if I handle serpents. And they don't want to come or they make remarks, like they're going to be like Wendy Bagwell, they'll make 'em a backdoor or something or other. He has a song about that." The

latter reference was to a recording made by a popular gospel group
after showing up for a singing engagement at what turned out to be a
serpent-handling congregation—a recording Fish now called "Some
foolishness."

Mary Fish had also been the butt of jokes, like men coming in to
where she worked and making comments about "snake sandwiches."
But that didn't happen much anymore. As the editor for the *Newport
Plain Call* had told me, unless something happened to call attention
to the church, most local folks ignored it and its members, just as few
were inclined to join its ranks.

John Fish estimated this particular church might have fifteen members. "I doubt that many," he was candid. "Most of the time it's me
and Mary and John Brown and his family and Andrew Click and Robert
Grooms and his family, and that's about all there is." Liston Pack had
quit coming, Fish said, taking inventory of the church's founders and
some of its staunchest members. Alfred Ball had started his own church
up on Cosby Highway, and until last night's service, his former wife,
Eunice, had been "out in the world" since their divorce three years
ago. Even Nellie Pack, Liston's first wife, had left the area several
years back, taking her two children with her. And Clyde Ricker was
here awhile and then off somewhere else.

"So the revival has been a larger turnout than your regular service,"
I observed.

"Sometimes, now, it's different. Sometimes there may be fifty people
here. Course don't have to get too many to have fifty," he said with
an uncharacteristic touch of humor. "I think Robert Grooms got seven
young'uns, ain't he?"

The little clearing had begun to fill. I had thanked the Fishes for
their help and was preparing to put away my tape recorder when John
Fish spoke up, with what I felt sure had been on his mind throughout
the interview, indeed since my arrival the first night. "I've read articles
where they said that they get in a frenzy and all this other, and there's
nothing to that," he said, looking me more directly in the eye than he
had at any time before. "We don't get in a frenzy," he insisted, "and
we're not a cult. We just believe the Bible like it is. That's all there
is to it." He paused only briefly before pursuing his defense, the
evidence he felt would prove detractors wrong. "Most of the people
like to say that they're a bunch of illiterate people, but they're not.

I've been a couple of semesters in college and didn't have any trouble passing the entrance exam. And Alfred Ball, I'd say, could pass the entrance exam without any problem. It's just that we believe in the Bible. People like to make excuses for not handling serpents. They say it's taking up a man, but I don't know how you're gonna take up a man."

I interrupted to ask "What do you mean?"

"They say that handling a serpent is some man that is a sinner, see, but that's not what the Word means," he was firm, all vagueness having long since left his voice. "It meant literally a serpent. They omit this part of it, and they call us a fundamentalist church," he said with the sort of disdain most often provoked by terms like "hillbilly" and "white trash." "We just believe what the Word says," he said, "and let it go at that."

Most people had taken seats in the tabernacle when Rayford Dunn entered and placed the battered gray box on the floor, next to the pulpit. I had been interviewing John and Mary Fish when he glanced out their car window and in his usual offhand manner announced, "He's got a serpent box an' there's probably a serpent in it." Word that it contained a copperhead had spread quickly among the folk milling about the clearing, and now a bridled, unspoken excitement filled the air.

The singing was more spirited than the nights before, at times bordering on rambunctious, and I could not tell whether it was because of the snake's presence or that of Carl Parton and Sister Eunice. The latter was a buxom woman with shoulder-length black hair and a liking for dark stockings and flashy colors. Last night's service was the first she had attended since her divorce from Alfred Ball three years earlier. By her own admission she had not been living right, though that was not apparent from the way she took up a guitar and launched into the singing.

By contrast, Carl Parton was a tall, lean man who might have gone unnoticed had it not been for his enthusiasm and considerable talent for music. During Brother Perry's opening remarks, he tapped restlessly, rhythmically on Andrew Click's drum, eager to get on with the singing. He along with Sister Eunice and his wife, Willene, brought a new electricity to even the old standbys, and their energy was infectious. The crowd sang full throttle, clapping and tapping their toes to the beat set by Parton and Pumpkin Brown on the guitars and Andrew Click's drumming.

For more than an hour the music continued, the emotional fervor building with every song. Rayford Dunn interrupted just long enough to take prayer requests and to make a teasing reference to the copperhead and the jar atop the pulpit. "We got snakes up here an' we got strychnine," he told the congregation. "If you git the anointin', come on up here an' handle 'em, but if you don't feel it, don't bother 'em because they're deadly. Hallelujah, the anointin' will do all thangs, but I can't do nothin'." He gestured toward the first pew. "C'mon, Brother Glenn, an' sing."

A man in his thirties hurried to the platform and took up one of the guitars, strumming as he approached the pulpit. He and two other men had arrived from Chattanooga during the singing, shaking hands with the local brethren as they made their way to the front. Brother Glenn himself was a bit of a showman, quickly taking to an audience and in no apparent rush to get on with singing. He strolled casually back and forth across the platform as he testified on the obligations of loving one another and doing God's work and anything else that seemed to come to mind—including the way he operated.

"I start singin' an' I listen," he said, running his fingers across the strings. "If a lotta people don't help me sing, I figure they don't like it so I jist put it up. I'm not gonna waste my energy, my strength, tryin' to pull a boatload of people that don't wanta be pulled."

The crowd shouted *Amen!* but Brother Glenn still did not sing, continuing to strum the guitar and witness for another ten or fifteen minutes before he called to Sister Eunice, "Git your guitar, Eunice, an' help me out." With her backing and that of the people, he sang confidently about judgment day. And when that song ended, he went through two more before finally relinquishing the microphone to Mary Fish and a young blond woman.

The sisters stood with backs to the congregation, their nasal voices leading the rest through stanza after stanza of "I Can Almost See the Light of Home," the rhythm punctuated by the swaying of the people's bodies and their clapping. They had entered another chorus when I realized Rayford Dunn had removed the copperhead from its box. The snake squirmed and its sharp tongue lashed out toward Brother Rayford as he held it high, his face contorted as he spoke to the serpent in unknown tongues. *"Eeee-lolola-masata-satamotayah."* The song was a lively gospel waltz, and yet it and the singing seemed tranquil compared to the rousing selections earlier in the service. Certainly the people had not reached the emotional crescendo I had thought necessary for them to feel compelled to take up serpents. But once the copperhead came into view, they burst into a cacophony of screaming and shouting that grew in volume as Rayford Dunn clutched the struggling serpent with both hands, stomping up and down the aisle and praising God. All the while, Mary Fish never turned around nor did she and the young woman let up on their singing, their voices competing with Dunn's glossolalia and the loud, strong exclamations by Brother Fish and Andrew Click. The bedlam continued to rise until Rayford Dunn returned the serpent to the box, where it remained through two selections by Eunice Ball and an introduction by Perry Beetis of Brother Muncy and Jimmy Selly, who had driven in from Logan, West Virginia.

When Brother Perry called on the latter to testify, the balding blond came to the pulpit with great reticence. He was a thickset man in still-stiff jeans. At first he addressed the congregation in a soft, meek voice, dutifully thanking them and God for allowing him to be in their midst. The people listened with a polite quietness until Jimmy Selly got started about being raised Catholic and worshiping statues and feeling he was missing something before he happened upon a Holiness church down the road from where he lived. "I could tell," he cried, "there was somethin' they had I didn't!" The congregation came alive with shouts of glory, and Brother Selly seemed to gather confidence. His voice became hypnotic, each phrase marked by a loud, heavy *huh* as his testimony grew into a full-fledged sermon. For almost an hour he preached to the people, reminding them God had promised to save their souls, not their flesh, and that He hadn't said the way would be easy.

"But fear not," Selly comforted his audience, "He won't let you down. Jesus said, I'll never leave you even to the end of the world."

Suddenly Jimmy Selly grabbed the bottle of strychnine, and I felt myself tense. "This right here is what I call God," he shouted, holding up the jar for all to see before he set it back on the pulpit. "You don't see God with the natural eye," he said. "You wanta speak with God, you hear the Word first. You wanta see God—" He picked up the gray box and dumped the copperhead onto the pulpit. "This is the way you see God!"

As pandemonium broke out in the sanctuary, I kept my eye on the strychnine, fearful that someone might take up the bottle and drink from it. All around me the people moaned, shrieked, some shivering and jerking in what could best be described as a spiritual orgasm. I was reminded of an account by a journalist who happened upon such a scene in the 1940s. It had, he wrote, "the strange, unreal—and disturbing—quality of a fevered dream." And I can find no better words to describe those moments in the Carson Springs church when Preacher John Brown scooped up the deadly copperhead and raced around the pulpit in the midst of what that same reporter would have termed "delirium."

I sat mesmerized as I watched timid individuals suddenly become bold and uninhibited, taking control not only of their own destinies but of deadly copperheads and rattlers. Under the "anointing," I realized, they spoke to and for God, prophesying and speaking in tongues, and during those moments were viewed not as illiterate but wise. Men considered losers by the rest of society became strong, brave, important, big, as they challenged deadly snakes and drank strychnine. And preachers were accorded added stature, which surely must have a bearing on the claim by eight out of the twelve men I interviewed that they had been "called" by God.

For a people who had experienced the harshness of life, heaven and hell were real, and God was like an ever-present father they talked to and about as casually as they would an earthly parent. He was both loving and a strict disciplinarian. Once Rayford Dunn told the congregation: "Junior Porter needs God back in his life. He had a heart attack. You jist can't back up on God an' not git caught." And members of the congregation frequently made remarks such as "God woke me up this mornin' " and "When kids is sick, if a guy can't git aholt a God he oughta take 'em to a doctor."

God was the source of all knowledge, the giver of power. And with that power, He bestowed a sorely needed sense of pride and of self-worth on people who, in the eyes of the outside world, were meaningless. But perhaps, as Robert Coles noted, God was most merciful in choosing the kind of life He led on earth. As Clyde Ricker told me,

"We have to live a life that's pleasin' to God, not to man. Man thinks we're crazy. Man thinks we've lost our mind. Let's git rid of him—That's what they did with Jesus. They said, Let's do away with Him. Let's crucify Him. Jesus lives in us. The Spirit, the Holy Ghost lives in this ol' flesh right here."

For Brother Clyde and his fellow believers, serpent-handling was not only a form of excitement, it was carrying on the work of Jesus, Who—like them—was poor, persecuted, and the child of God.

The next morning when I arrived for the homecoming celebration, the door to the church was still locked and a calm lay over the hollow. To one side, a sheet of plywood had been stretched across two saw-horses to make a table. Next to that, under a tree, canned soft drinks were iced down in a galvanized tub, and Preacher John Brown knelt beside it adding more. Except for Brown and the Morrows, the clearing was empty and quiet, with only Jimmy Morrow's voice occasionally rising in a ripple of excitement. Yesterday God had given him victory over a large rattlesnake on Hall's Top. When Preacher Brown suggested he show it to me, Morrow obligingly brought out a rust-red box and removed the serpent, its furious rattle ruffling the quiet.

"God tol' me whar he was at," he said, holding the snake where I could get a good look at it. "He give me vict'ry over it Saturday mornin' an' He tol' me to brang it to church an' He'd give me vict'ry over it today." As he grasped the wriggling creature, Jimmy Morrow seemed to fall under the anointing, his speech becoming rhythmic and repetitive as it often did when he witnessed during the services. "We're servin' a mighty an' a livin' God if we only trust in Jesus Christ's name, thank God. He's the light of the world an' He tol' us that we'd be the light of the world after He goes back, thank God, an' the Jesus Christ people, thank God, *are* the light of the world."

Occasionally a car or truck would straggle into the clearing, with Jimmy Morrow repeating the story to anyone who would listen, each performance accompanied by the whirring snake and no less animated than the first telling. When he finally ran out of an audience, he directed his restlessness at a water snake sunning itself on a rock in the creek. With slow, deliberate aim, he began chunking pebbles at the snake until, reluctantly, it slithered back into the stream, and his attention returned to the rattler in the box.

Earlier, on my way to the hollow, I had passed John Fish's pickup heading back toward town. Now the green truck returned, bearing another pair of sawhorses, and as I watched, Fish and Preacher Brown assembled another table, next to the first. Over the years the two men had become friends. Although John Brown was pastor of House of Prayer in the Name of Jesus Christ in nearby Marshall, North Carolina, his family—like John and Mary Fish—had been among the revival's most active participants. His wife, Peggy, was one of the lead singers and the woman I approached that first night for help. The curly-haired guitarist was their seventeen-year-old son John Jr.—or "Pumpkin," as most folks knew him—and Mark, their eleven-year-old, had been coming to services since he was born. Brown himself often gave lengthy testimonies and animated demonstrations of the signs, speaking in tongues, sometimes wringing his hands and running up and down the aisle and circling the pulpit. An upholsterer by trade, he was a slight man in his mid-forties, born and raised in Newport with an on-and-off-again upbringing in the Freewill Baptist Church. He and Peggy Brown had been brought into the Jesus Name faith by Liston Pack shortly after this church was founded, when it was still just a house with the partitions removed and the congregation had yet to handle a serpent.

Now Preacher Brown fondly remembered how the members had prayed for God to give them a sign if snake-handling was right and then one night, during service, a copperhead crawled up the church steps and the late Jimmy Williams took it up.

"A year later the Lord give me a rattler serpent," Brown said, "an' He let me handle that an' I been in the faith ever since. It is right, the signs of the Gospel is," he was positive. "A lotta people like to go around that part of it, but it's there an' it's the truth. If that's not the truth then it would give me room to doubt some other part of the Bible. It's a good way an' it's the only way we'll ever reach the kingdom of God, I'm persuaded in my mind." He focused his attention strictly on me. "I'd like to see you baptized in the name of Jesus Christ before you go back home. I certainly would. Receive the baptism of the Holy Ghost."

"It looks like it feels good," I said nervously.

"It is good," he was emphatic. "It don't only feel good, it'll keep you. It'll make you feel good all the time." He hesitated, then explained, "Now, I'm not sayin' you won't have trials an' afflictions because you will, but it's to temper you into the faith. To make you strong."

John Brown watched as a car rattled into the clearing. Then he smiled as he remembered lighter moments, like the time his then-four-year-old son Mark picked up a snake from the middle of the road and proclaimed, "Praise God!" That story reminded John Fish of still another occasion when the youngster pursued a rattlesnake under the Browns' home, demanding "Come on back here, you belong to my daddy."

The three of us laughed at those more humorous episodes, and for a while longer the two of them continued to reminisce, the group in the hollow essentially remaining the same. And when those stories were exhausted, when there was nothing more to do but wait for the others to arrive, we talked quietly about the week's events and about the weather—the idle conversation that fills so many days, so many lives.

Andrew Click had to stretch his short, little neck to its farthest reaches to see over the steering wheel of his shiny black Volkswagen, revival notices taped to both rear windows. Each night, without fail, the car would bounce into the clearing bearing him and his son Tracy and the silver drum Click had contributed to the musical ensemble. With the help of the boy, he would lug it and a loudspeaker into the sanctuary where, seated between the guitarists, he banged on the drum, reproducing the sound of a rotary washing machine.

At thirty-seven he was a wiry little man with a dust-color crew cut, birdlike features, and a cantankerous disposition exaggerated by a whiny nasal accent. In spite of his size, he was not one to hold back. His clear, clipped responses rose above all the rest, and once when he felt Brother Perry had allowed the witnessing to continue a bit too long, he complained sharply. "Ever'one's testified enough," he said testily. "We need the Word!" Even before the drum first arrived, he had sat up front rattling a tambourine, sometimes letting out a pained wail. The news editor for the local paper had described Click as well respected in the community. For a time he had worked for the state road department and today operated a service station midway between Newport and Parrottsville, a community seven miles to the east, where he was born and raised. Besides him, there were three preachers in the family. The others were Missionary Baptists, as Andrew had been before joining the Carson Springs church.

"I always wanted to come an' see it done," he told me as we waited for the church to be unlocked. "Then I was invited to come, an' that's my motto, fer 'em to come one time an' see it done. After they come one time I believe they'd wanta come back."

"When you came that first time, did you think you would join?" I asked.

"Never did have no idear," he said. "Sure didn't." However, he had soon become involved in the church and now served as a deacon. "It's been about eight or ten years," he estimated. "I don't know jist direct, but it's been quite a few years."

Meanwhile, his wife remained active at Victory Baptist Church, taking their two daughters with her and allowing only their ten-year-old son to accompany Andrew Click. "My wife she come one time. She said that was her last, which I still believe she'll finally start comin' with me. The Bible says He hears the desires of the heart, so that's my desire to have my family with me."

"Do you handle snakes?"

"I've handled copperheads an' rattlers an' cottonmouths, but I never have handled the others 'cause that's all we got around here," he said, volunteering "an' I drank quite a little bit of strychnine. I've always thought that was one of my signs, that I drank so much strychnine, which I believe that a lot of churches, they partake in that praying for the sick but I believe if God is able to heal the sick He's able to do the rest of it."

Several church members had singled out Andrew Click as one of those who drank the most strychnine, thus far without any apparent ill effects. And he attributed that to the Lord. "I'm not braggin' on myself, but God has let me do all the signs, all five of 'em. I've been under the anointin' of God so bad, so strong, in the church here that I couldn't even walk across the floor. I believe I been in the shape to where I could—if anybody'd shot me, it wouldn't've hurt me," he insisted in a tone of both wonder and pride. "I used to be a drinker an' done a little bit of ever'thang, but it's somethin' diff'rent from anythang the Devil has ever thought about offerin'.'"

Andrew Click had dropped out of school because of nosebleeds when he was only two weeks into the eighth grade. "Back then whenever I quit it wasn't like it is now," he explained. "You could go if you wanted an' if you didn't, you didn't have to. I was sickly, an' Daddy never did make me go because he thought my nose might bleed, which he had to come git me I don't know how many times."

"Are you sorry you didn't go farther?" I asked.

"Sure ain't. Never have regretted quittin'," he said, then he conceded, "If I had went on to school, why, they probably coulda been a lot more better thangs I coulda done."

When I asked if he had always done the same type of work, Click answered with the pride of an elected official. "I've dealt with the public, yeah. I always said I would like to have a little farm or a little business, which the first job I started on, public job, why, I started workin' with the public at Rock's Open Air Market. I worked up there an' then I started workin' at Newport Drug Store. I worked there fer I don't know how many years. I quit there two or three times an' would go back."

I glanced at Andrew Click's right hand with its four perfectly formed fingers but no thumb, not even a stub. Watching him play the drums, I had wondered if it was a birth defect. But now, without flinching, he recalled the accident.

"I got my thumb cut off in the meat chipper at the Super Dog," he said. "It lack ten days being a year there that I didn't do nothin'. When the doctor released me, I went back to git my job back an' they didn't have nothin' for me to do, so I started back workin' as a guard where I worked before I went to the Super Dog."

He described the incident without any evidence of self-pity that I could detect. It was just another event in a life that seemed ill fated from the beginning, though from the way in which Andrew Click talked about the past I got no inkling that he viewed it as such. He was happy with his family, his church, his community, his work—all the mundane jobs he had held over the years. Especially operating his gas station.

Quite a few people Click dealt with at the station were aware he was a snake-handler. Sometimes they even asked him to describe how it was done.

"Do any of them ever make fun?" I asked.

"Yeah," he said, "they make fun like the rest of the brothers up here git made fun of, but, I mean, I've got used to it. Back when I first

started comin' it kinda hurt me a little bit." But now Andrew Click
drew tall, and he brightened. "Over there I don't have to worry about
the boss comin' an' checkin' up on me. I enjoy people comin' over an'
talkin' to me about the Bible. You don't find too many people that
wants to do that, but I don't think anybody can talk about any better
thang."

Other than at the station, Click said, he hadn't been preaching as
much as he would like to. Nevertheless, he was confident he was getting
to the point where he didn't feel anything could hold him back. "I
know what it takes to preach the Word, an' if I'm livin' it I'll stand on
it an' preach it an' if I'm not I can't tell somebody what to do 'cause
I'm not doin' it myself."

From across the clearing I could hear the guitars and Eunice Ball
singing, and Andrew Click and I started toward the church, continuing
to talk.

"How many nights do you go to church during the week?"

"I've jist been goin' one night a week, Sunday night, an' try to go
Saturday night, not very often," he conceded, adding with new resolve,
"But I'm gonna try to git started back in the weekend services, 'cause
the more you do for the Lord, the more God's obligated to you."

It was almost eleven before the morning service finally got under
way. The jar of strychnine remained next to the Bible, and the serpent
boxes had been placed on the floor beside the pulpit. For all the
excitement the arrival of each box had created, the congregation seemed
oblivious to them and their proximity to the younger children crawling
about under the pews. Compared to the previous nights, the sanctuary
seemed empty. There were fewer than twenty adults and a half-dozen
or so small children. Neither Allen Williams nor Pumpkin Brown were
playing guitars, and many of the regulars—including Mary Fish and
Peggy Brown—were absent. Still other of the sisters were outside
fussing with the picnic lunch. During the singing and Rayford Dunn's
sermon, a few more people trickled in, but overall the audience remained small, the mood almost tranquil. Carl Parton and Sister Eunice
led the congregation through four songs, and even with those the usual
string of endless verses was cut short. Except for the two of them, the
singing was more dutiful than heartfelt, and I suspected the people
were physically and emotionally spent after last night's energetic wor-

ship. Only when Jimmy Morrow lifted the rattlesnake from its box did the crowd come alive. Shrieking and moaning filled the church ar d Andrew Click banged furiously on the drum, his own wailing rising above the rest. The din intensified when Preacher Brown stepped forward and took the serpent from Morrow, who then moved on to the gray box. Once Rayford Dunn joined in and the three men took turns handling the snakes, it was impossible to make out Jimmy Morrow's words as he jumped up and down shouting, the copperhead held dangerously close to his face. In less than two minutes, it was all over, with Brother Perry briefly taking up the rattlesnake, then flinging it back into the box.

After one final song Rayford Dunn lectured the folk on obeying God, reminding them it was a sin not to do something the Holy Ghost told them to do. "You can mistreat me," he said, "but, glory to God, you better not mistreat that Spirit." Andrew Click called out, "Jesus!" And Brother Rayford continued. "Whenever a brother takes them serpents up an' he ain't got that glory that comes from Above, he better be careful." He leaned over the pulpit to warn "They's danger in it. It'll cause you to collect your insurance, I'll guarantee you, if God's not in it." He went quickly from his sermon to the altar call, and by twelve-thirty the service was over, with the brothers up front embracing one another and then moving through the congregation shaking hands as they made their way to the door.

The church emptied quickly, and the people gathered about the picnic tables, shifting anxiously, eyeing containers of fried chicken, home-grown beans, potato salad, freshly baked cakes and cobblers. Once thanks had been given, they crowded in to fill their plates, men and children first, the womenfolk holding back for fear there wouldn't be enough food to go around. Then in twos and threes they clustered in the shade of nearby trees and next to the creek to visit and eat.

And when plates were empty and stomachs full, some headed home and others drifted toward the church for the final afternoon service. Two more rattlesnakes and four copperheads had arrived from North Carolina during lunch. Nevertheless, the crowd was smaller than that morning's, the service briefer still. And in less than an hour, the little church was again empty, save for the bottle of strychnine.

CHAPTER V

ERNEST ANGLEY:
"Win the Lost at Any Cost"

The procession by crutches and canes and wheelchairs had begun long before I arrived at Washington's Constitution Hall, crowding the space between the stage and the seats and extending back into the aisles. For almost an hour they waited, a collage of twisted arms and legs and faces mirroring hope and disappointment. To one side a young woman lay propped up on a stretcher. Her expression—like her frail body—was fixed in that moment when numbness deadens pain, her eyes open and staring yet seeing nothing. A middle-age couple took turns fanning her, the three of them seemingly oblivious to the more mobile members of the audience who already filled the orchestra level and spilled over into the balcony. No limousines or Mercedes-Benz circled the ornate hall of federal blues and gilded stars, where presidents and heads of state are sometimes entertained. Instead, on this Sunday afternoon in July 1982 the crowd was a racial anthology transported by public transit and chartered bus and dusty, dented cars from the cramped bungalows and dismal tenements of Washington and Baltimore, even from as far away as Atlanta.

In the excitement of congregating they appeared to forget the burdens that had brought them together: the arthritis, the diabetes, the debilitating doing-without. Fragrant with colognes and after-shaves, they became increasingly excited as a gospel group entertained while drawing the divergent *I*'s into an emotionally charged *we*, ready for the arrival on stage of the main attraction—Ernest Angley.

Although the Akron-based faith healer confined his appearances to weekly services at Grace Cathedral and on television and to one-night stands in big-city auditoriums, his beginnings had been in tents pitched along the two-laners that led from his native Gastonia, North Carolina, to the outer reaches of the South. From within twenty miles of the same red-dirt lowlands that produced Billy Graham, Angley was raised hard-shell Baptist, one of seven children born to a poor farmer-turned-textile worker who shepherded his family to church every time the doors opened. Young Ernest did not experience salvation until he was eighteen, when in the midst of his adolescent angst he felt as if God were dangling him over hell, threatening to drop him into the eternal inferno if he didn't surrender. Shortly thereafter he answered God's call to preach and headed for Cleveland, Tennessee, to the Church of God Bible Training School, known today as Lee College. For the next ten years he preached throughout the South and in 1952 chartered Healing Stripes Evangelistic Association, Inc. Two years later he—like Rex Humbard—followed the Southerners who migrated to Akron to work in the rubber plants that sprang up during World War II. Under his tent, Angley and his wife, "Angel," offered the dislocated a taste of home, attracting a following that enabled him in 1957 to build what an expensively printed booklet refers to as "a Modern Day Solomon's Cathedral," a garish orange-brick tabernacle with a price tag of more than $2.5 million. A year later he changed the names of both the church and the association to Grace Cathedral. After his wife died in 1970 and Akron turned from tire making to research and development, Angley again took to the road, conducting his regular Friday-night services at the cathedral, then immediately setting out for the civic centers of America in pursuit of his dispersed flock—the homesick, the hopeless, the hungering locked into inner-city poverty—offering them healing, religious fulfillment, and more: an afternoon of entertainment, of belonging, of feeling important. Now in the confines of the opulent hall, exhilarated by its star-studded carpet and plush curtains, and surrounded by their own kind, they swelled with uncharacteristic confidence and pride. Strangers before they arrived, drawn into fleeting friendships, they talked animatedly among themselves, the most mundane details of their existences seeming to assume new significance in the sharing.

As I made my way to the balcony, the quartet, in three-piece suits

color-matched to the auditorium's carpeting, performed vigorous selections, each singer stepping forward, in turn, to propel the song on.
The familiar, repetitious lyrics stirred the people until they too hummed,
clapped, and tapped their toes, ready, eager to give the evangelist a
welcome fit for a rock star. Shortly before two o'clock the baritone
raised his hand for silence. "Now get ready for the service that will be
following," he called to the crowd. "Reverend Angley will be coming
to the platform shortly. Be praying and thinking and be goodly always."
He and the other musicians exited, leaving behind only the pianist.
In a long, gauzy blue gown, the fragile young woman seemed to float
from the baby grand to an organ that had suddenly appeared on stage,
and then the music softened to a funereal quiver.

The woman next to me watched the transition with quiet anticipa-
tion. She was in her late fifties, I speculated, a slightly plump woman
neatly dressed in peach-color banlon. When I looked her way, she
smiled shyly and we exchanged names. A cleaning woman from sub-
urban Virginia, Mattie Farmer, like many in the audience, watched
Ernest Angley's weekly telecasts—for three or four years, she
estimated—and had attended previous services.

"I jes' like his meetin's," she replied when I asked about his appeal.
"They make me feel good."

"Have you ever been healed by him?"

"That's what I'm here today for," she said. "I got a allergy."

"I do too," I symphathized.

"You do too?" She brightened at our common bond.

As we talked, the baritone reappeared and the audience quieted.
"Let us stand all over this great congregation!" he exclaimed. "Get
ready for the services this afternoon and the honor and the glory which
is God." His arms swooped upward. "Regardless of what man says,
God says, *All* things are possible! So get ready to go away with armfuls
because God—loves—you! And at this time it's my happy privilege
to introduce your favorite evangelist—"

The introduction was overcome by cheers and applause as Ernest
Angley swept onto the stage, waving grandly and strutting back and
forth like religious royalty. "Thank you! Thank you!" he cooed in a
lingering North Carolina drawl. "And God loves you too!" His stubby
arms embraced the air, then hugged himself. "*Ouuuuuuuu!*" he squealed.
"That was some welcome! Now let me hear you say Praise the Lord."

The audience responded with an energetic hosanna, and Angley pushed for more. "Say it again!" The crowd's thunderous response set off a chain reaction:

Praise the Lord!
"Say it another time!"
PRAISE THE LORD!
"Again!"
PRAISE THE LORD!

The litany was repeated more than twenty times, each round growing louder, more intense. I sat fascinated by the exchange. In *The Art of the American Folk Preacher*, a study of black chanted sermons as an art form, Bruce A. Rosenberg observed: "The quality of the congregation appears to have a great effect upon the sermon, influencing the preacher's timing, his involvement in his delivery, and sometimes even the length of the performance." I had come to understand that the crowd at a revival had a similar impact on an evangelist. At the most practical level, the crusade could not occur *without* the audience, nor could Angley succeed in his self-proclaimed role as God's "right-hand" man without the congregation's acceptance of his right to that position. His ability to stimulate excitement also hinged on the audience's willingness and its desire to anticipate and to experience miracles. Just as his repetitious, somewhat hypnotic litanies fanned the crowd's emotional fervor, so the audience's amens encouraged his performance, as it did now, with Angley's commands and the people's responses overlapping like breakers crashing against the shore until the evangelist cut them off with a sharp *Hallelujah!*

"It's good to see you this year, all enthused, and sounds like you're prayed up and ready to go, ha-ha-ha." He gave a short, hollow laugh. "Isn't it wonderful to be on the Lord's side, and you know, the Lord's side is the *winning* side and when you're on the winning side you have nothing to fear, nothing to worry about, so you should be happy. Are you happy today?"

The audience shouted *Yes!*

"It's great to be happy," he said brightly, his delivery developing an exaggerated beat. "Well, I'll tell you, Jesus is alive. Jesus is alive . . ." His words were drowned out by a honky-tonk rattle and roll led by drums and the baby grand, with the young woman, having abandoned the organ, playing a piano that would have rivaled Jerry Lee Lewis.

As the music gathered momentum, the four men stepped forward singing "Jesus is alive and well . . . Jesus is alive and well."

Angley moved to the side, standing behind a gilded lectern on which a red Bible rested. The music blared from towering stacks of amplifiers that flanked the stage. In the invalid section, the more able-bodied tapped their toes to the lively beat, but many, like the young woman on the stretcher, seemed lost in a private, inaccessible world. Just below where I was sitting, an elderly black woman, her hair in neat corn rows, dozed on a rollaway bed, oblivious to the musical calisthenics. She registered no reaction when the song ended with a drumroll and a flourish or even when Angley strode back to center stage.

"Is the music and singing loud enough?" he asked.

The crowd returned an enthusiastic *Yes!*

"Is it too loud?"

Noooooooooo!

"Is it okay?"

Yesssssssssssss!

"Well, we wanta do it right for you," he said in the best Madison Avenue tradition. "And aren't you glad we are those children the Bible talks about? One day we will enter our Canaan too. By God, what a time we're going to have then. But we're having a time down here today, aren't we?"

Yessss!

"Yes we are. We are—those children—the Bible—talks about." His voice overtaken by a clinkering banjo, he stepped aside as the piano notes pranced and twirled like a prissy majorette directing the marching voices into the Promised Land.

As Angley clapped to the spirited beat, he reminded me of a flashy used-car salesman. Or, as one journalist once anointed him, "the Liberace of Pentecostalism." Like Billy Sunday and some of his other, more flamboyant predecessors, Angley was a spiffy dresser, the jacket of his gray suit elaborately stitched, a red carnation in the lapel. His bald head was discreetly covered with a too-carefully coiffed toupee. And his loafers—Gucci's, the press has reported—looked spit-shined. He was short and squat, the features of his Moon-Pie face fitted together like the distorted reflection in a fun-house mirror. It was difficult to determine his age. At first he appeared younger than I had expected. Late forties, maybe. But as the hours wore on he aged to his almost sixty years, the lines forming an unpleasant countenance that seemed inappropriate for a man who claimed such close communications with God.

"I have been one of those fortunate people to have such a close relationship with Him, for Him to come to me and talk with me," Angley boasted as the musicians eased into the wings. "The Angel of the Lord will always stand by my side in each miracle service, and I can hear what is being said. To behold His glory and be in His presence and feel the fire of His glory will make my face burn, His glory is so tremendous. The heat of it." Similar references were to pervade the service: "The Lord reminds me again and again . . ." and "the Lord took me into His head, His brain, and I saw what was wrong." At times the evangelist's voice assumed an authoritative, eerily emphatic tone as if to imply that God—not Ernest Angley—was speaking: "I am the *Lord* that walketh with thee. *I* am the *Loooooord* that walketh with thee." As the members of the audience became increasingly convinced of the evangelist's personal encounters with God, affirmations of *Amen! Hallelujah! Thank Ya, Jeeeeeezus!* resounded through the hall.

With God's mantle firmly on his shoulders, Angley edged into his appeal for money. At first the pleas were veiled as he casually related his travels abroad, to Germany, Hawaii, the People's Republic of China. "We live in a crucial hour," he warned. "It's almost going-home time. We are the Rapture generation. The Lord will come in our day. We *must* evangelize the world in this final hour." The gold lectern and the Bible had disappeared, and Angley stood alone, his arms sweeping through the air to emphasize the magnitude of the task. "This is the last time God's going to visit the nations before Armageddon, did you know that? This is it! This is it!" he said in thunderclaps. "And then Africa, dear, dear Africa. I left a part of Ernest Angley in Africa. I *must* go back. Such poverty. You here in America, *you're* so blessed. Oh, I know you say we're in need, but not in need like those people. Millions living in shacks you wouldn't want your animals to live in." With exaggerated pity he described the bleak existence of the African people and their great capacity for loving and giving—to the Ernest Angley Ministries. "That last night after they'd seen so many miracles and healings, when I walked on that platform it looked like a sea of faces of people instead of water," he sighed. "Countless thousands were there. And did you know, the heavens just opened. The glory of the Lord came down. In about ten or twelve minutes time, twenty thousand miracles and healings took place. The Great I Am is on the throne." The audience burst into applause. "The Great I Am is on the throne."

Angley virtually shamed the audience into giving by relating the "sacrifices" made by the poor people of Africa who, he claimed, put their wristwatches into the offering buckets. "I thought this must be the most priceless gift they have—or *had*," he said. "They had to work ever so long to get that one watch. Now, a watch doesn't mean that much to you Americans. They're not that hard to come by, but with them—Think about it." He let the thought weigh on the crowd's conscience. To reinforce his point, he related the story of an old woman who presented him with a hen's egg. "I don't know how many miles the little lady might have walked through the heat of the day to carry that one little egg," he said. "It might have been their breakfast they had to do without, determined to get that little egg there to drop it in the collection."

The monologue shifted from "I" to "we" as Angley shared the responsibilities of his missions as well as the rewards. "You're the partners of this ministry," he told the audience. "*You* sent me to Africa, and *you* will send me back. *You* sent me to Germany, and *you* will send me back. You will help send me all over the world, and *we're* gathering souls for Jesus, you and me. It's you and the preacher working together with the Lord. *Your* reward is going to be so great. You are going to be so astounded when the Lord shows you how many souls you've helped Him save."

The final pitch was aimed even more closely to home with the promise of financial prosperity to all who would give. "I don't care how low your wheelbarrow might be," Angley said, "God will fill it." With practiced humility, he interrupted himself to apologize, "The Lord reminds me again and again—Twice the Angel of the Lord has come to me on the platform to remind me I had forgotten to tell you what the Lord told me. This is what it is: The Lord is searching for special people. He said He is going to bring them into a *laaaarge* sum of money, either through gifts or through businesses, but—He said—the bulk of it is to be used for this Jesus outreach. That person will have plenty, but the bulk of it goes for the Lord."

As Angley told of a man who suddenly became a millionaire after agreeing to financially support this ministry, the people began reaching into their pocketbooks and wallets. "Give God a chance to move," the evangelist urged. "If you're out of work, put in your application at four or five places where you'd like to work, and then sit by the telephone expecting it to ring."

Failure to make a "covenant" to the Ernest Angley Ministries was likened, by implication, to refusing to obey God. Anyone willing to give was instructed to stand and to wave the money or checks, making it uncomfortable for those who would have preferred not to. "If God would prosper you with a large sum of money, either by gift or from businesses, would you share the bulk of it with Him through this ministry?" he pressed. "Raise your hand if God can really trust you. Can *God* really trust you? Can God *really* trust you? Can—God—really—trust—you?"

While the people stood, silent and with hands raised, Angley prayed on their behalf, instructing them, with eyes closed, to look into the face of Jesus. "Let Him speak to you and tell you what to give to this outreach," he urged. "Whether He tells you it's ten thousand, give it. Whatever He tells you. If you don't have it today, give Him part of it and say, Lord, prosper me and I'll send in the rest. I'll do it, Lord." Angley's tone was soothing, almost hypnotic, as he suggested what would please God. "You can send it in as tithes and offerings, or you can give it as a one-time gift. Any way you want to do it. If you don't have a job, say, Lord, I'm gonna make a covenant for a thousand dollars, now I want You to get me that job. How many's got that kind of faith? Just wave at the Lord. Wave at the Lord." A few hands went up, and Angley persisted, "And how many of you will make a covenant for five hundred dollars? Through faith, lift up those hands. Say, Lord, I will. I will."

On and on the evangelist prodded the people to make a pledge: three hundred, two hundred, fifty dollars. As he lowered the ante, the raised hands thickened. "I'd love for ever'body to make at least some *weeee* covenant with God of twenty-five dollars, ten dollars, five—" he said, assuring the people, "I don't use any of it for me. No, sir, my services are free. I'm working for Jesus, working for Jesus, and you couldn't *put* money in my hands tonight. I use it carefully to win the lost at any cost."

As the people rummaged through wallets and handbags, Angley reminded those unable today to give their entire pledge to write on the envelope what they planned to send later. "We'll never dun you for it," he promised. "The reason I want you to do that, that's an act of faith, and I say, Lord, remember what they wrote down? Bless them, prosper them, give them much above their expenses so they can send in the desire of their heart. The Lord does that to people week after week," he vowed. "It's *mar*velous. He'll do it. He'll make the way. Trust Him."

It was after three o'clock, but the push for money was not over. There was still the matter of the auditorium rent. "Now I want you to look and see if you have a one-dollar bill. If you don't have a one-dollar bill, give that five or ten or twenty. That'll be even better. But ever'one give at *least* a dollar." The audience chuckled as men and women carrying plastic buckets positioned themselves in the aisles. "Get ready to wave that dollar or five or ten," Angley called out. "I want to see if we have an invitation to come back to Washington. Wave hard."

Most members of the audience were standing, waving in one hand an envelope containing their "covenant"—cash or check or a written IOU to give a certain amount within a given time—and in the other hand, a contribution toward the auditorium rent. "These are your loaves and fishes you're holding," the evangelist singsonged. "The Lord will take them and multiply them. Whisper how many times you want Him to multiply what you're giving today. He's listening!" Angley looked out over the audience of flapping envelopes and bills and smiled. "You're so sweet! So wonderful! And we love you very, very much." He glanced over his shoulder at the musicians, who had reappeared on stage. "And now they're going to sing another good number. My —Lord—Will—Send—a—Moses—to—Lead—Us—Out. Let's go, children!" He clapped twice to set the beat and, stepping aside, reminded the crowd, "The ushers are coming!"

The financial pitch ended with the sale on stage of large green Bibles embossed in gold with "Ernest Angley Ministries Healing and Salvation Edition" and the evangelist's "crown of life" trademark. Although the Bible went for a hundred-dollar donation, Angley invited anyone with a down payment of twenty dollars to come onto the stage to collect the book and shake his hand, affording each buyer the chance not only to own this "special" Bible but to receive public recognition and to touch God's special envoy. Angley acknowledged the tome was expensive but explained, "I didn't want to put the Word of God out in cheap form." In a businesslike tone he extolled the Bible's features: "It's giant print. People that use reading glasses, they say they read this without glasses. That's beautiful!" Ushers moved through the aisles showing off opened copies. "We want you to have it, but you can't buy one," Angley said. "It isn't on the market for sale. No, that wasn't the reason we had it made up. What I'm using this for, I'm giving this as a gift to people who help me with something special." As he continued, he attempted to strengthen the audience's identification with him by portraying himself as human and fallible—like them. "I'm so busy praying for the sick, helping people find God that I didn't intend to get involved with raising monies to feed the starving, but the Lord reminded me one day, how could I go to these countries, how could I tell them the story of a man called Jesus and His great love, and them starving, so that's what I'm doing. I'm raising money to feed the starving. And the underprivileged countries we're going into, some of the countries—it's pitiful." His tone turned doleful as he appealed to the crowd's conscience. "Did you ever see little children with their stomachs bloated and starving to death? Their lips dry and parched? And they look at you with such longing eyes. You'd give 'em your last crust of bread, I'm sure. You're *that* kind of people."

A jazzy recording suggestive of a 1940s' boogie blared from the amplifiers as people began making their way toward the stage, a stooped, white-haired man leading the procession. "God bless you, kind sir," Angley said as he exchanged the old man's money for a Bible. "Because you care, they're going to be fed and hear the story of Jesus." Mattie Farmer looked on enviously. "If I had the money I'd sure buy one," she murmured, watching those with at least the down payment file onto the stage. Excitedly they shook Angley's hand and with equal delight basked in the public limelight as the revivalist in his flat, nasal monotone repeated to each: "Because you care, starving children are gonna be fed. Because you care, they're going to be fed and hear the story of Jesus." The attention and the chance to touch Angley was infectious with more than 150 people coming to the stage to claim their "gift."

The offering and the sale of Bibles took up half of the almost five-hour service. Aside from Ernest Angley and his business manager, no one can guess with any degree of accuracy how much money was collected or what was brought in before the service from the sale of records, taped sermons, and books. But the figure had to have been substantial. The approximately 2,500 people in the audience probably each contributed at least a dollar toward the $1,650 rent, alone. The sale of Bibles could have grossed a maximum of $15,000; a minimum of $3,000 if all those who came forward gave only $20 and never paid the balance. Although a spokesman for a major Bible publisher refused to discuss either the volume or the price paid by evangelists, insisting the matter was "privileged information," an employee in its sales department told me a Bible that seemed to match Angley's retailed for $39.95, plus two dollars for the gold imprint. A Washington, D.C., book dealer quoted the retail price for a quality leather-bound Bible at $50; the very top of the line, he said, sold for $85. To purchase the most expensive by the truckful—as many big-time evangelists do—would considerably lower the price so that the "down payment" covered, at the very least, Angley's cost. There is no way even to estimate what he collected in the form of "covenants," for evangelistic associations—considered nonprofit, tax-exempt organizations by the U.S. Internal Revenue Service—are not required to file annual returns or reports of any kind. The status is granted automatically, without their ever having to file any request or application or notice with the government. If the revivalist receives "love offerings" or a salary from the association, he is supposed to pay taxes on whatever money he spends for personal use. But, although the IRS has a special audit group to keep an eye on nonprofit organizations, until the sex-and-money scandal that brought down Jim and Tammy Bakker, the agency was reticent to question the finances of a church or an evangelistic association. In the early 1980s, a spokesman conceded that such matters were considered "delicate" and admitted, "we tread very carefully." Because of the separation of church and state, he said, "we don't want to look like we are telling them what to do." That attitude came under scrutiny in March 1987 with the disclosure of the Bakkers' use of tax-exempt, charitable contributions for everything from mink coats to Belgian truffles. The revelation that $265,000 of PTL club funds had gone as "hush money" to former church secretary Jessica Hahn, Jim Bakker's partner in a sexual tryst, seem to be the last straw. By the end of the year, the IRS, the Justice Department, a Congressional subcommittee, and a Federal Grand Jury had launched investigations of the Bakkers and the television ministry as a whole.

In spite of his following, Ernest Angley, to me, had no charisma, nor was he a good speaker. Even with his "good ol' boy" delivery he seemed removed, almost aloof, and I wondered why the people had attended. The answer was soon obvious. Most had come in search of a miracle, to be cured or to receive a financial blessing, and Angley was eager to please. Dispensing with a sermon and a reading of the scripture, he went directly from fund-raising to the healing portion of the service. Members of the audience were asked to stand or to come forward, making it awkward and somewhat embarrassing not to conform and "claim God's miracle." At first the evangelist called out the afflicted by categories: the deaf and dumb, the arthritic, cancer victims. With each appeal, scores of people crowded onto the stage, shepherded into lines by the musicians. Angley moved down each row, questioning the infirm about their smoking habits and their spiritual status and demanding they renounce cigarettes and publicly ask God's forgiveness for their sins before he would pray for them. Then shouting what sounded like *"Wooooo!"* or *"Ooooooouf!"* he forcefully tapped their foreheads. Some staggered to regain their balance, but many fell to the floor "slain in the Spirit," remaining on the ground only briefly before being helped to their feet by the male musicians.

That was not the case on New Year's Day 1978 when Minnie Brown collapsed after Angley prayed for her and other heart patients at a crusade in Charlotte, North Carolina. Jim Ray, a fire inspector on duty that day, reportedly attempted to assist the sixty-five-year-old woman but was told by an usher to leave her alone. "She's in the Spirit," Ray later quoted the usher as saying. "She will be up in five minutes. I have been in that same position and I know." When the woman didn't budge, Ray finally called an ambulance. On arrival at a local hospital she was pronounced dead of a heart attack. Shortly after the death, Angley told the *Charlotte Observer*, "Church is a wonderful place to go to heaven from." Two months later, however, during another Charlotte service, the evangelist lashed out at the city's newspapers, branding as "lies" their accounts of the incident. "That woman did not die in my service," he told the audience. "She lived ten minutes after she got to the hospital. . . . I've always told you never to die in one of my services. If you feel like you're going to die, please ask God to get you out of here."

Such an occurrence seemed remote now, as the men and women straggled from the stage and Angley looked out over the crowd. "There's a heart miracle taking place," he said matter-of-factly. "Over there you are." He pointed to his left. "You with the white hat on. Yes, you.

Stand up. Lift your hand. Put it over your heart, and call that a miracle. Call that a miracle." The audience applauded, and the evangelist concentrated on the rear of the hall. "Another heart miracle back there. Lift your hand and call that a miracle. Up here's a person with sugar in the blood. Raise your hand. Call that a miracle. Call *that* a miracle." Angley's eyes darted across the crowd as he proclaimed one healing after another, from diabetes, rheumatism, bad nerves. His tone grew urgent as the miracles came in multiples. "There's five hundred and seventeen people who came in here with a back condition," he announced. "You have been healed. If you have back trouble, stand up. Twist, turn, and see if you're one of the five hundred and seventeen who got the miracle." The auditorium resembled a health studio as twice that number stooped and stretched. "Ever'one that there's a difference in your back, wave at the Lord. Wave at the Lord."

On and on Angley called out what seemed to be random numbers and ailments: 897 people with "low blood, high blood, poor circulation, or poor blood"; 414 men with "trouble in the lower part of your body"—"Stand to your feet," he urged, "don't be ashamed"; 1,507 with "terrible battles of the mind"; 91 with "bunions or growths on the bottom of the feet." With each revelation, scores of people—eager both for a miracle and to demonstrate their faith—stood, waving, cheering, and praising God. They responded in like numbers or more, while the rest of the crowd applauded as though those claiming a miracle had given a stellar performance. When Angley announced 197 who had been "seeking God desperately about something special," the entire audience rose. Undaunted by the discrepancy, the evangelist prophesied, "Part of you in the next three days are going to know the exact will of God. In the next three weeks, all of those, of that number will know the will of God, thus saith the Lord."

In 1975, during a rare interview, Angley told Darrell Sifford, then-executive editor of the *Charlotte News*, that X-ray vision and revelations from the Angel of the Lord enabled him to determine infirmities. "I'll close my eyes and sometimes it'll be just like I'm looking at an X ray," he told Sifford. "I may see a kidney being re-created, a bone being straightened. I'll see that the person has no eardrum, but then I'll see an eardrum floating into that person's ear canal. But sometimes I have no vision at all. It's something I can't control. I give my mind over to the Holy Spirit. Sometimes, instead of a vision, the Angel of the Lord

will whisper to me, tell me what's wrong." The evangelist described the
Angel as having "the most holy, sacred" countenance. "There is no
human face with such a sacredness," he said. "I want to fall down and
worship. The eyes are so soft. I feel as if I could look into them forever,
those pools of peace and understanding. I see the face and I feel loved."

Now Angley interrupted the revelations long enough to explain to
the audience the source of his inspiration. "The Angel is standing by
my side, and he gives me the numbers of these miracles and healings.
It's *mar*velous. He knows exactly how many is being healed and he
gives me the numbers and I just pass them on to you." He held his
finger to his head, his expression intense. "There are fourteen people
who came in here with one leg shorter than the other. It's the same
length now," he proclaimed. "Ever'body that had one leg shorter will
you stand up." A gray-haired woman to my left stood, shifting her
weight from one leg to the other. "Check yourself," Angley directed,
"Even-Steven. Put them together, put your knees together. Check
your hips. Check your heels." The elderly woman looked down at her
ankles. "Ever'one that something's happened to you, seems to be a
difference in you, wave at the Lord." The old lady smiled as she waved
along with the crowd. "Praise the Lord," the evangelist exclaimed.
"Why, if God couldn't lengthen a leg He wouldn't even be God."

Angley had been on stage more than three hours, yet in spite of the
feverish pace at which he proclaimed the miracles he was not even
perspiring. His jacket remained buttoned; each hair of his brown toupee was neatly in place. Coolly he focused on the 1,497 eye problems
that would be corrected, he said, in a matter of minutes: glaucoma,
cataracts, crossed eyes, nearsightedness, blindness. Patiently, methodically, he directed anyone with vision problems to place two fingers
over the bad eye. "Even if you have an artificial eye, put out your
fingers and let God give you your sight," he urged. "He's done it
before in this service. Why not today? What God will do for one, He'll
do for two million or two hundred million. He is God. He is God.
Now, I want you to feel the presence of the Lord comin' down over
you just like a blanket. Feel it wrapped around you." A woman screamed
once. Then the huge hall became quiet except for Angley's voice, his
delivery slow, soothing, hypnotic as he commanded damaged eyes be
re-created, all cataracts shed. "Take this unbelievable power from the
gift of miracles that has now come upon your fingers and massage your

eyes gently. It's the same power that God used to make the universe. The same power God used to make the first man Adam, the first woman Eve, and He is remaking eyes today. Do not open your eyes until I tell you to open them. The diseases are cursed, in the name of Jesus."

Softly he decreed that all damaged eyes be re-created and cataracts shed. Like a divine optometrist, he instructed the people to remove their fingers from their eyes and look toward him. "Just look this way while God makes the correction. Your vision is getting clearer and clearer and brighter and brighter." His voice grew louder, his pronunciation more precise, as if he were verbally imitating the visual improvements. "Sight's coming to blind and sightless eyes. In the name of Jesus, it is happening. In the name of Jesus, it's taking place. Oh, hallelujah! Look around and check those eyes. Everyone that there's a difference in one or both eyes, wave at God. Stand up and give God all the praises, so much has happened here, and that power is still working. Let the Lord work with your eyes until they're just like you want them."

It was almost six o'clock, and the hall had grown noisy with the restless shifting of grownups, the fretting of children. Below me, in the invalid section, the old black woman impatiently patted the sheet that was pulled up about her. If Angley had interpreted the Angel correctly, there had been at least five times as many miracles as there were people in the audience, and the end seemed nowhere in sight. As he summoned those who drank or used drugs, Mattie Farmer grimaced.

"When is he going to get to us?" she asked.

"We've been here a long time," I said, glancing at my watch.

"We sure have," she grumbled, "and I've gotta go to work."

I asked if the mass healing for allergies had helped her, and she shook her head. "I don't know," she said irritably. "I still itch like the devil."

People of all ages crowded onto the stage, their eyes never straying from Angley as he lectured them and the audience on demonology. "Just like you see people, God lets me look into people's souls and absolutely see the demons that bind them," the evangelist declared. "The Lord even numbers the devils to me that's in a person. They're real. They are not a myth. They have eyes and ears and noses. Jesus taught demonology when He was here on earth, and He said believers would cast them out. The Lord has given me this special gift to deliver you countless thousands. Those demons will go out of you. You won't crave your habit anymore. Isn't that wonderful? You will be free. But you have to want it. You have to want freedom. So get your mind right on the Lord."

He stepped in front of the first man and asked, "How long have you been on your habit?" The man's answer was inaudible, but Angley boomed into the microphone, "Twenty-one devils bind this man, saith the Lord. *Yeaaaaaa!* Come out of him, you foul devils!" The audience cheered. "Yes, and forty-one devils bind you, saith the Lord," he informed the next man. "You want 'em out?" The man nodded. "You want 'em out— *Wooooo!* O my God, they came out!" Three times the stage emptied and again filled with Angley exorcising each person's demons. "Yeaaaa! Come out, you foul devils! Out!" Finally he administered a quick oath to keep the evil spirits out and Jesus in, delivered another stageful from smoking, dipping, and chewing, then signaled to a young man standing near the wings. "All right, Lou, start lining 'em up."

With the younger man leading the way, Angley hurried down the stage stairs toward the invalid section. From their wheelchairs and stretchers the people watched anxiously. For almost five hours they had waited, and now the faith healer moved quickly through their midst while the musicians sang a lively rendition of "I'll Fly Away." From time to time the short evangelist became lost in the crowd as his young business manager steered him toward individuals apparently singled out in advance. When Angley reached the old black woman on the stretcher below where I was sitting, he clapped his hands once over her head, shouted *"Wow!"* and stepped toward the next cripple. Soon the evangelist disappeared through a stage door without offering a benediction or a good-bye. Without missing a beat, the singers launched into "Amazing Grace," and the people too began their slow exodus from the hall, the lame, sick, and disabled leaving as they had entered: on crutches, wheelchairs, and stretchers.

While I saw no evidence of anyone being genuinely or dramatically cured, probably few among the 2,500 present would admit to not having experienced a miracle. And because of his claims of being empowered by God, Angley—like many revivalists—was a unique speaker in that he offered nonfalsifiable claims. Who could challenge his boasts of conversations with God? Who could dare say that God had not told the revivalist to instruct the audience to contribute to the Ernest Angley Ministries? To doubt Angley would be to doubt God Himself.

If a person failed to be cured, the possible causes were endless. The individual may have simply not claimed his miracle, or perhaps his faith had not been strong enough. Certainly neither God nor Ernest Angley could be held accountable.

The family of Gracie Rogers typified the audience's unshakable faith in the evangelist and his ability to heal. The fifty-seven-year-old woman, dying of cancer, had driven from Petersburg, Virginia, with her husband and daughter, the three of them confident she would be cured. For more than four hours Gracie Rogers dozed on a folding bed the family had brought with them. When I asked her husband, Charles, why they had driven almost three hours to attend, he replied, "The doctor said he had no cure for her. Nothin' else he could do for her. So she wanted to come here today and see if she could be healed." I asked if he believed she would be healed, and he answered firmly: "Yeah, 'cause I already saw it. I seen it with a nine-year-old boy in Petersburg, and I saw it in New York. I know God heals."

A little more than a month later, I telephoned the Rogers' home in Petersburg and was told by Loretha Dodson that her mother had died two weeks after the service at Constitution Hall. Yet the daughter's faith was unshaken. "My mother told me her cancer was all right," she insisted, "but when we carried her to the hospital her blood pressure was real high." She remained confident that Ernest Angley could have saved her mother's life. "I felt if he had just put his hand on her a little longer," she reasoned, "but there were so many people he had to pray for."

"They're through," the man said firmly, blocking a stairway leading to the stage, where the male singers were packing the musical instruments. I was attempting to approach Angley's business manager as he headed for the side door when the middle-age man stopped me. I explained I merely wanted to speak to Lou Spangler about interviewing the evangelist, but the man refused to budge. Both his presence and his negative attitude surprised me. Although I had read that some evangelists were accompanied by bodyguards, this was my first encounter. Thus far in my travels the revivalists and their teams had been extremely cooperative, freely granting interviews and encouraging me to mingle with their audiences. For the most part, they were equally accessible to their followers. Only Angley and the somewhat extreme David Terrell had eluded me. A letter to Angley had gone unanswered, and shortly before the Washington service, a long-distance call to Akron got no farther than a secretary. I had then decided that if I could talk to a member of his team I might succeed. But now I was stymied. While I was pondering my next move, Laddy Knight, the blond baritone who doubled as platform man, stepped to the edge of the stage to visit with friends. I waited, finally managing to attract his attention. At his suggestion I telephoned Lou Spangler the next week, and again a secretary intercepted, turning down my request for an appointment with Angley during an upcoming crusade in Baltimore.

Over the next two years I made other attempts, to no avail. Even a call to his younger sister Bea Medlin, also a revivalist, went unreturned—although it was rumored the two did not get along. In 1978 Medlin told the *Charlotte News* she and her brother didn't contact one another "except when Dad gets sick," although both lived in Akron. "Ernest was preaching before I was, but the Lord taught me about demons first," she said competitively. "We built the tabernacle [Grace Cathedral] in Akron, but I felt like going out on my own preaching. I didn't want to preach, but the Lord decided for me." At the time, she had a church in Rockingham, North Carolina, and another under construction in nearby Mount Holly. She planned to build still another in Uniontown, Ohio, conceding "I don't know if he's too happy about [my building a church close to his] or not."

In the intervening years, I sought out journalists who had interviewed the evangelist. They offered little encouragement. Angley, they explained, was not pleased with his less-than-flattering image in the press. Their own impressions ran from one extreme to the other. Few were neutral. One writer described him as "distasteful" and another, as "grotesque," revealing a flip side to the saccharine-voiced evangelist rarely seen by the public—what the reporter labeled "the wrath of Angley." Yet Darrell Sifford, a former executive editor of the *Charlotte News* who had interviewed the revivalist, admitted without reservations, "I liked the guy. I found him to be an engaging, honest fella." Initially turned off by Angley's platform manner, Sifford discovered the evangelist was quite different off stage and subsequently invited Angley to his home. The newsman also agreed to appear on Angley's television show to talk about an ear problem that had seemed cured after the evangelist's laying on of hands—only to later recur. Looking back, Sifford, now a columnist for the *Philadelphia Inquirer*, regretted that appearance. "I feel, I guess, a little bit like a charlatan because I was talking about something that hadn't really happened," he told me. "It appeared that it had, but it hadn't."

The evangelist had a profound influence on Sifford's then-sixteen-year-old son, Jay, who eventually followed Angley's footsteps into the ministry. Even after his parents divorced in late 1975, Jay frequently turned to Angley for advice, including the choice of a Bible training school. "He's one of the most high-quality people you'll find in the profession," Jay Sifford said during a telephone interview. He described Angley as a quiet, private person, amazed by his own success. His flamboyance, the young man speculated, was the product of necessity. "I think a lot of the people who come to hear him expect that to some extent and it holds their attention. His services are very long, and if he talked in a monotone voice he'd really lose the people quickly."

Several others I spoke to shared the Siffords' view that Angley was sincere, or at least *thought* of himself as sincere. Peter Geiger, former religion editor for the *Akron Beacon Journal*, described the evangelist as a good showman. "It's a little hard to do that act and not appear on a level with a silk-suited, used-car shark," he commented, "but it's just him. He's on, he's up. Nobody has to give [money], and they get a pretty good show—or what for them is a show." One of the few journalists Angley considered fair, Geiger portrayed him as "an overcomer," explaining "He's short with no neck. Bald. He doesn't let these things get in the way."

I was surprised to find *anyone* with favorable views of Ernest Angley. True, I had been repulsed by Schambach's platform performance, only to find him quite likable when we met. Would it be the same with Angley? In April 1984 I decided to try to reach him again. I wrote the evangelist, then telephoned Spangler's secretary. The next day she called to say Angley would see me the next month before a service in Baltimore. I was pleased but somewhat concerned. Barring any interruptions, I would have at most an hour, scarcely enough time for a good in-depth interview. If this would be my only opportunity, I was worried about coming away without broaching some of the controversies that surround him. I was equally uneasy about asking something that might squelch my chances of getting another session.

When I arrived at the Baltimore Civic Center that May Sunday in 1984, Lou Spangler suggested I wait in the auditorium. At a quarter past one, a scant forty-five minutes before the service, the business manager instructed Woody Young to escort me to a tour bus where the evangelist was waiting. Young, the lead singer, had been a school teacher before the quartet began traveling full time with Angley in 1976. He had come by both interests naturally: his father was also an educator; his mother directed the choir at the Church of the Brethren, which Woody Young—like the rest of his family—attended until the late 1960s when he became acquainted with Grace Cathedral. In his forties, Young could have passed for a mortician. He was tall, stiff, somber in appearance, his skin a cadaverous white against his dark hair. A slightly raised eyebrow was the only outward clue to a mischievous bent that surfaced as we eased through the disabled already lining up at the stage entrance. As the quartet's lead he sang the melody. The females, he joked, "just sort of fill in. They sort of do the shoo-be-doos."

At the bus, he entered first to introduce Angley, who invited me to join him at a built-in table behind the driver's seat. During the 1982 service, I had been at a loss to understand his appeal. At close range, I was even more puzzled. In my estimation, he seemed just plain dull, and his *oooh and-ah* delivery made his accounts more humorous than inspirational. He exhibited none of the characteristics inherent in most leaders, yet his team and his fans spoke to and about him with a reverence that went beyond ordinary respect. Everyone referred to him as "Reverend," seldom using his last name. On stage there had been moments when he reminded me of a small boy all dressed for Easter. But without benefit of the glaring lights and, I suspected, makeup, he was a credible sixty-two. The one interesting feature of his otherwise homely face was his eyes. The color of fresh coffee, they sparkled as he regaled me with an animated account of his family's evolution from Baptist to Pentecostal and his first visitation from God.

I had read abbreviated versions of that night when young Ernest's bed was whisked out the farmhouse window, into the heavens. Now in a breathless, gossipy little voice, the evangelist embellished the event, describing how his bed commenced to move. "It began to go around and around like a merry-go-round, and I'd never been on a merry-go-round," he recalled. "And then the furniture joined in and then I was in the stars. It was some sight to behold. There were *millions* and *millions* of stars and no way to number them. I don't know how long I was in that vision or whatever it was," he said guardedly, "but when I came to myself it was like I had been flying, and I lifted my head and I looked—and to my astonishment the furniture was all in place and the bed was in place, but it was just like a giant hand took one poster of the bed and lifted it up about twelve inches and dropped it with a thud, and that was the end of the visitation."

"You mean the poster actually fell off the bed?" I asked.

"It seemed to be lifted from the floor," he clarified, "just the foot of the bed. One side lifted and with a *thud!* it went down, like someone dropped it. Well, I thought I did something to my brain, that I moved my eyes some way or another—This is the reasoning of a seven-year-old," he was quick to explain. "I couldn't tell anybody about it. How *could* you explain anything like that?" He shrugged. "And I'd go to bed early ahead of my brother again and again. I'd bury my face in my pillow and concentrate. I'd do my eyes *allll* kinds of ways," he said, demonstrating, "and move my head to the left and to the right—"

"To get it to happen again?"

He nodded. "I thought I'd turned on my brain, I did something that caused this to happen, and it was *some* fantastic experience."

That was the beginning of what Angley and his staff clearly regarded as a very special working relationship which he constantly referred to in both his services and private conversations, dropping God's name as nonchalantly as he did those of talk-show celebrities on whose programs he has appeared. "I see Him just like I see you," he told the *Atlanta Constitution*'s Jim Auchmutey during a 1978 interview, casually adding "He looks more or less like the pictures you've seen of Him." The evangelist himself told me he spent more time with God than with people. "See," he explained, "I have to be so yielded to Him that He can use my mind and my hands like I use them." When I asked Lou Spangler about the composition of the evangelistic association, the business manager informed me, "God is the head, and He's put Reverend Angley next and Reverend Angley gets the mind of God and gives it to me and I go forth to accomplish it."

In spite of such a portentous visitation and his strict Baptist upbringing, Angley did not consider himself saved until he was eighteen. In a 1975 story in the *Charlotte News*, he recalled, "I was just miserable, couldn't enjoy anything anymore. The Spirit wouldn't leave me alone. It was like He was holding me over hell and threatening to drop me in if I didn't surrender." He received the baptism of the Holy Spirit and, he said, in the weeks that followed began preaching in German, Latin, and Hebrew—languages he had never studied. "The Lord was pouring out His sermons through me," he said in that 1975 article. "I didn't realize what I was saying." In 1941 he enrolled in Lee College, an affiliation he and Church of God officials prefer to ignore. Some reporters have suggested a falling-out, with one article quoting a secretary in the school's admissions office as saying "We'd appreciate it if you didn't mention our college in connection with him too much." A past president of the institution, also enrolled there at the time Angley attended, would neither confirm nor deny the rift. "He just doesn't appeal to me," he told me, conceding the church didn't look favorably upon revivalists who ventured out on their own without seeking to cooperate with local churches. Angley attributed his reluctance to name the school to his preference to remain nondenominational. However, it is public record that Angley attended Lee College, where he met his late wife, the former Esther Lee Sikes of Tampa, Florida—affectionately called "Angel." Upon graduating, the two traveled throughout the South.

"We had some *mighty* tent crusades," he said of their decade on the road, "and then we came to Ohio and opened in the tent. In Akron, Ohio, that was the beginning of Grace Cathedral," he noted proudly. "It started in a tent."

"How did you come to go to Akron?" I asked.

"The Lord sent me," he answered simply. "I was visited in a divine visitation, and the Lord told me I was to go to Akron."

In truth, Angley was only one of many Southern evangelicals attracted by a ready-made audience hungering for a taste of home in a city where, for a time, more West Virginians lived than in that state's own capital. Old newspapers chronicle how he and his wife sold their belongings to make the move, arriving in 1954 with little more than their evangelical fervor and a tent they pitched on a hill near the current site of Grace Cathedral. The driver of Angley's tractor-trailer transported them and then embarked on his own soul-saving mission, leaving the couple to carry on alone.

"We started from the very bottom, in a tent, sawdust or shavings on the floor. Without a member," the evangelist singsonged. "Now we have about seven *thou*sand people on the membership rolls, and we have *thou*sands for outreach partners."

"Those must have been hard years in the beginning," I commiserated.

"They were," he said, "but delightful moments and rewarding moments as God built the work."

Within three years, the Angleys dedicated a $1.5 million cathedral replete with two four-hundred-pound crystal chandeliers imported from Europe; a pulpit, grand piano, and Hammond organ encrusted with twenty-four-carat gold leaf, and multicolored exterior lighting, which a tour book boasted was "engineered by the same skilled technician who executed the lighting of the White House Christmas Tree and the General Electric World's Fair Display." Angley was not the only transplanted cleric to do well in a state whose official motto is "With God, all things are possible." In 1958 Rex Humbard opened the doors to his $2.1 million Cathedral of Tomorrow, the first church designed specifically for television productions with a hydraulic stage, audiovideo studios, and an overhead fifty-by-one-hundred-foot cross studded with red, white, and blue lights to provide virtually any lighting effect. When a severe slowdown in the automobile industry began to cut into the blue-collar work force, claiming a thousand jobs a year between 1970 and 1984, it took its toll on church attendance—and giving. By 1980 Humbard was on the brink of bankruptcy. Construction on a tower designed to rise 750 feet next to the Cathedral of Tomorrow progressed no farther than its concrete base. For Angley, the mass exodus of rubber workers coincided with his wife's death from colitis and a directive from God that he bring the multitudes to the Lord before the "Rapture"—when Christ is to return and take all the believers back to heaven with Him. Shortly thereafter, the evangelist again took to the road, conducting his Friday-night healing services at the cathedral before heading out on the interstates.

Now Angley watched as one of his workers entered the bus with a single red carnation, apologizing for the interruption. "Here's your flower," the young man said as he placed it in a small, under-the-counter refrigerator.

"Whoever brought it, thank them," the evangelist told him, returning to our conversation as the man exited.

Initially, Angley confided, he had set out merely to preach. "I didn't want the gifts of healing," he said. "I thought they were wonderful and I believed in them, but I asked God to give them to others. I'd preach healing to the people, but I knew to have the gifts of God I'd have to stay shut away from people so much and I *am* shut away so much in prayers and fasting and seeking God." His plans changed, however, when at age twenty-two he developed an ulcerated stomach. "My body went down to just about a skeleton," he recalled, "and it looked like I was going to die in spite of everything. I was getting worse and worse all the time and then one night the Lord came and He healed me. Made me whole all over. The skeptics can say whatever they want, but maybe they've never been to the edge of the grave and wanted to live so very much and *then!* suddenly in that intense pain you're never going to have it like that again. You're never going to have one of those terrible nights of terror and horror that seems like it'll never end. I used to pray, O God, if You won't heal me—I would just be suffering so—I'd say, Please, God, would you let the dawn come, just this once, early," he said theatrically, "and you know, He brought the dawn between ten and ten-thirty that night."

In spite of Angley's weakened condition, God instructed him to go on a forty-day fast after which he would emerge with the gift of healing, the evangelist elaborated, his excitement mounting. "When I came out of that fast, I knew I had the power. I knew I had it. I was like Elisha with Elijah's mantle," he said, referring to the Old Testament account of Elisha using Elijah's cloak to part the waters of the Jordan River. "I wanted to touch somebody. I knew it was *God's* power. I wanted to touch a crippled person and see them walk." He squinched his shoulders, thrilled. "And at last these people had gathered together for service, and a lady stood there with two crutches and I just knew she'd be healed! I just knew it in my heart! Before I touched her, I knew she'd drop those crutches! I lifted my hands and the Lord just made her whole." Excitedly he raced on. "Later, a little deformed baby was miraculously healed as I held it. One side of its face and head was normal and beautiful; the other was small and ugly, and as I held it, it was just like a breath of fresh air breezed over it and it was made whole, and so many people knew it. We passed it around like a collection plate. People wanted to hold it. They wanted to touch it. Miracles," he declared grandly, "bring people to God."

Angley likened his X-ray vision to the laboratory technique, enabling him to look beyond a person's skin and see his affliction. "Maybe I'll see a curvature of the spine," he said to illustrate, "and then the power—the miracle power appears in royal blue, the healing power appears liquid fire. It usually comes from the left, and the miracle power comes from the right. Many times both are in the vision. At other times it'll go all out miracle power. And it'll come down just like a cloud and it covers the spine and it'll lift, and when it does, the spine is just as straight, and it's illuminated."

He described the angel referred to during so many of his services as having peaceful eyes and the shape of a man. "They speak in the first person because they speak as God speaks," he said.

"Is there more than one angel?" I asked.

"There's just one that stands by my side, but angels will come in and minister to the people in the congregation. Oh yes, oh yes, the blind receive their sight—"

"When you say the angel that ministers to you, or speaks to you, is he—"

Before I could finish, Angley answered, "He's the messenger from God. The Lord called him my Big Angel, that's all I know. He's never given me his name. I believe he was the one sent from God to bring about that experience when I was seven. At the time, of course, I never dreamed—I didn't know anything about an angel. Mama taught us they protected us, but I didn't know one stayed around me." He laughed mischievously. "As naughty as I was sometimes."

"When you held up your hands and when the woman was healed, what did you feel?" I asked.

A smile cut across his face. "I just felt jubilation," he bubbled. "I was just *thrilled* from the crown of my head to the tip end of my fingers to the tip end of my toes, that God had done it!" His voice deepened. "That *Gaaawd* had done it!"

It was a quarter to two. There was a lot more ground I wanted to cover, but Angley was beginning to fidget. "It's a long service," he said plaintively. "It'd be better to see me in Washington." In the meantime, he suggested, "you digest this."

Three weeks later I found Angley's team members in jeans and T-shirts, setting up Washington's Convention Center for the evangelist's crusade that afternoon. Lou Spangler was in the stands marking off a reserved section for ushers. He was an average-size man of thirty-seven who looked conscientious and hurried. Since 1979, his assorted titles had come to include that of executive director of Ernest Angley Ministries, a position that placed him third in command—just after God and Reverend Angley. Although somewhat reserved, he was pleasant and polite. Still, I sensed that if the need arose he could be ruthless to protect the man who had replaced the father he had not seen in thirty years. In Baltimore we had arranged to meet an hour before my interview with Angley. Now he glanced anxiously at his watch. Because of a boxing match in the Convention Center the night before, preparations for the service were far from complete. He himself had to finish labeling the special sections and change clothes before local volunteers began to arrive for their assignments. I suggested he might be more relaxed if we postponed our conversation until after the service, and he agreed.

While I was waiting for Angley, I wandered about the hall observing the preparations for the service: several men hanging a blue-velvet curtain at the back of the free-standing platform, others hooking up three television cameras, still others checking the behind-the-stage monitors and sound equipment. In the center aisle, Laddy Knight climbed a ladder to adjust the floodlights. Mark Latham, the tall blond bass, and Bob Boyle, the drummer, were arranging an assortment of records, tapes, and books at a sales table just inside the entrance.

"Everyone has other jobs," Latham explained as he unpacked back issues of *The Power of the Holy Ghost*, Angley's bimonthly magazine. "I'm not talking about *other* employment. We're working right for the cathedral. For instance, myself and Bob and Bruce who does the audio work—" He pointed across the hall to a young man in an orange shirt. "We take care of the buses. We wash 'em and wax 'em and clean 'em up. Woody, our lead singer, he helps our mechanic."

"Does the mechanic travel with you?" I asked.

"He's on the stage now," Latham chuckled. "See, *everyone* has different jobs."

The Baltimore service differed greatly from the one I had attended two years earlier. The Civic Center with its concrete floor and plastic chairs lacked the elegance of Constitution Hall, and recordings—rather than live musicians—accompanied the quartet. But more than that, Angley's performance was quite unlike the one I witnessed in 1982. Both the evangelist's entrance and his reception were considerably subdued in comparison to the first ovation in Washington. He spoke in a deeper, more controlled voice. Stock lines like "The Lord is delicious" were delivered with considerable restraint, and he scaled down the *Praise the Lord* litany, after a couple of rounds simply drilling the crowd to "Say it again and again and again," leaving the audience straggling behind. Even his money pitches were played down. I wondered if his restraint was because of the three cameras televising a future segment for his weekly show, because of what many Pentecostals interpret as the leading of the Lord, or because of his awareness of my presence—which I suspected was partly the case. When Angley and I sat down for our second session, he attributed the variations to divine guidance.

"The nine gifts of the Spirit work for me and they work in different ways," he explained matter-of-factly, "and I don't know rightly how they're going to work. I'm just an instrument He uses."

"Sometimes you give a sermon and sometimes you don't," I noted.

"It all depends," he said. "If He moves on me to have testimonies, I have testimony time. I think it's very good to let people of all walks of life testify. There's no little people or big people in the eyes of God, and I feel that, for instance on television, people with higher educations and people that are actors, actresses or whatever, they've had a chance to tell their story. But what is known as the little people, they've never had a chance, and sometimes their story is much more rewarding and brings more people into the kingdom than someone that's made it what America calls big or some famous person. What we call fame in America may not be fame in heaven at all and what they call big here on earth may not be big in heaven."

"*Will* there be fame in heaven?" I inquired.

"Well, I think there's—" He cocked his head and considered the question. "As such we may not call it fame, but there's degrees of rewards, you know, because there'll be a day of rewards and some will be greater than others. Many people are going to be shocked because some of the laymen are going to get greater rewards than some of the ministers and priests and rabbis, and that's something to think about."

"Are there any special people you want to talk to when you get to heaven?" I asked.

"Oh, yes!" he said with enthusiasm. "I'd like to talk to Jesus and of course my wife." He smiled coyly. "I'd like to be hand in hand with her all over heaven and walking around the throne the first time, she was so dear and so precious and still is in my heart," he rhapsodized. "I would like to talk especially to the prophets of old, and I'd like to have a good chat with Noah, of course, and Abraham and Moses and

Isaiah, Jeremiah, Daniel. I'd like to talk to the Hebrew boys, and I'd like to even talk to Jonah and the apostles—especially Peter and Paul. I'd like to talk to those two for a long time. John the Revelator, it'd be of great interest to talk to him." He listed the Bible greats, scarcely omitting a one. "And I would like to talk to Lazarus too. How he felt and where did he go. Was he conscious during the time his spirit left the body? And I'd really like to hear the story from Jesus of Calvary. I'll never be satisfied with the written story of Calvary because it can't be written," he insisted. "No human being—think if you'd been called on to have written such a story."

"This is hard enough," I agreed.

At both services I had attended, I had wondered about Angley's thoughts as he swept on stage to the standing ovations, especially in view of his upbringing in rural poverty. Throughout each crusade and on the telecasts I had watched, he made repeated references to his unique "in" with God. Nevertheless, when I raised the question, he brushed aside any desire for personal fame.

"I accept it more for the Lord than I do for myself," he insisted. "I'm so set apart from it, even the praises, the applauding. I'm conscious of the fact it isn't really Ernest Angley that's being applauded. It is the power of God and the spirit of the Lord and the gifts of God that work in my life and that's what draws them to me, not because I'm so special. Special is because the Lord is so special in my life."

"Are you still amazed at God choosing you?"

His eyes sparkled. "Oh, forever I shall be! Ever, ever, and ever."

"Why me?"

"Yes, that's what I was asked on one of the big talk shows on television one time," he recalled, mimicking the moderator: "Well, why did the Lord choose you?" He leaned across the table and in an exaggerated Southern accent replied, "I said, You know, I don't rightly know, but that's one thing I'm going to ask the Lord when I get to heaven, why He chose me." His laughter evaporated into a sigh. "Oooooh, to say why? I don't know. There was a time I didn't want to be a preacher. I could have chosen a thousand professions and not been a preacher. The way people criticize the ministry. Some of it is deserved, I'm sure, but so many people, they look at the ministry as a charity case and it's such a *thankless* profession."

When I asked about his personal life, Angley insisted he had none.

"I spend more time with God than I do with human beings," he said piously. "I really didn't want the healing ministry."

"There's no such thing as an evening off?" I asked.

"Well," he hedged, "sometimes in business it's required of me, and sometimes going in to where my family lives, welllll, there's an obligation to be with them for a dinner or something. But I don't have a life-style like an average person would have. The Lord wants so much of my time and He needs me to prepare me for what I must do for Him in the services."

"So you're on twenty-four-hour call," I observed.

"That's right," he said. "It's twenty-four-hours duty around the clock and in His presence and yielded entirely to Him, to His will. My spirit day and night is, I have come to do Thy will, O Lord, just like the Master, and I feel that's what it must be if I'm going to wear His shoes and do His work."

That left little time to get together with other ministers, not even his evangelist sister, he said, and while he and his late wife "Angel" had occasionally visited in restaurants with Rex and Maude Aimee Humbard, that was the extent of their socializing. "Wife and I, see, she helped me pastor Grace Cathedral for seventeen years and we never had a Sunday off except for the day I preached my mother's funeral, so that tells you something," he said. "We didn't take vacations, a couple of weeks like some people, and go off to rest."

Former *Beacon Journal* religion editor Peter Geiger agreed the Angleys "were never that big in town." He described the evangelist's life-style then and now as "fairly simple." The various Cadillacs driven by Angley over the years—sometimes pink, sometimes gold—have been registered to a Columbus, Ohio, dealer, according to Geiger. And while the evangelist lived in an upper-middle-class neighborhood of homes built around a man-made lake and each surrounded by at least a half-acre of land, his was owned by the cathedral and among the smaller houses in the area. Two others who have written about Angley felt he neither lived luxuriously nor was accumulating great wealth. Both cited his hectic schedule, which, they theorized, would leave little time to enjoy special amenities. "He doesn't have time to live too high on the hog," speculated Margaret Poloma, a sociology professor at the University of Akron and author of *The Charismatic Movement*. She reviewed his travel schedule and the intensity with which he prays over people, concluding "It's really hard for me to look at the man and say he's making money. He is, but the money goes back into the ministry, it appears. I think his not having a family makes a lot of difference." Caren Goldman, who profiled Angley for the Cleveland *Plain Dealer* (Sunday) *Magazine*, agreed. "No matter what the motivation, whether it's strictly an egotistical kind of thing or it is truly a religious motivation, or a combination, his time is almost totally involved. It could be that material things satisfy him," she speculated, "and now these things are personified in the cathedral itself as opposed to his own individual life-style."

Their views, however, were only a matter of speculation. Angley's home has been off limits, at least to journalists. When Darrell Sifford visited Akron at Angley's invitation, he asked to go to the evangelist's home and was refused. "He made it clear that, in effect, his house was private and nobody went there," Sifford said. "I think there are a number of things you could read into that, but it would only be speculation." While the newsman considered Angley neither a con artist nor someone on an ego trip, he didn't share the opinion that the evangelist lived modestly. "He's rather ostentatious in his dress as well as his gold Cadillac, and I think that sort of fits with the kind of personality he projects," Sifford said. "The temple is ostentatious. I would have been surprised to find he lived in a modest home because it didn't fit with the other stuff."

Over the years, Angley has been equally sensitive about discussing finances. Once after Sifford pressed the matter, the evangelist described the high cost of a television ministry and of buying time on a number of stations. "That was his sort of indirect way of responding to my jibe about his hustling for money, saying, Hey, it takes a lot of money to support the kind of ministry I'm conducting—and it does. There's no question it costs a lot of money." With Jim Auchmutey, the evangelist was less diplomatic. According to the Atlanta reporter, he and Angley talked about various topics for at least forty-five minutes before Auchmutey broached the subject of money—how much he made and how it was spent. "Angley immediately got disturbed and said that was all reporters wanted to talk about and we just didn't know anything about God's Word," Auchmutey said. "He got real snitty about it." The interview was abruptly terminated, and the evangelist refused to talk with him after the service and at another crusade two years later.

I too did not get far into the tightly guarded world of finances, either with Angley or with Lou Spangler. During the crusades, Angley repeatedly assured the crowds that none of the offering went to him. "I don't use any of it for me," he told the audience at Constitution Hall. "No, sir. My services are free: I'm working for Jesus, working for Jesus, and you couldn't put money in my hand tonight." In our conversation he insisted he had no interest in personal wealth, and as for the cost of his various projects—that was determined by the Lord. Just as his own illness taught him compassion for the sick, Angley told me that growing up in poverty had enabled him to understand the needy to whom he ministered.

"What about people in this country?" I asked. "Do you have any missions here?"

"No, not missions in the States," he said, explaining "We have more help in the States. When you go into some of the other countries—if you've never been there—you'll find that it's hell on earth for those people. You can't describe it. And to see them. Those eyes looking at you. They just haunt me, and I just want—if I could just gather all the hungry of the world, all the starving in my arms and love them and feed them and clothe them and tell them the story of Jesus. You know Jesus had such love for the poor," he reminded me, "and too, we had so much happiness, so much fun growing up, seven children—"

"I bet you had a lot of ice cream," I suggested, hinting at one of his favorite indulgences.

The evangelist blushed. "Well, I love ice cream. I was ready to eat ice cream any time I could get it. Any time. Uh, but in growing up not associating money with happiness," he said, picking up his train of thought. "Money has never been my god, and money doesn't bother me, for me to crave it and desire it and want it for self. See, I have given everything to the Lord. I don't own any properties. I don't even have a bank account. And I just take a part of a salary from Grace Cathedral, and I don't take *anything* for the crusade services in America or Canada. The Lord is my source of supply and the Lord will give me what I need daily. He didn't put me on earth to be rich—only in His riches. You know, Jesus, the most wonderful personality on planet earth, His riches were from heaven. He didn't even own his own bed."

"And you don't own your own bed," I interjected.

"Well—" He stopped, somewhat taken aback, and we laughed as he looked around at the bus's interior. "This belongs to Grace Cathedral." While not plush, the bus and an identical vehicle parked next to it obviously had not come cheap. Nor had the huge tractor-trailer that housed a storage area, a generator for emergencies, and a miniature television studio. For the most part, Angley and his workers slept in the buses en route to a town and then checked into a motel because there were no showers on board. On longer trips, the evangelist sometimes flew by commercial airline—as he had a few weekends earlier to Ontario—with the team leaving ahead of him with the three vehicles.

"It takes time getting the equipment across the border," he explained, "so the team went ahead of us and I stayed and had the big Friday-night miracle service. Have you ever visited Grace?" When I answered no, that I'd like to, he smiled. "You ought to," he said coquettishly, "even before you finish your research."

A source of pride for Angley and his flock, the cathedral has been the object of as much ridicule by outsiders who have described it as "gaudy" and "garish"—"a gold-leaf palace." It was, in the words of one visitor, "not marked by moderation." Nor was an elaborate seventy-two-page brochure that took the reader all the way from the "dazzling beauty" of the sanctuary, with its seating capacity for three thousand, to the "well-appointed ladies room." The text doted on the most minute details and referred to the cathedral as "the House God told Reverend Angley to build." The booklet put the total value "well in excess of two and a half million dollars." In front of the cathedral, a circular "Fountain of Blood" was alternately spotlighted in red, blue, amber, and white, a large cross rising in the center with the word LIFE inscribed on the arms and an open "Bible" at the base. The building itself was orange brick and Carrera marble with GRACE CATHEDRAL spelled out above the portico in neon. The furnishings were rococo, in a setting of foil and flock wallpapers and yards of "cathedral blue" and "royal ruby" velvet and silk-satin brocade.

When his wife died in December 1970, her three-hour funeral cost an estimated $25,000, with the silver-plated casket alone priced at $12,000. She was buried on the cathedral grounds within view of Angley's office in the "Angel Memorial Garden." Near her grave, the winged marble angel—shown at the beginning and end of the evangelist's weekly telecasts—rises twenty-three feet above a red-granite base and the "Flame of the Holy Spirit," which, shortly after her death, a brochure said would "always be ablaze," only to be snuffed out by the 1975 energy crisis. Within the cathedral, her Bible and the elaborate robes she wore to direct the choir are enshrined in "Angel's Robe Room," an ornately furnished salon used as a bridal parlor for weddings held at Grace.

Ernest Angley's motto was "Win the Lost at Any Cost," and he seemed to work toward that endeavor. The Washington service cost roughly $8,000, including rent of $6,000 for the Convention Center, utilities, transportation, and his staff's salaries. While he had no ready figures for his television bill, he estimated the show—consisting primarily of segments taped during regular services at the cathedral or on tour—appeared on "over a hundred" stations in the United States, Canada, Africa, Haiti, and the Philippines. Even nonprime-time rates were not cheap. While most stations consider the exact amount paid by a client "confidential," Chuck Cowdrey, manager of WDCA-TV in Washington, indicated the cost for Angley's Saturday-morning time slot fell somewhere between $3,000 to $6,000 a week. Since Washington is the ninth largest market in the country, the figure for other stations would go up or down considerably depending on the market.

Whatever the total, Angley was not concerned. He was, in fact, in the process of buying Rex Humbard's television building and putting together a one-hour talk show to be aired five days a week on a limited number of stations in the United States and Canada with other cities to be added in the future.

After he had outlined the extent of his plans, I remarked, "That will be very expensive."

"It will be," he said, "but you know Jesus held the worth of the whole world in one hand and one soul in the other one time, and He said this soul is worth more than all the wealth of the world, so I don't consider dollars and cents when it comes to souls."

"Do you have *any* idea how much it will cost?"

"No, because I just take it by faith," he said nonchalantly. "When the Lord tells me to do something, He'll supply the need, and I use all the wisdom He gives me. Some people would try to cover all the nation at one time. I don't believe in that. I believe in paying as you go."

Others attributed Angley's casual faith in finances to more substantial planning. In Darrell Sifford's estimation, the evangelist was "a shrewd businessman" who surrounded himself with competent people. Lou Spangler put it in slightly different terms. "God gifted him with his business ability, and he's a fine business person." Spangler himself had been a foreman for General Tires before joining Angley full time in the mid-seventies. After completing three years in the army, he said, he attended the University of Akron, taking mostly business and history courses. Although he dropped out before receiving a degree, Spangler considered business his area of "expertise" and insisted he had no aspirations of becoming a preacher.

Angley had made reference to the purchase of the Humbard facilities during the Baltimore service. In calling for new partners to "help us evangelize the world," he told the audience with more than a little pride, "You've heard about the new facility we're getting. It's Rex Humbard Foundation's television studio, offices, and so forth. All set and ready to go, and some people's wondering, What's happened to Rex? Well, he's moved to Florida—didn't you know it? He doesn't need that building any longer. *I* need it." The people applauded. "And Rex told me he'd rather not hand it to anybody else in the world. Isn't that nice?" Again the crowd sounded its approval. "He said he knew it would be used for Jesus. And it will be. It will be. And you'll have to come see us sometime. We'll be putting on all kind of live telecast, and you can get right in on it."

I first learned of the planned purchase via a "telecom" dispatched by Angley's computers. The communiqué detailed a "visitation" not unlike the now-famous call Jesus paid to Oral Roberts directing him to construct the controversial City of Faith medical center in Tulsa. Marked "AN URGENT, URGENT MESSAGE FROM THE LORD," this dispatch spelled out the heavenly mandate:

. . . GOD IS POURING HIMSELF OUT TO ME LIKE MIGHTY RIVERS AND I MUST HAVE CHANNELS TO FLOW HIM TO THE PEOPLE. SOME PEOPLE IN AMERICA AND CANADA CANNOT GET THE ERNEST ANGLEY HOUR. ALL SHOULD HAVE AN OPPORTUNITY TO HEAR AND SEE WHAT THE LORD IS DOING FOR PEOPLE THROUGH THIS JESUS MINISTRY. . . . JUST AS GOD GAVE NOAH A PLAN TO SAVE HIMSELF AND HIS FAMILY, HE HAS GIVEN ME THIS PLAN FOR YOU AND ME TO HELP GET OUR LOVED ONES SAVED AND BRING MILLIONS TO GOD THROUGHOUT THE WHOLE EARTH. WHAT IF NOAH HAD FAILED?

The letter detailed the features of the building with its 140,000-square feet of floor space: a seven-hundred-seat television studio complete with special lighting and a computer-controlled lighting board, an audio studio for professional recording, plus offices. While the $2.1 million price tag was not mentioned, the "telecom" urged the reader to "PLEASE RUSH BY RETURN MAIL YOUR COVENANT PROMISE" and listed multiple choices ranging from $100,000 on down to $25 and "$OTHER." The donor was given the option of sending the entire amount or making a down payment with up to two years to pay the balance. "THIS IS GOD'S PLAN, NOT MINE!" Angley wrote. "LET HIM TALK TO YOU NOW. HE SAID TO TELL YOU THAT WHAT YOU WRITE IN [as] A COVENANT PROMISE TO HIM FOR HIS PLAN WILL COUNT FOR ALL THE TIME AND ETERNITY. OH, CHILD OF GOD, THINK OF IT! INVEST, INVEST IN THIS PLAN OF GOD."

In Lou Spangler's estimation, the building was worth ten times the purchase price. "It's a gorgeous building," he said during an interview after the Washington crusade. "We'll renovate that building and make it something wonderful for God." The structure, he said, would be used strictly for television and recording sessions with the regular healing services still to be conducted at the cathedral—by Angley on Friday nights, by an assistant pastor on Sundays. The evangelistic association would move its offices to the complex and lease the remaining ones and a commercial "buffet" to outside tenants.

The overall plan called for shifting the emphasis from domestic crusades to more television and foreign travel. "The Americans and the Canadians have had God-God-God, *just God*. You can tune in on your TV and find some preacher anytime," Spangler reasoned. "He may not be right or he may not be correct in what he's saying, but you can find God, and there's been opportunities for Americans and Canadians to have God all over the place." He outlined the hectic schedule of leaving immediately after the Friday-night services and sometimes not returning to Akron until the following Thursday. Now, he said, "God's moving in a different direction." Or to be more direct, the foundation had been laid. The name Ernest Angley had become a household word.

The changes, of course, would require more money. Hence the urgent "telecom." Since the 1982 service in Washington, in addition to Angley's bimonthly magazine, I had received almost forty pieces of mail, reminding me of upcoming crusades in Washington and Baltimore but most of them asking for contributions. "Fill up Jesus' stocking with your best offering," one missive beseeched as Christmas approached. Thanksgiving, Easter, the evangelist's birthday, the thirtieth anniversary of the day he and his wife first pitched their tent in Akron, all brought messages. The "anniversary" letter encouraged me to send a dollar for each year Angley had been in Akron to help send the Gospel "to people who have never heard." If I could send more, so much the better. At the beginning of each year, he sent calendars with the monthly photographs in the form of envelopes that could be returned with contributions. Some of the requests offered gifts in return: an eight-by-ten color photograph of "God's servant," a two-by-three-inch cross made from an olive tree grown in the Holy Land and prayed over by Angley, a mother-of-pearl dove pin. Several urged me to "invest" in sending video tapes of his telecast to other countries: $200 would pay for an entire tape, $100 for half a tape, $50 for a quarter—or whatever I could spare.

The correspondence was expensively printed, sometimes with photographs and always on multicolor letterheads. The stationery usually included Angley's trademark, "the crown of life"; his motto, "Win the Lost at Any Cost"; and a photograph of the evangelist displaying a toothpaste-ad grin. Sometimes the letters addressed me as "Dear Friend" or, most often, by my first name. They were filled with messages that Angley claimed God had told him to pass along: that the end of the world was at hand, that the evangelist was to buy a building or travel abroad. Always the missive included a divine directive to give.

While Angley came across in the interview as unpretentious, he was definitely in the spotlight, the focus of adoration and attention. I thought about all the other evangelists relaying essentially the same "message from God": that we sheep follow His designated "servant." How was someone to know *which* man—if any—God actually wanted us to support? How could anyone be sure that God had not indeed spoken to Angley, as unlikely a candidate as he might seem? Certainly no mortal could prove it had or had not happened.

Up to now, Angley's television audience had not been large. In their 1981 book *Prime Time Preachers*, Jeffrey K. Hadden and Charles E. Swann described Angley as "the lunatic fringe" of religious broadcasting and estimated his weekly audience at 314,600 viewers, compared to Oral Roberts's 2,719,250 and Rex Humbard's 2,409,960. Just how many viewers watched Angley for spiritual sustenance and how many for sheer entertainment was impossible to determine. While revivalists, especially faith healers, have long been the butt of jokes, Angley— perhaps more than any single evangelist—has attracted a sizable "subculture" following. Steve Martin, Johnny Carson, and Robin Williams have done "Ernest Angley" take-offs, and many ordinary folks who could scarcely be described as "followers" tune in weekly simply to be amused. A Washington lobbyist confessed to keeping an Ernest Angley scrapbook, and two house painters told me they taped the show's soundtrack each week in order to perfect their impersonations of the evangelist while they worked. A religion editor, who preferred to remain anonymous, said he occasionally invited friends to "Ernest Angley Brunches," the show being the main entree.

Over television and on the platform, there indeed were times when the evangelist himself seemed to be doing a take-off on "Ernest Angley." *Los Angeles Times's* Howard Rosenberg once called Akron "the Yankee Stadium of TV evangelism" and described Angley as "the Joe DiMaggio of TV preachers, the heavy hitter." The television columnist lamented that only thirty-two thousand households in the area tuned in to Angley. "Everyone should see Ernest Angley, at least once," he wrote. "Ken Copeland tells a story so well he could make the telephone book sound spiritually breathtaking. Jimmy Swaggart sings a mean spiritual. Rex Humbard brings along his kids and grandkids. Oral Roberts has singers and a prayer tower. Frederick K. Price has the gift of street talk ('You're goin' down the tube, Jack')." Still, the columnist insisted, "all others pale before the Rev. Ernest Angley."

As two o'clock neared, Angley glanced at his watch.

"Can I have ten more minutes?" I asked.

He chuckled uneasily. "A couple more, because I really need the time."

"I wanted to ask your reaction to some more critical things," I proceeded cautiously. "You said you don't read the critical articles—"

"They're worthless, so why should I?" he said coolly. "Just like if I would start to read your book and you had critical things about the ministry, I wouldn't even finish it. When you drop on God's work, then I would be through with you if you couldn't edify Jesus."

Like a number of the more flamboyant evangelists, Angley often lashed out at the press. "If they write something good about the Lord, God bless them," he told a 1976 Charlotte audience. "If they write something bad, God will get them." Jim Auchmutey felt the full brunt of Angley's fury when he asked about the evangelist's financial affairs and again after his article ran in the *Atlanta Constitution* with a separate story on a $4 million lawsuit brought by a Charlotte couple. The parents accused Angley of turning her then-twenty-two-year-old daughter against them and luring her to Akron. They also claimed he publicly slandered them on at least three occasions—including Tom Snyder's "Tomorrow Show" when the evangelist branded them as "demon-possessed" and "liars." After Auchmutey's articles appeared, Angley's supporters deluged the reporter with angry letters and telephone calls, and the evangelist devoted an entire telecast to lambasting him. At a subsequent crusade attended by the journalist's mother, Angley whipped the crowd into such a frenzy that Mrs. Auchmutey later confided she would have feared for her life had the audience known who she was.

It was a side of the evangelist Roger Baerwolf, general manager of KXTX-TV in Dallas, also witnessed after the station elected not to renew Angley's contract because of an increasing number of complaints. At the time, the *Dallas Times-Herald* quoted viewers as saying Angley was "an abomination to the Lord" and "too effeminate." The evangelist in turn threatened to sue and encouraged his backers to bombard the station with angry letters and phone calls. "There was a tremendous amount of reaction," Baerwolf recalled. "I don't know whether saying they [the calls and letters] were hostile is accurate or not, but there were certainly some harsh tones in some of the letters."

When I brought up the tirades and criticism of the media, Angley responded without hesitating. "Oh, I've really given it to reporters," he boasted, a bit of vengeance in his voice. "I've said to them, You don't need to think your poison pen will do anything against this ministry."

"One reporter referred to the wrath of Ernest Angley and said there was a side that people didn't see," I observed, citing the Dallas incident as an example. "*Is* there a wrath of Angley?"

"I tell people the truth sometimes, especially when they lie, and *that* was a lie there," he said flatly. "That was a made-up lie, see, and when I stand against things that are wrong, and that reporter that had written the story then, well, he was vicious. We made him leave our building one time, so he waited until he got in a position that he could get that story published and then he was as vicious as he could be. It was in the Atlanta paper, wasn't it?"

I nodded.

"He was *very* vicious, but he'll have to give an account to God."

I asked if it might not be better to ignore an unfavorable story and turn the other cheek, but Angley insisted, "Sometimes I have to stand up to be counted when things are not right, and of course part of what that newspaperman had written and that station, that man that was manager had lied. We had it investigated. There was no mail to that effect, see, so I let him know and my attorney let him know if there was anything more he could expect a lawsuit."

In another vein, television comedians have been no less critical. Robin Williams made "The Right Reverend Angry" a staple of the "Saturday Night Live" repertoire, and Johnny Carson has frequently suggested if faith healers were genuine why did they wear toupees instead of growing hair—an obvious reference to Angley. Yet the evangelist took no offense at their jabs and indeed considered them good advertising.

"I don't feel like Johnny Carson's making fun of God, making fun of the ministry when he's doing it, although I've never heard him," he said. "I feel he's on there to make people laugh and it draws attention to the program . . . I feel no matter what they try, people try to write, God will usually get some good out of it."

Besides, he ended on a positive note, "there's no need for anybody to be on front-line duty for the Lord if they can't take criticism."

A little more than a month after our Washington meeting, Angley was arrested in Munich, Germany, and charged with suspicion of fraud and healing without a license. Three days earlier the death of an elderly woman during his crusade in Zurich had stirred up a controversy in Switzerland. But while West German authorities were aware of that incident, it was an advertisement in the Munich newspapers and *Der Stern* magazine that led to the arrest. The ads billed Angley as a "wunderheller" (wonder healer) and "wunderpediger" (wonder preacher), and, according to public prosecutors, the practice of physical "cures" by anyone without a medical license is prohibited by West German law.

The evangelist had held services in Frankfurt earlier in the week but apparently did not come to the authorities' attention then, just as he had escaped notice during a visit in 1982. At the first service I attended, Angley had, in fact, boasted about his German reception. "When I walked through the crowd of people and hit the platform," he told the audience at Constitution Hall, "I fit just like I was in Washington, D.C." But on July 11, 1984, after witnessing Angley's five-hour service in a hotel ballroom, thirty law enforcement officers placed the evangelist under house arrest and confiscated his luggage, thirteen video cassettes from the meeting, and an undisclosed amount of cash. He was held in his hotel room for five hours before being taken to police headquarters and booked. The next afternoon after posting a bond of 40,000 marks (roughly $14,000), he rejoined the 186 American and Canadian supporters who had gone on ahead of him to Paris for the final service in a five-city European tour that had been widely promoted on his weekly telecasts and in his magazine.

When Angley returned to Akron three days later, an estimated 1,500 followers greeted him at the airport with placards proclaiming WE LOVE YOU and WELCOME HOME PASTOR. The crowd cheered as he likened his ordeal to that of Christ and disclosed plans to file lawsuits—at God's behest—against the West German government, the city of Munich, its police department, and prosecuting attorneys. "I wasn't going to seek revenge," he insisted, "but the Lord said He wanted the suits."

I first learned about the arrest from a "telecom" sent by his headquarters. The communiqué detailed Angley's apprehension and requested a special offering to help "fight this great conflict in Germany for God." It was accompanied by a prepared letter, which I was urged to sign and mail to the German embassy in Washington protesting Angley's arrest. That same day I telephoned the embassy and was told that at least 2,000 copies of the protest letter had already arrived. Two weeks later the letters numbered 6,500, and by September the tally reached 15,000 with each day's mail bringing an average of 150 to 200 more. When I asked press attaché Christoph Bruemmer if this was a first for the embassy, he chuckled. "Television evangelists are nothing new for me, but fifteen thousand letters—*yes!*" By the end of October the letters were still coming in at a rate of fifty a day, and Bruemmer and his staff stopped keeping a count.

Outside of Akron, where the story was page-one news, Angley's arrest got little media coverage. But the evangelist more than made up for that on his own telecasts and in his magazine. The December issue was devoted to the incident, with color photographs of his arrival at the airport and another of him clad in a T-shirt, showing off what he said were bruises caused by a West German policeman. The cover was headlined GOD RAINED JUDGMENT ON MUNICH and carried a picture of a snowplow cleaning up from a severe hailstorm that struck several hours after Angley's departure. A superimposed caption read: "After Munich was hit by a disastrous storm of Old Testament proportions, snowplows were needed to clear the hailstones off the streets. More than 1,000 fire fighters and 250 policemen were used in the cleanup." The caption was an almost-verbatim version of the tongue-in-cheek account written by Stuart Warner for his *Akron Beacon Journal* humor column after he read an Associated Press story about the storm and, aware of Angley's arrest, tied the two events together. The storm had not been mentioned in the telecom and, according to Warner, the evangelist was unaware of it until he read the *Beacon Journal* column. Nevertheless, in his magazine Angley insisted that upon leaving Germany he had a visitation during which God took credit for the disaster. "When I shined my light upon my son in his cell, I was moved with great anger; and when I am moved with great anger I move with judgment," Angley quoted the Lord. "I want the inhabitants of the earth to know I take full responsibility for the calamity in Munich. I, saith the Lord thy God, did it."

According to the wire-service story, the storm was indeed awesome. Hailstones the size of tennis balls injured three hundred people and caused what was estimated at "tens of millions of dollars" in damage. At the Munich airport the hail and high winds broke two thousand panes of glass in the terminal and knocked ten Lufthansa planes—including five 737s—out of service. Several small planes were declared total losses.

"It was like the end of the world," said one man who got caught in the storm. "The sky paled, then got very dark. As the first chunks of ice fell like granite from heaven, people fled in panic to house entrances and overhangs."

An Akron travel agent who happened to be in Munich on business later told Stuart Warner the hail was more the size of grapefruits and that after the cleanup, damage estimates were raised to billions of dollars. While the man was not an Angley follower, he admitted the whole ordeal was scary. "It makes you wonder," he told Warner, "what kind of power guys like that [Angley] might really have."

In his humor column, Warner himself counseled the West Germans: "Better ye should have invited General Patton back than risk the wrath of the righteous Rev. Ernest Angley!"

CHAPTER VI

H. Richard Hall:
"Reading the Thoughts of Men's Hearts"

From outside, the meeting house known as Stepney Faith Center was singularly unimpressive, an accumulation of white stucco boxes added one onto the other as the membership and its finances had expanded: first a small, somewhat traditional churchlike structure, without the spire; next a rectangle, evenly marked with utilitarian windows; then a Sunday-school-type building, and beyond all those, a trailer where the widow of a previous pastor lived. A neon-embossed cross—which when illuminated alternately flashed JESUS SAVES / JESUS HEALS—rose above what appeared to be the entrance but wasn't.

It was very early April, the night too chilled to venture out into the tents, and so most evangelists continued their rounds of civic centers and off-brand tabernacles such as this one located at the ragged edges of Aberdeen, Maryland. I had made the three-hour drive from Washington to meet H. Richard Hall, a veteran of almost forty years on the sawdust circuit who—from what I read—fit my preconceived notion of an old-fashioned tent revivalist. While one scholar likened his appearance to that of a small-time politician, my initial impression, from the photograph in Hall's bimonthly tabloid, was of a mean-mannered, fire-and-brimstone preacher whose words could virtually pummel the soul.

When I arrived that evening in 1981, the gravel parking lot had begun to fill with cars, their occupants lingering in the deepening dusk to talk in twos and threes before drifting indoors to visit among the polished pews. For the most part, the people were as modest as the sanctuary, with its unadorned walls and its windows barren of stained-glass Madonnas. Their most prized possession, I surmised, was a dog-eared Bible; their closest friend, Jesus. The revivals that passed through town with monthly, sometimes weekly, regularity brightened their lives with music, miracles, and the "stars" of their galaxy—the revivalists they listened to on radio, watched on television, read about in slick evangelistic publications. There was a festive air. Laughter, animated conversations that would have been frowned upon by mainline Protestant churches. Two middle-age sisters in a pew near the front sat sideways waving to friends, and young girls wearing Saturday-night clothes smiled coquettishly at the boys. And in the midst of the visiting and the sharing of recipes and scripture, a stout old woman with gray hair and multiple chins hobbled up the aisle greeting those to either side—including me—with a sprightly "Purr-raise Gawd!"

Some wept, their arms raised, their faces troubled and tormented as Brother Hall directed his finger and his voice across the crowd like a divining rod detecting agonies of the flesh and of the soul, then pronouncing those who would believe, delivered *in the name of Jesus!* And yet it was as if God were reprimanding rather than relieving the people of their suffering. Only the aging black woman next to me appeared serene and at peace. Throughout the service her voice had warmed the singing, punctuated the sermon with a calm, confident "Thank You, Jesus," a soft, simple "Yes," a harmonious *hmmmmmmm.* Sometimes she sat with her eyes closed, her face as radiant as her multicolored tam, while all around her a hushed, hurting hallelujah circulated through the sanctuary, gradually rising with the evangelist's building fervor.

He was a tall, gaunt man in a black three-piece suit, its somberness reduced by the fabric's slight sheen. The jacket had been removed in the fever of the moment, and strands of his long, dark hair fell across his forehead. His face was as creviced as the North Carolina hills of his birth, dark and menacing when in repose, like a rubber mask that changed with his mood: brooding, smiling, glaring, winking, condemning, brightening, bantering. At the moment his expression was intense, his deep-set eyes trained on a hefty man in the first pew.

"See this brother here, the Lord's speaking to him," Hall said, gesturing for the man to stand. "In the last three months you've been walking on toward death. The things of yesterday are not enough. You know you have to walk into a deeper realm, and I feel it now moving over me the same thing you feel." The organ played softly as the evangelist addressed the man in a mournful tone. "It started when you were praying before God on Thursday. He's coming to you before another week's out. You'll have a visitation of the Spirit like you've never had before. There's been a personal problem, sir, and God's working it out."

A chorus of supplications overwhelmed the man's own thanksgiving, and Hall moved on. "Man settin' next to you—stand, friend." The man rose and waited expectantly. "You've got a condition in the center of your chest, like a pressure pushing in right here," the evangelist informed him, bearing his fist against his own breast. "Tell the folks if I'm telling the truth." The man faced the crowd and, with eyes lowered, nodded. "You'll never have it again. You're healed in the name of Jesus!"

Oh, praise God! the audience sighed as the evangelist's eyes shifted to the rear of the auditorium. "Beautiful little black woman waving her little hands—it's in your breast. You're healed. Praise God, you won't have to have that operation. The Holy Ghost just took that thing right out!" The woman's cheeks were slick with tears, her hands grasping for heaven, but already Hall's attention was focused on the balcony. "Little lady in the gray dress, praise God, the Lord's touching you. It's in the upper part of your back, going into your head. Did you ever tell me about it?"

The woman in gray's lips formed an inaudible no.

"Did *God* tell me?"

She nodded.

"You'll never have it again!"

A concerted *Praise God!* rose from the crowd.

And Hall shouted, "Can you believe? Can you believe?"

Oh, yes, Jesus!

"Magnify the Lord with me," the revivalist urged. "Believe in the name of Jesus for the glory of God. If thou canst believe, *all* things are possible for them that believe!"

The people responded in a universe of tongues, one urgent, repetitive *"Praise God—Praise God—Praise God"* rising above the rest. The hosannas fell like soft, steady rain until Hall's pace suddenly accelerated and he shouted, pointed, moved through the crowd, heralding the miracles that burst forth like bolts of lightning: healing, divine deliverance from "low blood," "passing-out spells," "that trouble in your ovary." The outburst of miracles had caught me by surprise. Except for random speaking in tongues, the earlier portion of the revival had differed little from black services I had been to or from livelier Sunday evenings in the Southern Baptist churches I grew up in. There had been spirited congregational singing, impromptu testimonials, and a sermon—albeit unlike any I had ever heard. It was almost going-home time when Hall began his account of God removing a tumor from his side, the recitation virtually evolving into a ballad. As he ended, the evangelist approached a man near the front and requested he touch Hall's side.

"What do you feel?"

The man answered, "A hole," then after pressing his hand to the other side, responded, "No hole there."

"He melted it out," Hall said. "He took it out. All I know is that He did. All I know is that the way I feel right now I wouldn't mind to join the others on another shore, and that's the truth. I feel His presence." Sighs stirred through the sanctuary. "And at this moment —and this is the truth—God, bear me witness. Prove to these people if you have to—I couldn't care less if I ever returned to Cleveland, for we're in a great realm of His anointing. *Hate-samo-ah-pora-ti-ahto.* His anointing is here."

Hall's expression was solemn as he looked out over the congregation. "Praise God," he declared, "I feel the Holy Ghost." And suddenly the miracles began. The people's murmurs and moans rose in a simple symphony of hope with the organ's soft strains of "Only Believe, All Things Are Possible," the hymn played at so many services where, with the Word of Knowledge, William Branham had read "the very thoughts of men's hearts," as he expressed it. This special anointing was said to have enabled the late evangelist to discern sins, illnesses, even past and future events in a person's life, with the individual reportedly receiving deliverance as soon as he asked forgiveness for any unconfessed sins. The operation of this gift of the Spirit was not confined to the platform. Branham's followers claimed he frequently was aware of conversations as they took place thousands of miles away and could meet a person he had never seen and immediately call him by name. Hall himself traced the origins of his own long association with Stepney Faith Center to seeing the name of its former pastor spelled out above the man's head during a service in Washington, D.C.

But for the most part, both evangelists exercised the Word of Knowledge to reveal to people their divine deliverance from problems of the body and of the soul, as Hall did now. Each wonder brought a new outburst, even from those not singled out, with the evangelist skillfully though ever so gently orchestrating the congregation's emotions, raising, lowering, leveling, lifting passions until the ululations became strong and constant. At times his own spirit seemed to soar, and he urged the people to follow. "Now we're reaching out, praise God. Reach out with me," he beckoned. "Tell the Lord I'm reaching out in the name of Jesus for the glory of God."

The audience drifted with him on a cloud of hosannas. And then, without warning, a strangeness settled over the sanctuary, a quiet, heavy foreboding. Hall stopped, abruptly. "There's something moving in here," he said, an eeriness creeping into his voice. "Praise God, we're walking where the angels can't even walk—the angels don't have the Spirit of Discernment—the angels don't have the Word of Knowledge," he chanted in the rhythmic, rattling monotone of a fast freight train. "The angels don't talk in tongues—the angels don't get the Holy Ghost." His own spirit seemed to rise and swirl and settle, to again inhabit his flesh, as he gestured toward a woman near the center aisle. "This pressure that comes, you'll never have it again," he informed her. "Praise God, you like to think of it as nerves but it's beyond that, but you're healed. Drop me a letter if you ever feel it again."

In the midst of the awe and adoration the evangelist turned on the crowd and glowered. "Now, Mister Hall, you're guessing," he mocked the skeptics. "Okay, you may have the microphone. Anyone may have it. Come on and guess the next one." His eyes darted across the crowd. "Anyone, anyone here, come take this microphone." There were no disbelievers, or at least none who would come forward, and Hall railed, "See, you won't move, but you'll point a finger of scorn at one that'll be bold enough to speak in the name of Jesus! *Ha-bee-ya-kapaya-ka-hoyah!*" Utterances that were unintelligible flowed from his lips, yet the people responded as if their hearts were speaking to one another.

"Weeping, son—" He motioned for a young man in a blue shirt to stand. "Weeping, I mean weeping. Such loneliness, and it's the truth and I just now feel it! Weeping—*ah-keya-pa-koyah-sha-na-hoya*. Little casket." Anguish filled Brother Hall's voice as he cried out, "Weeping, God, why? *Why* my baby? *Why* my child? God, *why?* Right, son?" The young man wept uncontrollably, for among Pentecostals tears are not reserved for women, and Hall too spoke in a sobbing tone as he addressed the grieving father. "God's gonna take that awful weeping away from you tonight and let you know you're going where the child is."

The supplications grew strong, steady, unrelenting, as the evangelist started toward the rear pew where I was seated. "Young man with the mustache," he called to the man next to me, leading him into the aisle. "Praise God, we're strangers, right? Don't know ya?" The man's voice was barely audible as he confirmed Hall's statements. In a conversation before the service, this man called B. J. Stanley had spoken reverently of the evangelist as "a man of God," recalling how at a previous revival Hall had detected the young laborer's preoccupation with suicide and on still another occasion had proclaimed him healed of coronary problems and a tumor. When I asked if the growth had been malignant, Stanley shrugged, "He just said it was a tumor." He was in his mid-thirties, with the burdened shoulders and brooding eyes of a man for whom heaven and hell were real. It was not in Stanley's nature to question Hall's pronouncements any more than he would have God's, and now he clung to the evangelist's words. "Praise God, there you are on your work, your job, but all the time your heart's not with it." As Hall reached into the inner recesses of B. J. Stanley's soul, drawing out a lifetime of hurts and unfulfilled dreams, tears welled up in the young man's eyes. "Your heart is seeking out. Praise God, you feel a call of God upon your life. You don't know how to start it, but you know you're going to preach to your people, praise God. Yes—you—are! Randy West comes along and preaches to some of 'em, other brothers, but one day they're gonna have a prophet—yes, sir, praise be unto God—and let you be that prophet to your people! *Habeya-kapaya-kahoyah!*" The evangelist held the microphone to B. J. Stanley's lips amplifying a howling, haunting, windlike sound that rose and fell and faded into a greater rush of moans and murmurs and wails dominated by Hall's harsher tongues. *Kumbeko-yah-lohoyah-tehoya-teyakahi-ah.* Stanley slumped into the pew and buried his face in his hands, sobbing.

As the evangelist started toward the pulpit, an atmosphere of other-worldliness descended upon the sanctuary, and he turned and looked about, as if he had been placed in the midst of space and was only now discovering the stars about him. "I don't know whether you see it or not, but there's a light hanging over this boy, praise God," Hall said, bewilderment in his voice. His eyes tracked something that at first only he seemed to see, then they swerved to the rear of the room. "There's one hanging over the little fella settin' back there in the yellow shirt. See him? There's one over the big boy that sung awhile ago. These are men of the most high God." The evangelist's eyes were flashing, and the words came quickly as he heralded halos that I could not see nor could I be certain other members of the congregation actually saw. Their supplications had long since reached hurricane force, strong, steady, and without words, one lone *"O God!"* rising above the rest. "There's one over the little woman settin' over yonder waving her hand—see her?—with the black hair, praise God? It's all over the building here. My God, why don't somebody magnify the Lord?"

A great noise and confusion filled the sanctuary, but Hall did not wait for it to subside. "There's one over the brother that came up here a while ago. Brother Dill. See him yonder? There's a light over that man, and God told me to tell him his greatest anointing is ahead. My God, lay your hand on the woman next to you, will ya? Put your hand on her, and she's healed by the power of God." The woman cried out, *"O God!"*—just that—and Hall exclaimed, "Blessed be God, that's the anointing of God that's moving her. Raise your hands and magnify the Lord. Touch the woman in front of you there, praise God. You're healed by the power of God, in the name of Jesus, it's gone for the glory of God. Why don't somebody magnify the Lord?"

In the midst of the pandemonium the black woman next to me softly murmured, "Oh, thank You, Jesus, thank You, Jesus, thank You, Jesus," as if she were repeating a Pentecostal rosary. Hall's own voice was like a gathering storm, swooping down and swirling the people to an emotional high. "Everybody's getting away from me now. You're just looking like just a body there. That's the truth. The Spirit moves in to take away the natural. The Holy Ghost is saying to you, Come up a little higher. Get away from that which you can see. Get out of the carnal. Come up a little higher. There's some things I want to show you. There's some things I want to speak to you. There's some things I want to reveal to you. Come up a little higher. I want to show you some things that will surely come to pass."

OH, PRAISE GOD! HALLELUJAH! THANK YOU, JEEEEEEEESUS!
Hall paused, letting the congregation release its emotions before he
proceeded in a calmed voice. "Up to now it has been Word of Knowledge, but at this moment I turn around—" He stopped and surveyed
the audience. "Is anyone here that's got a deaf ear?" The man next to
me raised his hand, and Hall beckoned him to the front. "The young
man God spoke for. Now then, if that was God awhile ago, why would
God not remove that deafness out of his ear?" he asked, then mimicked
the doubters. "Oh, you say, you're getting yourself in the corner. Come
on, get in the corner with me!"
    Yes, Lord!
    "Watch God make a noise!"
    Praise God.
    "Where's another one, a deaf ear?" He scanned the audience. "Any-
one else?"
    "Right here, Brother Hall," a man called out as he encouraged a
teenage boy to step forward. "Here's one."
    Again the evangelist canvassed the crowd. "Is there anyone else?
It's okay if you don't want to move, but there's somebody else has
deafness in their ear and I want to pray for it."
    In front of me an elderly woman nudged her husband. "Why don't
you take that thing out and go on up?" she nagged, but the old man
brushed her aside, refusing to budge or to remove his hearing aid.
    "Just a minute," a woman from across the aisle called.
    "That's it," Hall said as the woman hurried toward him.
    B. J. Stanley watched intently as Hall concentrated on the woman,
instructing her to cover her good ear and repeat what he said in a
whisper I could hear from where I was sitting. When the young laborer's turn came, he at first responded in a deep, steady voice.
    "Praise the Lord," he repeated the evangelist's words.
    "This ear?" Hall asked, feigning uncertainty.
    Stanley nodded.
    "Are you sure?" the evangelist pressed. "You told me you were deaf."
    "I know I did," Stanley said, his voice quivering. "I know I said it
was deaf."
    "Well, is it deaf now?"
    "No."
    "Are you hearing me?"

"I'm hearing you."

"Turn around and tell these folk."

"I can hear Brother Hall," he wept as he echoed the evangelist's words. "I can hear, praise God. I can hear."

Amid hallelujahs and amens, Hall stepped back to study the teenage boy before facing him squarely. When the evangelist spoke, he did so as if he was addressing God as well as the congregation while continuing to take in the youngster's wholesome appearance. "What sin's in this little boy? What evil's in him?" he said sternly. "Why don't somebody say God's touched these people that's much older than him, why not him?" Supplications rippled through the auditorium. "Well, you say, now you shouldn't—but I'll say to God, Why—not—him!" he demanded with mock indignation. "If I could do it, I would! But I can't do it! I want God to come on in here, son, and touch you!" he said forcefully. "I don't want you to go through life like this!" Then, lowering his voice, he had the boy place a finger in his ear, inquiring "How old are you?"

The boy replied, "Fourteen."

"Are you sure it's this ear?"

He nodded and, like B. J. Stanley and the woman, repeated what Hall said to him in a whisperlike tone that was audible from where I was sitting. The litany ended with a declaration from the boy that he could hear. The evangelist called the mother forward, instructing her to whisper into her son's ear, "Tell him you love him."

The boy responded, "I love you too."

"Oh, dear God!" the mother wailed.

The congregation's hosannas were cut short as Hall, accompanied by the organ, burst into song. "My God can do any-thi-ing . . . anything, oh anything. My God, my God can do anything." The congregation was swept up along with him. *"He made the earth in all its glory . . . my God can do any-thi-ing!"**

The sanctuary, in its morning solitude, seemed even starker than it had the night before. The drums and organ were covered and quiet; the blinds drawn against the sun's steady climb toward noon. There was an

---

*"My God Can Do Anything" written by Vep Ellis. Copyright © 1957 by Lillenas Publishing Co. All rights reserved. Used by permission.

aura of a room not yet awakened, a smell of waxed floors and polished pews and seldom-opened hymnals that, from midweek intrusions of my youth, I somehow associated with empty Protestant churches. Footsteps that would have been lost among the amens and hallelujahs resounded with unreasonable clarity, arousing childhood guilts of being where I should not be, of intruding on God during His private meditations. I felt myself wanting to tiptoe as we made our way past the pews toward the pastor's office, Brother Hall, followed by me, then Craig Strain.

The latter, in his early thirties, had not outgrown the lankiness of youth, and I could envision him strutting about a football field in a brass-buttoned band uniform. He had sung in the choir at the Methodist church his family attended in Indiana, where his father sold farm equipment. But like many of his generation, he had abandoned God—just as he did his studies—in a quest that led him through the drug culture and finally to Hall's organization. There, he carved out a position for himself by doing odd jobs and setting up a print shop before he earned a spot on the evangelistic team. Now, in addition to playing drums and supervising the newsletter, he oversaw the licensing of ministers.

In the study he pushed aside the rumpled blanket from a makeshift bed and settled into a sofa across from the desk where Hall was seated. At close range the evangelist looked no less sinister than his photograph, and, in the course of my stay in Aberdeen, some of his most devoted workers confided that on first encountering him they too had found him frightening. One associate compared his face to Frankenstein's, and yet, as we talked, his manner and voice were gentle, kind, and at times witty. He wore the three-piece suit from the night before, his dark hair combed straight back to the collar. His face was so crumpled I couldn't determine whether the creases were permanent or due to fatigue from last night's service.

On the platform he had freely woven anecdotes from his past into a rambling monologue, relaxed—as most evangelists are—before an audience. But one on one, he was visibly uncomfortable. Persistently, though politely, he evaded my first requests to talk about himself. "You don't want my background," he would protest, "I really like to give this." And then he would expound on the history of Pentecostalism or on the late forties and early fifties, those many-miracled, pretelevision days of mammoth tents and magnetic men when revivals attracted tens of thousands and evangelistic publications abounded with testimonies boldly headlined WOMAN RAISED FROM THE DEAD, ONCE TOTALLY BLIND SEES AGAIN, GIRL WITH SEVERED VOCAL CORD SINGS OVER RADIO. But gradually Hall's withered face warmed, and his account was no longer that of an outsider. He had been there. He had known the thrill of a packed tent and of watching the lame walk and the blind see at the laying on of a hand—*his* hand. His own mother had been among the first in the western hills of North Carolina to receive the baptism of the Spirit and to speak in tongues during the developing days of Pentacostalism. For a time that occurrence caused her father, a Baptist preacher, to bar the widow and her five-year-old son from the family home, but the stern rebuke did not stop the mother from embarking on her own ministry and from surrounding young Homer Richard with the fervent new converts. From then on, Hall had been captivated by voices and visions.

"I had some strange experiences when I was a child," Hall mused, quick to add a good-humored disclaimer, as he so often did as the interview progressed. "And of course children do, they experience things, so whether it be a figment of my mind, I don't know, and it may be because Mom got in the charismatic move—I mean to be as honest with you as I can—and it might have been hearing them so much. They was really carried away with dreams and visions and interpretations and speaking in tongues, interpretation of tongues, and the whole body movement. Ecstasy, elation, emotions—that was the thing more than it is even today. At nine I had a feeling I should go into seclusion, and I wanted to go into the woods or someplace and my mother wouldn't let me, but for three days, just to satisfy me, she let me stay up under the house, and she'd bring me food and quilts and things." He paused to study my reaction before acknowledging "That's way out, isn't it? But I think that's what you wanta hear." Again he stopped and canvassed my face, growing increasingly relaxed, introspective when he resumed. "Before I was born she said she had a dream—course people don't believe in dreams—but she had a dream she was going to have a son and he was going to be a minister, and she dreamed I would be born with a veil over my face. Now that don't mean anything to city folk, but to mountain people that's out of this world. Born with a veil over your face!" He attempted to explain a caul, a thin membrane that sometimes covers the face of a newborn baby and in Appalachian lore marks a person as special. "I was born at home, and sure enough I was born with that veil over my face just like Mom told them I'd be."

Caught up now in his recollections of the voices and visions that had captivated him the way fairy tales fascinate most youngsters, Hall no longer needed prodding. "When I was thirteen, just as sure as I'm sitting here, there was a light came into my room and swung over the old iron bedstead. It was about one-thirty or two o'clock in the morning, and it was light as noonday in the room, and that's the truth! I wasn't asleep 'cause I jumped from my bed and went running to my mother's room and told her. Course I was all uptight, upset, shaking, so she walked with me all night long. She told me the plan of my life, and it turned out just exactly—She said she had seen it all in a vision before, and it was a sign from the Lord."

Several months later he received the baptism of the Spirit and at fourteen began preaching on street corners and in prayer meetings and churches when the elders would let him. He smiled, remembering those early, eager ambitions, especially the Sunday he preached barefoot to a crowd of six or seven hundred people at what loomed in his memories as a big Church of God. "There was eleven people converted that night, *grown* people. Maybe because I was a child," he conceded with a chuckle. "People kinda go along with a child."

After high school Hall attended the Church of God of Prophecy Bible Training School, and at age twenty-four he was ordained. Over the years he also studied at the Atlanta Institute of Speech and Expression and a Knights of Columbus school in New York and picked up an honorary doctorate from the William Carter Bible College in Goldsboro, North Carolina.

"That's just little things in life," he said, after completing a résumé of his education. "I don't think it amounts to much, but it all adds up in the end. We in Pentecost like the term we're totally ordained and the Lord speaks to us, but, again, the Bible says Study to show yourself approved unto God and He'd bring all things to remembrance," he reasoned, "but if He don't bring all things to remembrance, you have to learn somewheres."

"Do you get to read very much?" I asked.

"That's my hobby," he said. "Mathematics or history—I like history, but just anything. I've got a feeling if you learn something you won't go too many years but what you won't pick it off the shelf and use it."

"Didn't you study some law?" I asked, remembering a reference from a book.

"Yes, but not to any degree," he replied nonchalantly. "I wanted to be a lawyer."

"In addition to preaching?"

"No, I really wanted to be a lawyer," he said. "That was my dream all my life, and then politics—And I'm still carried away with politics, am I not, Craig?"

"Guilty," Strain agreed.

Hall sighed wistfully. "Aaaaah, yes, but I'm a preacher."

At the time, he explained, an individual could study under a private attorney and take the Georgia bar exam without attending a college or university. The speech and expression classes were to prepare him for the courtroom, to teach him articulation and body movement to enable him to communicate with a juror without actually speaking. His studies were cut short when he developed tuberculosis and was told by doctors he could never again speak publicly. After three months, however, he resumed preaching.

"I just got up out of the bed and started," he said. "I got all right." He hesitated, then proceeded haltingly. "Again, I had a strange— you'll call it a figment of the mind, but I call it a vision, appearance of—and it could well have been in my mind. I don't know. I'm not all that hide-bound. All I know is that it worked, and I did experience, I felt like it was the Lord, a transparent figure at the foot of my bed. He spoke to me, said He'd healed me. I went back to preaching and then that ended this other idea in my mind."

"Did you feel after you saw God, or the vision, that was a sign He wanted you to preach?" I asked.

"Yes, I knew it was," he said. "I *know* that the first sign of insanity is hearing voices," he chuckled, "but I did. I heard voices, so call it what you want to."

Hall was state overseer for the Church of God of Prophecy in Colorado, Utah, and western Texas when what he summed up now as "seven years of tremendous move" burst forth. A young man, still in his twenties, he had long agonized over why the miracles he read about in the Bible no longer transpired, why the crippled, the lame, the deaf, the blind were not healed as they had been in the early church.

"That was almost a torment in my mind, that if God is the same, then why—not—now?" He pounded the desk for emphasis. "And then came this charismatic move of forty-six, forty-seven, forty-eight, forty-nine, fifty—you'll only read about it, but it's the truth," he said, his excitement growing as he recalled those electric days of tent revivals and his own decision in 1952 to leave his denomination and join the sign-gift ministry. "Roberts with a twenty-thousand-seat capacity tent. Jack Coe with a twenty-two-thousand tent. Roberts and Jack would build their tents one above the other just to be the largest. Then Allen comes in. Then us lesser lights like myself and Brother Grant and Brother Nunn and Brother Dunn—I don't think they'd appreciate me terming ourselves lesser lights," he chuckled, "but I just hit the issue head-on. When that's what you are, that's what you are. If you can't be Jupiter and Mars, then maybe you can be another little star, but you're still there, in the same realm. That's the good part about it."

Craig Strain listened intently to what I felt certain was not his first time to hear Hall's account of the glory days of tent revivals. "You had to have no advertisements. You had to have *nothing*," he was adamant. "You'd come to town, set up a tent, and the first night—" he snapped his fingers, like *that*—"you'd have a thousand people. The second night, fifteen hundred. Before you left, maybe fifteen, twenty thousand. I guess Brother Branham did more to attract the people and *real* miracles than anyone. He preached to as large a crowd as two hundred thousand people at one time in Africa, and, honest, the dead were absolutely raised in his services, and people screamed to the top of their voices, totally healed that were blind, totally blind."

Hall's eyes reflected admiration as he recalled the man he still looked up to. "William Branham superseded anything," he said, awe in his voice, "and yet he was the most simple speaker and nonassuming man of all of Pentecost. I never heard him speak with tongues. Never heard him *hallelujah!*" He mimicked a shout. "None of that. But he was the champion of the time." During last night's service Hall had described Branham as "the senior prophet" of his day. "There was none that measured to the man," he told the congregation, adding with an edge of humor "Oral Roberts might get to blow a flute for Brother Branham. Billy Graham—they might let him beat a tambourine. He walked as close as I've ever seen a man walk to God."

* * *

It was William Branham who resurrected the Word of Knowledge, bringing that "gift of the Spirit" to the public's attention as Oral Roberts did the healing line. Although Branham conducted his first tent revival in June 1933 and that same year built a small tabernacle in Jeffersonville, Indiana, he did not gain national prominence until May 7, 1946, when, he said, a two-hundred-pound angel relayed a directive from God to take "a gift of healing" to the people. As proof that God had commissioned him to deliver the people, he would be given two signs: first, an ability to detect and diagnose diseases by vibrations in his left hand; second, the gift of the Word of Knowledge by which he could, Branham later wrote, "discern the secrets of people's hearts." The visitation was not the first for "Brother Billy." According to the evangelist, God had spoken to him when he was three years old and again when he was seven. Even in the early days when he worked at assorted jobs to support his family and his ministry, the simple Baptist preacher was considered "the man sent from God." His small band of followers often claimed to see supernatural lights or halos about Branham's head. Beginning in late 1945, with increasing frequency he told his disciples of new visitations. Then, during one Sunday-evening service when he was describing the angel's visit and revelation that he would soon be standing before thousands in packed auditoriums, Branham was summoned to St. Louis to pray for the sick daughter of a minister friend. With borrowed money and clothes he immediately embarked on a trip that would begin, in the words of one evangelist, "a healing itinerary such as perhaps was never paralleled outside of Christ's and the Apostles' sojourns with the sick of their day." After the girl improved, Branham returned home to his job as game warden only to journey again to St. Louis a month later to conduct a revival. It was then that word of his miraculous healing powers began to spread. By midsummer when he held a revival at the Jonesboro, Arkansas, tabernacle pastored by Rex Humbard's father, an estimated twenty-five thousand people from twenty-eight states and Mexico descended on the little-known city. Long after the revival ended, a caravan of cars and campers wound its way through the Ozarks, "reverently tracing the path of this Twentieth-Century prophet."

Soon Branham's associates were hard pressed to find buildings large enough to hold the burgeoning crowds drawn to his services amid reports that he had miraculously straightened clubfeet, cured leprosy, and raised the dead. The population of Vandalia, Illinois, doubled in a single day when he came to conduct a healing service, as the reports became increasingly sensational. During one campaign *The Voice of Healing*—a periodical launched to promote Branham's ministry—wrote that "invalids arose from their cots in transfiguration as the illuminated messages went forth." A woman, said to have been blind in one eye for ten years, "received full sight and straightening of the eye while at home preparing to come to the service." By 1950, when it had become almost impossible to find halls large enough to accommodate the swelling audiences, Branham ordered a tent to seat five thousand.

Long after his death, his ardent followers continued to marvel about how the vibrations caused Branham's left hand to become red and swollen and his wristwatch to stop. Fred F. Bosworth, a popular healing revivalist in the twenties, likened the sensation felt by Branham to picking up a live wire. "When the oppressing spirit is cast out in Jesus' Name," Bosworth wrote in 1950, "you can see Brother Branham's red and swollen hand return to its normal condition." But it was the Word of Knowledge that most impressed his peers and fascinated the crowds. With this gift he was said to have discerned the thoughts, sins, illnesses, even past and future events in a person's life, making him not only a channel for healing, Bosworth wrote, but "a Seer as were the Old Testament Prophets." Adamant that Branham was never wrong in the often-detailed statements he made, the elder evangelist wrote: "Just as clearly as one sees material things around them, Brother Branham, while in prayer during the day, sees in vision some of the principal miracles before they take place that night. He sees some carried in on ambulance cots, or sitting in wheel chairs, and can describe how they look and how they are dressed . . . Not once during the more than three years since receiving the gift have these revelations failed to produce perfect miracles exactly as he had already seen them in visions." When Bosworth asked how he saw these events before they took place, Branham replied, "Just as I see you, only that I know it is a vision."

The crowds continued to grow. In January 1950 a crusade in Houston had to be moved from the City Auditorium to Sam Houston Coliseum to accommodate the more than eight thousand people who turned out nightly. During this revival, the Reverend W. E. Best, pastor of the Houston Tabernacle Baptist Church, challenged Branham to prove that miraculous healings had not ceased with the apostles. Bosworth agreed to take on Best in a debate that received considerable coverage in the press. But still another incident was to garner even greater publicity. Best hired two professional photographers to take pictures of him during the debate. When the photographers returned to their darkrooms, all the frames of Best were completely blank. The one shot of Branham showed a halo above his head. Branham was not surprised when informed of the photograph. Similar phenomena, he and his followers attested, had appeared since the time of his birth. The incident was enough to make a believer out of Ted Kipperman, the then twenty-one-year-old photographer hired by Best. In 1984, during a telephone interview, Kipperman described the experience as "the most amazing thing I ever saw."

Unlike the more flamboyant revivalists of his day, Branham was described as "gentle and quiet spoken in all his dealings with the people," seldom raising his voice or becoming excited. He had a "quiet mastery" over his audiences, and his sermons—like the man himself—were simple, and yet, according to historian David Edwin Harrell, "the power of a Branham service—and of Branham's stage presence—remains a legend unparalleled in the history of the charismatic movement."

Just as A. A. Allen left his mark on R. W. Schambach, Brother Billy made a lasting impression on Richard Hall. Although I never heard Branham preach, from talking to people who did encounter the late evangelist I gathered that Hall's style, both on and off the platform, bore striking similarities to Branham's—which some observers considered more by design than accident. The two men indeed had much in common: Both were raised in Appalachian poverty—Branham, in Kentucky; Hall, in North Carolina; and both seemed to put little stock in worldly possessions. At the height of Branham's popularity, he frequently arrived at gatherings in a battered old truck, wearing a mismatched jacket and trousers. While Hall dressed in tasteful three-piece suits, a member of his evangelistic team likened him to Mahatma Gandhi, insisting "He doesn't have *nothing!* We buy him his suits, and his home is all broke down. Sometimes I think, Why doesn't he fix it up for his wife, but he doesn't have the time or the desire." Another worker confided that Hall usually cut his own hair or had a member of his staff do it. Like Branham, he seldom stressed money during his services. The night before, the offering was not collected until the end of the service, after many people had left. Even then, he told those who made financial pledges to his ministry, "If you can't pay, don't worry about it. You've got enough to worry about without worrying about some preacher." But the strongest bond between him and the late evangelist was their deep, religious mysticism, their frequent references to visions and visitations.

Hall was only one of many young deliverance preachers to follow William Branham into the sign-gift ministry. From the beginning, he patterned his ministry after those of the revival giants, though on a smaller scale, with healing and the Word of Knowledge a vital part of his services. He launched a weekly radio broadcast—on thirty stations by 1960—and published a periodical, the monthly budget for his entire operation a modest $3,000. Over the years he earned a reputation as a successful small evangelist, with a far-flung congregation of followers who eagerly awaited his regular visits and sometimes drove hundreds of miles to attend his meetings. He appealed to the unsophisticated, often to the social outcast, and was proud of the inmates his ministerial association licensed within prisons. That same desire to appeal to "those that have a need and don't fit" led him to detect in the youth rebellion of the late sixties a hungering he felt he could satisfy. "Those boys are waiting for this supernatural or charismatic move, mysticism," he told historian David Harrell, "and we have it." He soon surrounded himself with bright, young college dropouts who willingly sheared their hair, traded faded dungarees for three-piece suits, and joined him on the sawdust trail and at his Cleveland, Tennessee, headquarters. With a boost from the evangelist, some eventually went out on their own; others, like Craig Strain, Mike Shreve, and Pat Hayes, conducted meetings yet remained part of Hall's United Christian International. The bringing together of old-line Pentecostals and offbeat hippies was, in Harrell's estimation, "a striking accomplishment."

By the early eighties, Hall's organization included the branch that licensed independent ministers, a correspondence Bible school, a youth program that sponsored a two-week summer camp, a missions department, and churches in Cleveland and Asheville, North Carolina. His bills now amounted to $1,300 a day; nevertheless, he continued to work cautiously within his limits, confining his telecasts to fifteen stations and the *Shield of Faith* to a newsprint tabloid.

The heart of his ministry remained the arduous four- and five-hour revival services that kept him on the road all but one day a week—a day he, like the rest of his staff, spent cranking out newsletters, tinkering with automobiles, or working on construction projects. Since suffering what he diagnosed as "a little trouble in my body," a period in July 1980 when his heart missed every other beat, he no longer erected his own tent. Instead, he preached the last few services at Mike Shreve's and Pat Hayes's three-week tent meetings and in between conducted revivals in churches. Occasionally he ventured into Pennsylvania or Illinois or Iowa, even to larger cities like Chicago and Washington, but he traveled primarily in the South, logging a hundred thousand miles a year, most of them by car. Frequently he ended one service at midnight, then drove all night and into the morning to his next engagement.

Now when I asked what it was like to live on the road, out of a suitcase, Hall countered, "After twenty-five or thirty or thirty-five years, I'd say, My God, what would it be like to have to stay in one room!"

"I guess you've learned to be a good packer."

He shook his head, amused. "That's the sad part. A man never gets there, I don't guess. We just throw things together. The kids, they're all good to me. I'll go in and in three or four hours my clothes are all clean and in the bags ready to go."

Although Hall had made this trip to Aberdeen with Craig Strain, each member of his team usually traveled alone, in his own car. In the early days his wife, Amelia, led the song services, but she had long since gone out on her own, spending much of her time conducting revivals in the Caribbean Islands. The two had met at a prayer meeting and married when he was nineteen. In spite of her Methodist upbringing, she was as much a religious mystic as he: She too had been born with a caul and, at an early age, had been visited by God. When she was five, He had told her she would become a missionary.

"Miz Hall is tough as wet leather," the evangelist said in a tone that was nonchalant yet reflected pride. "Some of the rallies don't have lights or any facilities, no sanitation. She can take it. I don't want to, and I'm tough."

"Was she a missionary when you met?" I asked.

"No, she was a Methodist. Still claims to be Methodist with the Pentecostal blessing," he said. "She's right hard on doctrine. I guess you can see that I—whosoever will, let him come. She reaches an altogether different type people than me."

Amelia Hall's work had started with occasional trips to Jamaica and some of the smaller islands. She now remained "in the field" most of the time. Recently she had begun evangelizing in the western hills of North Carolina, but for the most part she concentrated on the Caribbean.

"With you both on the road you must not see each other very much," I observed.

"Ooooh, 'bout once ever' month or so," he estimated, without obvious regret, adding "but, honest, this becomes a way of life and it supersedes anything. It really does."

The couple had no children, and while the evangelist himself was reticent about admitting it, many of his young workers were like sons, especially Don Warren. A brochure issued on the thirty-fifth anniversary of Hall's ministry included numerous photographs of him with Warren's own children, one of them named Donald Richard. And when he discussed his team, there was an unmistakable touch of fatherly pride at the mention of the organist. Warren had joined the Halls when he was thirteen. With his parents' permission he had brought along his guitar and a cardboard box of clothes for what started out as a summer on the road. That fall, after the revivalist promised to see that the boy kept up his studies via correspondence school, his folks allowed him to continue.

"Don's been with us twenty-seven or -eight years," Hall said as we discussed his team, then unexpectedly his mind jumped ahead. "Will you ask Don how he started playing the organ?" he instructed me. "Don't ask me, because if I told you it'd be hard for you to believe. He'd never set down at an organ in his life. *Never*. Now this thing was so strong in those days until—" Hall could not resist telling the story. "My wife was leading services and the little girl that worked with us —you ask him. I'll tell you now, then you can go ask him. The girl that had worked with us had gotten married and now she was gone. So we were starting a new revival. No organist. Don picked the guitar. He was just a little fella, thirteen years old, and my wife came to me right before church, said, Whatever we going to do? Said, I cannot lead song service without music. Well, I had been out to pray and this *strong* impression from God—sort of like a voice, but not audibly— said, You have an organist, and Don in my mind just appeared before me. So I accepted it. Went on that night and right before church, she said, What are we going to do? I said, Just don't get uptight, we have an organist. She said, Well, praise God. Said, Now who is it? I said, Uh, it's Don. Came church time, I walked over to Don—you ask him—he didn't know a thing about it. I said, Put your guitar down. I raised my hand over his head. Said, in the name of Jesus, get to the organ—just like that—and start playing. He didn't even ask a question. Little fella thirteen years old went over and started playing the organ and played it then just like he plays it now. Can you believe that?" Hall didn't wait for me to register a response. "You don't have to believe it. You're objective. That's okay. Ask him. Never had played an organ before. Didn't even wanta play one. Didn't care a thing for it. But he's one of the best in the Pentecostal ranks," he boasted. "He really is. I mean, he can get that organ and go with it."

Such supernatural occurrences apparently were neither new nor unique. In *Like a Mighty Army*, a history of the Church of God, Dr. Charles W. Conn wrote that one of the many spiritual manifestations at early Pentecostal services was "someone playing a musical instrument—usually a piano or organ—he could not otherwise play." He related the experience of a Midwestern minister's wife who had no musical ability, yet played the piano beautifully while in the Spirit. Later, in my own travels, another young man told me how "God imparted the gift to play the organ" after Hall laid hands on him. A flyer promoting United Christian International's First Annual Easter Teaching Seminar and Revival, held the week after my first meeting with the evangelist, listed various workshops and noted that "Brother Hall will pray for you to receive a gift of music as others have by the laying on of hands. Don Warren will speak and demonstrate on flowing with the anointing of music."

Now the evangelist proceeded like a new grandparent showing off snapshots. "Don was in Lee College for two years, and he's a college man." He gestured toward the drummer, encouraging him to sketch his own scholastic background, at Ball State University and Lake Sumter Community College, but before Strain could finish, Hall's prowling, probing mind raced ahead.

"Did you know—" he broke in, apologizing "I know this don't fit, but did you know Mike's having difficulties, really a challenge, from the chief atheist, the woman—what's her name?"

"Madalyn O'Hair?" I offered.

"We got a letter today that he's gonna be challenged through the courts because he's going to the schools talking on drug abuse, and she said he's just using it for religion. So-o-o-o, I don't know what'll come out of it. But that's pretty good, to get the big shot in atheism to give him a fit, isn't it? I think we should write an article. When we go home Sunday," he made up his mind, "I'm gonna put that in our magazine."

During our interview I had watched his somberness give way to exuberance, his grimace change to a grin. "Oh, we enjoy life, we really enjoy life," he said at one point. "We get exuberant over nothing." The comment was intended to describe his young staff, but it was equally true of the evangelist. Mellow and easygoing by nature, he could become as excited about a new door being installed at his Cleveland tabernacle as he could by a jammed tent.

"You enjoy it," I commented.

"Oh, yes, I do," he said without hesitation. "I enjoy the challenge. Of course, I guess you see my type of preaching is unorthodox, *totally*. I want to get in rapport with the people. I mean, I want to reach the people. Okay if they're farmers, let's have some overalls. Let's go. Whatever. Honest, I want to be right in with them, and I've got to find a way. You see me seeking my way last night?" I nodded. "Looking for some way to get to this one. See this fella over here, I want to get to him."

Grabbing the air with one hand, then the other, he described his efforts to draw the audience into his sermon. Last night it had been obvious that Hall was having a good time, even fun. Shortly before the service ended he asked the crowd, "Who says you have to come here and be sad? Tell ever'one you came and had a good time." As I watched him singing, clapping, clowning, dancing in the aisle, it occurred to me that after his staid Pentecostal upbringing and almost forty years of conducting revivals six nights a week, he had turned the services into a night's entertainment for himself as much as for his audience.

I had also concluded that his style and many of his views were unconventional, different even from the other tent evangelists I had encountered. The late A. A. Allen had been heralded with a flourish not unlike Ed McMahon's nightly introduction of Johnny Carson. After the audience's emotional batteries had been charged, his platform man would boom, "And now, HERE—HE—IS—God's man of faith and prayer, BROTHER—A—A—ALLEN!" But last night, without fanfare, Hall took the microphone from his song director in the midst of the congregational singing, the elder evangelist's smooth, mellow voice soaring above the rest until the crowd stopped to listen. He was a showman, but of a different variety than the more gregarious Schambach. Hall mimicked and clowned, sometimes flinging his long hair over his face and parting it to play Indian or some other role, then removing a large comb from his hip pocket to slick it back into place, yet his humor was low-key, his delivery a leisurely, strolling-along pace. Even his shouting had a soft edge. His sermon began as a rambling epic laced with homespun philosophy, personal anecdotes, and folksy stock phrases like "Preach on, Brother Hall" or "Boy, that didn't set so well." But in the end his goal was that of all revivalists: to evoke response, to whip his audience to an emotional frenzy. He was like a conductor orchestrating the people's emotions, drawing them into a dialogue, encouraging them to complete his scriptural quotations and to punctuate his pronouncements with an exclamation, a gentle nod. As the altar call neared, his pace quickened and his delivery became rhythmic, repetitive, like the chanted sermons of older black ministers, unleashing a swarm of amens.

Some of his views were equally unconventional. In a sermon on creation he insisted, "I'm not worried about by what means. If it was a process, all right, or if it was a big *BANG!* that's all right. It don't bother me at all. God did it." He opened the altar call with a promise from God that all who came forward would receive a miracle within thirty days. "You don't have to be a believer," Hall assured the audience, "Bless God, if you get under the rain it's going to rain on you."

In spite of the role of divine healing in his services and in his own life, Hall also believed in medical science and had been hospitalized the year before during his heart ailments. He openly expressed doubts that manifestations of the Spirit—including speaking in tongues—were always genuine. Some people think they have a Spirit of Discernment or a Word of Knowledge, he cautioned, when in fact they have "a spirit of imagination." He was especially skeptical of what he termed "way-out religious fanatics," conceding "When I hear people start talking all the time about *God* told me, about every sentence or ever' three or four minutes saying God told me, I get a little leery. I get a little worried, a little afraid." While many Pentecostal evangelists attributed their seemingly impromptu sermons to waiting on the leading of the Lord, Hall readily admitted he didn't take a subject "because it ties me and it may not be the thing that would go." Instead, he carefully monitored the congregation's response. "I may have a subject in mind and may get to it after a while and they won't even know. After I see one start nodding his head or smiling, and I look around and I see two-thirds are listening, then, Okay, I'll go with it. But until I know I've got them with me, there's no use me trying to get my thought to them or give them another idea."

Frankly, he told me, it was easier to reach a person with emotions than with reason. "If you do not get to an emotional high, either in weeping or in exuberance or in so-called ecstasy, you have no place to move people, but after you one time get them emotionally, then you can give them points of reason, your reasoning, and they'll accept it. If the first thing I do is to start giving reasons, they're going to put up barriers. But if they have laughed with me and they have sung with me and they've clapped their little hands with me and stomped their feet, if they've got in the mood with me, then I come back and give them my reasoning. If two-thirds go with me I'm happy."

In the old days revivalists took great care to record the numbers of newly saved. To describe the success of a 1958 evangelistic tour to Latin America, A. A. Allen wrote: "The souls that were saved in that campaign cost only twenty-five cents each, or FOUR FOR A DOLLAR! . . . I read in a periodical of another evangelist that his cost of winning souls averaged $2.00 each. Another group estimated that their cost was even higher." The practice of determining the "cost per convert" came into vogue around the turn of the century when evangelists began to emphasize mass conversions as a means of justifying the growing expense that went into revivals. The success of a crusade came to be measured by a figure arrived at by dividing the cost of the services by the number of people saved. But Hall no longer had the newborn fill out "decision cards," nor did he keep score.

"That's something I got away from years ago," he said.

"In the Baptist church we had an invitation, do you do that?" I asked.

"In a different way. Everyone is included. I don't want to leave anyone out. If you make an altar call this way: And now then, Sister Mary is going to play a song on the organ, and Brother John, give us a song appropriate, we're going to give an invitation. Well, you know what's going to happen to the people you want at the altar? Out the door they go grabbing their cigarettes." He chuckled. "A hunter don't even go out to the fields beating through the bush, Little squirrel I'm gonna get you. You can work better on a mass invitation. There's no person even in school wants to get up and sing a song by themselves, but if there's fifteen or twenty little girls and boys singing, oh, well let's go. They like to belong."

In the brochure commemorating Hall's thirty-fifth anniversary in the ministry, there was a photograph of him as a young man, his deep, dark eyes bright with admiration as he stood next to the legendary William Branham. Now during a lull in the conversation, the quiet was laden with memories of those long-ago days when tents and miracles loomed large on the American horizon.

"None of us are touching that revival," Hall said. "We got all this television. We got all the radio. We got all of that. The Seven Hundred Club. The PTL, and power to it all. It's beautiful. And we've got the Schambachs and myself, but none of us are touching that revival of that seven-year period."

Before William Branham died, his crowds dwindled from thousands to a few hundred, his daily mail from a thousand letters to seventy-five. In *All Things Are Possible*, David Harrell speculated: "To a Pentecostal world that craved marvels in the years immediately after World War II, he offered his sincerity and his fantastic array of personal spiritual experiences. To the modish charismatic movement of the 1960s, Branham was an outdated figure." But others blamed the decline on financial problems and his growing insistence upon preaching the controversial "Jesus Only" doctrine, as opposed to the more prevailing belief in the Trinity, and Hall agreed. "When he just preached healing, he had all these people with him, but when he started preaching doctrine—and especially baptism—that made a problem for him. So that may have been part of the breakaway of the huge mass revival to Pentecost."

Many of the big-name revivalists of that day were dead. Others—like Oral Roberts, who had become a Methodist—had turned their attention to television and to Bible schools and universities. Those who remained on the sawdust trail had learned to content themselves with small tents and fewer people. Things had changed. Still, Hall was hopeful.

"I think there's gonna be a turnaround," he said thoughtfully. "There's an exuberance. You could see it here last night, even with this little crowd, there was an expectancy. You pick it up?" He didn't wait for an answer. "Or, I've come here to get freed—that's the attitude—I've left all my problems outside the door. So I go with that spirit. If there's something I can do—it may not be even praying, but just speaking to them to relieve their frustrations—I'm going to do it."

CHAPTER VII

MIKE SHREVE:
"Into the Highways and Hedges"

Sparta was nestled in the rolling North Carolina countryside at the junction of routes 18 and 21. Its courthouse square was surrounded by the usual pharmacies, hardwares, and dry-goods stores. Beyond those, unpretentious houses extended along the two arteries until the dwellings gave way to open land scattered with fields of late-summer corn and an occasional clump of trees. Except for a shopping center to the south of town, little had changed in the almost forty years Brother H. Richard Hall had been coming to the area. The population had hovered at a thousand, with most residents dependent on farming or the lumber industry for a livelihood, especially since Interstate 81 reduced the stream of motorists that once passed through on the way to nearby mountain resorts. A bowling alley and the bar at Bob and Marie's Motel provided the only commercial outlets for entertainment.

The tent was located a mile outside town, off Highway 18, not visible from the road, its presence marked by a small sign with an arrow and TENT hand-lettered in red. After I turned onto the dirt road and headed down and around, the vinyl expanse came into view. Its whiteness was so blinding in the summer sun that the surroundings seemed to recede like the blurred peripheral images in a photograph. The tent itself appeared larger than its actual dimensions, an illusion that gave way as I followed the road's winding descent. Even then, it stood taut and pristine between a green slope and a row of simple homes. To the

front sat a one-room frame church with electric cords extending from
an open window to a tractor-trailer truck parked next to it.

The grounds were virtually deserted except for one man in shirtsleeves rounding up a litter of puppies from under the church. When
I approached, he stopped long enough to accompany me to the trailer
where he rapped on a screened door, calling to Mike Shreve that a
reporter wanted to see him. A male voice invited me to enter.

The young evangelist was polishing shoes, several pairs of already-
shined loafers lined up before him in the dimly lighted truck. Emptied
of the tent and sound equipment, it had been converted into living
quarters for Shreve and the dozen teenage boys traveling with him for
the summer. Suits and blue jeans hung from a rod extended across the
far end, and a hot plate and an electric frying pan rested on a makeshift
table of plywood and cinder blocks. A slender woman introduced as
Wanda Rogers was ironing a man's shirt in the limited brightness of a
lone bulb that dangled from the ceiling.

In spite of the heat, Mike Shreve wore a vest and matching trousers
and a white dress shirt unbuttoned at the neck, the cuffs peeled back
once. At thirty he was what many young women would have considered
"a good catch": bright, articulate, engaging, with curly dark hair, clear
blue eyes, and an attractive balance of wit and determination. For the
ten years he had been associated with Richard Hall, however, there
had been little time or opportunity to date, let alone consider marriage.
All but one or two nights a month were spent on the road, traveling
much the same territory covered by the Methodist circuit riders of
frontier days and leading a life-style not too removed from theirs.
During the winter he moved to a new town every two or three days;
in summer, between tent revivals, he scheduled shorter indoor meetings. Each stop came as close to a "home" as he ever got. For even
though he had a room at the church back in Cleveland, Tennessee,
he carried his few belongings with him and slept most often in the
tractor-trailer or his car, as he had for the almost three weeks he had
been in Sparta.

While Hall had been coming to the community most of his career,
this was Shreve's first visit. He had spent the first day helping erect
the tent and then, while his crew made the final preparations, drove
seventy-five miles south to conduct a two-day meeting, returning in
time to open this revival. He had been joined two nights before my

arrival by Hall and his team who, after the last service ended on Saturday, would head for Grundy, Virginia, to wind up Pat Hayes's revival there while Shreve and his entourage traveled to Harlan, Kentucky, to begin another cycle.

The rugged life appealed to Mike Shreve. As the son of a now-retired naval officer, he had had a peripatetic upbringing, attending kindergarten in Cuba and living here and there around the United States, most recently in Orlando, Florida. He had also wandered about the mercurial worlds of alcohol, drugs, and eastern religion before joining Brother Hall. At first, Shreve had taken part in the elder evangelist's meetings, but now he too bore all the responsibilities that came with a tent.

"Taking the tractor-trailer around the country is a lot of sleepless nights," he said, dabbing a rag into a tin of black wax. "You just go from town to town and get in at five o'clock in the morning, sleep in the car, and get up around seven-thirty or eight and work eighteen hours. It's hard work, hard labor."

"Who drives the truck?" I asked.

"Don Warren, the organist, does most of the driving," he said. "He just drops the truck off and goes back with Brother Hall. It's a good two days to get a tent this size up, and this is our smaller tent. Our big tent—it's a good two or three days of hard labor for several men."

"How many people does this one hold?"

"Oh, maximum you could put around four or five hundred," he estimated. "We've got probably about two hundred chairs in there now. The big tent holds about twelve hundred."

Once the tent was up, Shreve's days were filled with overseeing repairs, preparing for the evening services, planning future meetings four or five months in advance, writing a column for the *Shield of Faith* newsletter, and riding herd over the boys who traveled with him as he and Pat Hayes had followed Brother Hall.

When I asked what he did the one day a month he spent in Cleveland, he replied, "About seventy hours' work in ten hours' time. Preparing for meetings, promotion, working on the buildings that we're constructing at any given time. We built our convention center on the Mondays when we'd come in from a revival. We'd get up early and work all day on the building, then go back out on the road."

"You mean, actually hammer nails?" I asked.

"Oh, yes," he assured me. "In Brother Hall's ministry, preachers aren't sissified. If you're a preacher, you get grimy and dirty just like everybody else. I think it does a preacher good to have to get out and labor and sweat."

Mike Shreve clamped the top on a tin of polish, then buffed the last loafer to a sheen and lined it up with the others. It was half-past four, and he was eager to drive into the nearby hills for a few moments' solitude before the evening service. After we had made arrangements to meet the next morning for an interview, he went to pray and I headed down the road to my motel.

By the time I returned for the service, cars filled the area between the tent and church and spilled out onto the road. The crowd consisted of salt-of-the-earth-type folks, somewhat older than those I'd met at other revivals and about 150 in number. Some had already taken seats under the tent; others milled about outdoors visiting among themselves and with Mike Shreve, dressed now in a pink dress shirt and gray pinstripe suit.

Brother Hall was still nowhere in sight. Not until the song service was already under way did he wander onto the podium and take a seat behind the drummer. His expression was distant and detached, as if his mind were somewhere else. At one point he stood, walked to the back of the tent, and began lowering the side curtains, slowly, and with the help of several men, not returning to his seat until the tent was completely enclosed. The service had been in progress almost an hour when Mike Shreve finally introduced the elder evangelist, and his team—all except Don Warren—replaced the young men on the platform.

The service was virtually a replay of those I attended at Stepney Faith Center, with Hall repeating some of the same anecdotes, even the same one-liners, in a rambling sermon that was equal parts parable, homespun philosophy, and down-home humor. The people responded, as they had in Maryland, with tongues and exuberant amens and pressing forward, in the late hours, when he announced the altar call.

It was almost midnight when I started back to my motel after joining Shreve and his crew for a spaghetti supper in the truck. Even then, the boys were tittering like youngsters at summer camp, showing no signs of winding down. The next morning I returned shortly after ten and found no movement in or about the tent. The side curtains remained down, and the door to the church was closed. The only person in sight was Wanda Rogers, slouched down in the front seat of her automobile, napping. At the sound of my car's engine, she looked up and motioned for me to join her. The boys, up until five o'clock telling ghost stories, were still asleep, she said. Mike Shreve had driven into the hills to pray, but she expected him to return soon.

There was a delicate goodness about her, about the way she moved and spoke. She was a slender woman with the resilience of a tender young shoot not easily broken by adversity. At twenty-one, she was in her own quiet way a bulwark for her husband and those around her. That inner strength had developed over the years, as a buffer against the hardships in her own life. At age two she had been abandoned by her mother and sent to live with first one relative and then another. When she was ten, she moved in with her father and his new wife until that brief marriage ended and she again went to stay with her grandmother and an aunt. The most constant aspect of her childhood was attending Pentecostal meetings, many of them Richard Hall's. It was, in fact, at one of his meetings that she met James Rogers, whom she married the day she turned sixteen. She spoke openly but without bitterness about her upbringing, dwelling on the happiness her religion brought her as a child and, now, evangelizing with her husband. Three years ago James had quit his job in a textile mill, first to join Mike Shreve's team and then that of his older brother, Ernest. For the past year he had been on his own, preaching in smaller churches throughout the area. Ordinarily he and Wanda spent five or six days a week on the road and one in Cleveland in their refurbished mobile home. But this week, because he had no engagements of his own, they had stopped by Sparta to assist Shreve, with James playing the organ and Wanda acting as big sister to the younger boys.

When James first broached the subject of going on the road full time, Wanda had balked. Now she talked of her obstinance openly but with embarrassment. "We had a seventy-seven Granada and that was a luxury to me, because we'd never had a brand-new car with an air-conditioner, and I said, No! I can't get rid of my car and my washer and dryer—luxuries, you know," she recalled with an uncomfortable laugh. "I got in the car and kind of spun out of the parking lot. But I got to thinking about it. I knew we could sell our furniture, but our car—I didn't want our credit to go bad. I went to his mom's and I was talking to her and his brother was over there and he said he was going to buy a car, a brand-new one, so he'd just take our car. I knew then that it was God working everything out. And so I went back up to the tent that night. I drove up real fast on the parking lot and I jumped out and I said, We can go! We can go! I was for it then, when I knew everything would work out." She seemed comforted, even now, by that assurance. "His brother gave us an old Chevy van, and we put a rod up and threw all our clothes in there. With what we sold we paid everything off, and we left with forty dollars and headed down to Florida to meet Brother Mike at his tent meeting."

"Do you remember your thoughts when you pulled out?" I asked.

"I didn't know what I was getting into," she said softly. "I thought, I don't know how long it will last, if it will last a couple of weeks or a couple of months or years, but I wouldn't trade what I have now. I've gotten used to this kind of life-style. It's kinda rugged for a girl, because she needs a lot of things, but you get used to it."

"Are you the only female most of the time?"

"With James, yes. We don't have anybody working with us," she answered, "but when we were traveling with Brother Mike my sister-in-law was there and her husband and the drummer and his wife. There were three of us. It didn't make it as bad, but it was still kinda rough."

Until a year ago when they bought a secondhand mobile home, she and James slept on the floor at the church during their brief stopoffs in Cleveland, and on the road they lived in the Chevy van. Now when the couple held their own revivals they usually stayed with the pastor or members of the congregation. But during Mike Shreve's meetings, they slept wherever they could. "A couple a nights we stayed in the tractor-trailer," she said, "and then a couple a nights we slept in the church. We stayed in that camper last night." She nodded toward a small white van parked next to the tent. The owners attended the revival on weekends so that tonight she and James most likely would sleep in the truck. "We've got a blanket," she explained, "and we sleep on a cushionlike thing."

"When you travel with Mike he sort of looks to you to cook and take care of people, right?"

"He doesn't make me cook," she was quick to explain, "but I see how helpful it is because he can be doing more important things. And

I feel like I don't play any musical instruments and I don't sing. I don't do that much participation so it gives me free time to do a lot of these things. I feel obligated in a way to do it for them, and I enjoy it."

Near the end of last night's service she had turned to me to ask the time and then left to go to the truck to prepare supper. Now I asked, "What would have happened if you had not been there?"

"They probably would have had sandwiches," she said. "Mike probably would've waited until the service was over and then just put the bread out and got sandwich stuff from the refrigerator across the street. That's usually what they eat mostly unless somebody brings stuff already cooked. They don't match anything together. Lots of times they don't have it to match."

"Do they eat breakfast?"

She shook her head. "When I'm here I try to have lunch ready by twelve-thirty and then a meal after church. And if they want something during the day, they can fix a sandwich."

Mike Shreve pulled up next to us in a light-blue Datsun with suits and dress shirts hanging from a rod across the backseat. As I watched him get out of his car, it was difficult to imagine him in faded jeans with long, straggly hair and a beard. He wore the pink shirt and pinstripe trousers and vest from the night before and in spite of having slept in them was meticulously groomed. Wanda Rogers glanced at him striding toward us and then turned her attention to my question as to whether she had prepared last night's supper or it had been brought by members of the church.

"I cooked the spaghetti," she started, her explanation cut short by Mike Shreve.

"Trial of her faith," he said jokingly as he climbed into the backseat. "Never had cooked spaghetti."

"You hadn't?" I asked.

"Uh-uh," she laughed. "First time. I never had cooked for that many either. Some people brought the green beans and macaroni salad, and I fixed the rest."

"You fixed the spaghetti and meat sauce all on that little hot plate?"

"Uh-hmmmm," she chuckled, "and an electric frying pan."

"What do you do when she's not around?" I asked Shreve.

"Let 'em eat peanut butter and jelly sandwiches," he said playfully.

"I came back this week after Mike had cooked for 'em a couple of days and they said, We're so glad you're back. All we get to eat is sandwiches when Mike cooks," Wanda Rogers ribbed him.

I turned to Shreve. "What did you cook last week, was it really peanut butter and jelly?"

He laughed good-naturedly. "I went to a little bit more trouble. I cooked a lot of eggs and bacon and things like that."

"*Lots* of eggs," Wanda emphasized.

"Yeah," he conceded, "I'm good at eggs."

Many of the boys were youngsters with Pentecostal upbringings who had stayed on after Hall's annual July convention, but others were recent converts whose teenage wanderings were not too different from those of Mike Shreve. He too had sampled garlic diets, LSD, and yoga in a gnawing quest for something—he knew not what. He had been raised Catholic, educated in parochial schools, and was an altar boy devoted to the church until he entered his teens and began his slow, quiet rebellion. From early childhood he always seemed to be searching, probing—more active than most. He made good grades, though they could have been better, and played the piano, organ, and guitar. In high school his musical compositions showed unusual maturity and promise, and his parents felt certain he would excel as a composer or a writer—his ambitions as a youth. They were equally confident he was capable of being accepted by most any school he decided upon, even Harvard, where his younger brother earned a degree in psychology. But less than six months after heading to Florida State University to study music and creative writing, he dropped out—the only one of four siblings not to graduate from college. Following a near-fatal overdose, he stopped experimenting with drugs and took up with an Indian guru, moving into an ashram, teaching yoga, and praying as long as fourteen hours a day. Still, the then-nineteen-year-old felt unfulfilled. Often he walked the streets, weeping and looking. When a friend wrote about being "born again" and urged Shreve to seek salvation, he rejected the idea. Nevertheless, the thought weighed on his mind. Finally, one day while standing on a street corner hitchhiking, he was picked up by Kent Sullivan, a young man who had been converted three months earlier. It was then that Mike Shreve found what he had been searching for. In the back of Sullivan's van, he knelt and accepted Jesus Christ as his savior. Six months later, after a revival in West Virginia, he and Sullivan—like many young people of that era—joined Richard Hall's ministry.

Earlier, when I had stopped in Grundy, Pat Hayes remembered those days as "wild." "Brother Hall had a bunch of hippies," he recalled. "Me and Mike and Kent were the first, and then we began to collect 'em everywhere we went. And for about two years we went with Brother Hall everywhere. Everytime he would go to a town, he'd drive in and for the next four or five hours we'd all be coming in behind him. Old trucks and vans just loaded with kids. We'd sleep in Sunday school rooms and be out on the streets every day, all day long, witnessing. How we lived I don't even remember, but somehow we did."

Now Mike Shreve reconsidered the evangelist's appeal. "Brother Hall is a nonconformist," he said thoughtfully. "During the sixties and seventies the young people were really rebelling against the status quo and against society as they saw it, and Brother Hall, we could relate to him because he didn't fit the mainstream of churchanity. He was his own person. He had longer hair—not real long, but long enough to where we thought Brother Hall was one of us. And he had his own way of preaching. It wasn't the set way of getting up there and opening the Bible and quoting scripture and then preaching for fifteen minutes. He'd just get up in the pulpit and preach for two hours in such a flamboyant way that he never lost your attention. And powerful miracles took place. My mother was healed of cancer in one of his meetings." Shreve described how, during a Word of Knowledge session, Hall told his mother she was being healed of a breast tumor that she was aware of but had not mentioned to her family. "So we saw things like that happening in the meetings which attracted us to him because we saw a reality of Christianity that we were searching for, something like unto what Peter, James, and John had."

It was exciting to be in those crusades, Shreve said. "We brought a little bit of different coloring, so to speak, to his ministry because it'd been very straightlaced and approaching things from a little bit more of a churchy direction. We were the Jesus Movement hippies."

"Did you still have long hair?" I asked.

"I cut that after I got saved," he said, "but still, the people had not seen anything quite like Kent and me. We always wore blue jeans and we had our blue-jean jackets with 'Jesus Saves' on the front and big emblems all over it. Brother Hall would let us testify in the meetings about how God had delivered us from the eastern religions and drugs. Kent and I would get up early in the morning—seven-thirty, eight o'clock—and go in the streets and stay out there ten, twelve hours every day, going into bars and the juke joints. It was a very exciting kind of ministry, not the drab kind of day-to-day normal pastoral ministry. We went out there where the Devil was really active and invaded his territory. In fact, we really felt like we were God's terrorists."

For three or four years, that, along with leading the congregational singing, was Mike Shreve's main role. It was, in fact, Shreve—along with Kent Sullivan—who won Pat Hayes to the Lord in a Louisiana shopping center. Eventually he began receiving invitations to preach, and at Hall's urging he went out on his own. Both he and Pat Hayes, however, had remained part of Hall's association and continued to hold joint services such as this one, though neither was bound by a contract.

"I never planned to preach in the pulpit or to hold revivals in churches," Shreve said. "It was something that developed all by itself. I had confidence in my ability to reach the lost out on the streets. I knew I could go to the bars and to places of drug traffic and where crime was abundant and I could reach these people. But I felt very inadequate when it came to standing in the pulpit and preaching to people that had been saved twenty years or longer than I had. But gradually God began moving me in that direction."

According to Shreve, he learned to preach by watching Brother Hall and by the leading of the Holy Spirit—not by taking special courses or attending a Bible college, as his parents had urged him to. "I didn't want to just be another preacher coming out of the mold," he insisted. "Some of the most successful men I've ever read about were self-made men that didn't go the normal route. They always forged a way through the wilderness instead of walking down a beaten-down path, and I've always been kind of a misfit and—how can I say it?" He hesitated, looking for the best way to describe himself. "I've just never fit in. I didn't fit in with the elite crowd. I didn't fit in with the other crowd. I never went to football games. Never hardly went to any school functions because I thought it was silly to jump up and down at a football game and go to some prom."

"Did you date?"

"I wasn't that much of a misfit," he laughed. "I still liked the girls just like every other teenage boy. But still, even as a teenager I didn't fit in with people, and I think it was the call of God on my life."

"Do you think you'll ever marry?"

"It's possible, but right now I don't foresee it in the future. Nothing would hinder me from getting married if I felt like it would be right, and the right time and the right person. It would have to be the right kind of person for this kind of life-style. Most women wouldn't be able to adapt."

"So in a way you are almost living the life of a—"

Shreve finished the sentence for me. "Priest—but I don't have the clerical collar and the titles. I don't have anything materially except a few suits and a car. I don't own a home, don't have any material possessions, and really my car is in the name of the church."

Like most of his team, he usually dressed during the day in the same clothes—except for the jacket and tie—he wore on the platform. While he sometimes wore blue jeans, this was how he dressed most of the time. He had gotten used to it, and was comfortable. When I asked how he got his clothes cleaned, he cleared his throat and smiled at Wanda Rogers. "We usually find one of the wives in the group and volunteer them."

"Like Wanda?"

"Yeah," he said thoughtfully, "she's real helpful that way. Or usually, there'll be somebody in the community that lets us use their washers and dryers. Most of the guys use laundromats, though."

"Do you ever find yourself sitting in a laundromat in a little town?"

"One of the least enjoyable things for me is washing my clothes at a laundromat," he admitted, "and if I can get out of it in any way, I will. If I can find some obliging person who will do it, I'll pay them a few dollars."

"What about shopping for clothes?"

"I rarely go shopping," he said. "Just don't. I hate to. I'll look for about a minute, and if I don't see what I want I split. Usually people buy me clothes. I believe the Bible. Jesus said, Seek ye first the kingdom of God and all these other things shall be added unto you. And it's worked. In fact, the two times I've bought myself a suit, either there was something totally wrong with it or I was allergic to the material. I thought that was God's way of saying See, you're trying to take care of yourself. Just let me take care of you. So a couple of years ago I quit even shopping for myself. I said, Okay, Lord, I'll just give myself totally to you, and when you want me to have a new suit, somebody'll bring one to me—and they have."

"Where did you get this suit?" I asked, eyeing the designer initials on the vest lining.

"Some folks in Tampa bought it for me."

"They just know your size—"

Wanda Rogers laughed. "He gives 'em a hint," she teased.

"No," he said, chuckling good-naturedly, "but if they ask me I'll let 'em know real quick."

Besides helping maintain the tent, truck, and musical instruments, the boys were required to devote two or three hours to studying the Bible and witnessing on the street. Still, there was time for playing chess, riding bicycles, hiking through the woods, or having a jam session. Shreve himself, however, had no interest in recreation, or even a vacation.

"I don't like things like watching television," he explained. "I don't like football, baseball, soccer, badminton, chess, or games like that. I don't like wasting my time, and to me that's a waste. I try to spend every minute constructively, doing something worthwhile."

"Do you ever reach the point where you're tired and you wished you didn't have a service tonight?"

"Sure," he readily acknowledged, "there's a lot of times I'd like to just take off into the mountains for a week, but you become in a sense—" He hesitated. "I don't like the word prisoner, but it's the only thing I can think of. You become a prisoner of the ministry. In order to be a success at it, you've got to keep at it. If I'm going to do something, I don't want to be a failure, and I don't want to fool around, so I don't see the need to give my time to recreation or a vacation. I haven't had a vacation in ten years. Don't want one."

He slept five hours a night and sometimes took a nap during the day, most often in his car. While I could understand sleeping in your car in an emergency, I couldn't imagine doing so night after night for ten years, or for a lifetime. Nevertheless, Mike Shreve insisted he had gotten used to it. "I'd rather sleep in my car as to sleep in a motel," he insisted. "I hate the feeling of a motel room. Cold. Inhuman." He shuddered. "I like a rugged life-style. Always have. From the time I was a teenager, I liked roughing it. And I never cared for a lot of luxuries."

There was another side to sleeping in cars and trucks and sometimes on the floor. While some of the more remote communities had no motels, the practice came more from a conviction that the money could be put to better use. Like Hall, Shreve and the other young men associated with the elder evangelist drew no salaries, preferring to take only what they needed for expenses.

"God's blessed us financially enough to where we could stay in motels, but we all have a common desire to use as much of that money as possible for God's work," Shreve explained. "If Pat was staying in a motel and Brother Hall was staying in a motel, and I was staying in a motel—that's hundreds of dollars every week that instead we channel into the work of God."

While Shreve said he was all the time surveying his goals, his priorities, when I mentioned the word *ambition*, he stopped me. "Ambition can destroy you, if you're not careful," he said thoughtfully. "I would rather stay small and have a simple ministry on a level of being able to love and relate to the people and see them grow spiritually as to get wrapped up in all kinds of programs and colleges. I just don't want that. Unless you can keep it on a level of real sincerity. Success can corrupt you and steal simplicity from you if you're not careful. Jesus was totally successful, but He was totally simple and sincere in His approach."

Throughout most of the interview Wanda Rogers had listened quietly. But as the sun climbed higher in the sky and the boys appeared on the grounds in growing numbers, her thoughts turned to lunch. Finally she interrupted, to ask what she should prepare, and Mike Shreve suggested eggs. She grimaced. "When I was going to fix eggs yesterday Richard said, Don't cook any because Mike cooked so many the other day nobody will eat 'em," she said.

"Why don't you make egg salad?" Shreve persisted. "I love egg salad sandwiches."

"We need some bread."

"Okay, I might give you money to go get some bread," he said playfully.

"You want me to fix deviled egg sandwiches and what else?"

"We got salad, don't we?"

"Deviled eggs with salad?" she groaned.

"Sure," he said, "why not?"

"We got some lettuce, but we'll need tomatoes, and I don't think that milk is any good. One jug looks like it's clabbered," Wanda Rogers added to her grocery list.

Mike Shreve reached into his pants' pocket. "That's supposed to have some change to it," he said jokingly as he handed her several bills.

"You wanta eat with us?" she asked.

"Yeah," Shreve said, "why don't you?"

But before I could respond, Wanda had reservations. "You probably want to see what it looks like first."

"I'm game."

"We haven't died from it yet," she assured me.

Mike Shreve laughed. "We do pray hard over the food, though."

"You ain't kidding," she agreed. "We say, Lord, sanctify this, and *again*. I'm okay until a praying mantis comes in or a moth. One got caught in there the other day."

"Wanda has a deathly fear of bugs," Shreve explained, deadpan.

"Well, see, here you are cookin', you know, and they open the door and these moths come in and you don't want 'em to fall in the food. We don't have any lids."

Later when I went to the truck to see how lunch was coming along, the menu had changed from egg salad sandwiches to chicken, then back to eggs. Wanda Rogers was standing at the makeshift table frying sausage and bacon, a towel pinned around her white cotton skirt to protect it from the splattering grease. Plastic plates, a loaf of bread, two jugs of milk, and one of red Koolaid were set out on the table, and a pot of grits bubbled on the hot plate. Before James became an evangelist she had worked as a waitress, one of the few jobs open to her after quitting school in ninth grade. Still, she had no regrets.

"I never was interested in school," she said, turning the browning strips of bacon, "and I don't need a lot of education to do what I'm doing."

"Do you ever wish you had a permanent home?" I asked.

"I guess it kind of gets in your blood, you know, traveling," she said.

"I enjoy it. I don't think I *could* settle down since I've had a taste of what I'm in now."

"You really don't *miss* having a home?" I pressed.

Wanda Rogers stopped turning bacon to reconsider the question. "I miss the luxury of a nice bathroom," she conceded. "You can take a shower any time you want to at home, but here we usually go to people's homes and you kinda have to work around their schedule."

"There's no such thing as sitting in a bubblebath for a half hour," I observed.

"No," she laughed, "and there's no sitting down just to relax."

Here in Sparta, Mike Shreve and the boys had been bathing at a nearby school, and Wanda and James Rogers had been going to a house across the road. During the day they used two cinderblock privies located between the church and the tent. "Sometimes they just have Port-o-Johns and sometimes they look really awful," she grimaced. "Up at Thomasville they were brand-new ones, and I was so excited. I kept sayin', These are so pretty!" She laughed. "Them women looked at me like, This girl's crazy thinking a Port-o-John's pretty, but it was the nicest one I've ever saw. I mean, when that's your bathroom, that's your bathroom."

"What about taking care of your hair?" I asked. "How do you get it cut?"

She ran her fingers through her dark hair, in the growing-out stages of a shag cut. "I've lost a lot of pride since I've been traveling," she said, "a lot of pride. Usually we'll shower in the afternoons. I wash my hair then if I have to and blow it dry and try to stay as neat as I can until church time. If we're staying at people's homes, it's more convenient because you have a nice place to get cleaned up and can roll your hair if you want to for service that night, but during a tent meeting, when you're living out of the truck, you really can't."

On their one day back in Cleveland, she and James worked in the stencil department at Hall's headquarters and at night they were seldom alone. What little free time she had there and on the road was spent washing and ironing, studying for a correspondence Bible course, and going shopping.

"What do you look for?" I asked.

"Just odds and ends," she said, cracking eggs into a large bowl. "Usually I shop at Goodwill stores or thrift shops because you can get skirts real cheap. That's mostly what I look for in a town because usually you don't have the money to go out and buy a dress. If someone gives me ten dollars and tells me to go buy me something, I see how much I can get out of ten dollars. If I need toothpaste I'll get the cheapest thing I can, an offbrand or something like that, and then if I've got anything left I'll go to a thrift shop and pick up a few odds and ends to wear."

The screen door to the truck opened, and Mike Shreve entered. "Eggs," he said, glancing over Wanda Rogers's shoulders at the yellow mixture thickening in the electric frying pan. "And you tried to talk me out of eggs."

"Well, I wasn't but once I got over there and I saw that chicken and the woman said, It's mornin' time, you don't eat chicken this time a day. You ought to save it for tonight."

Mike settled into a folding chair. "I like eggs," he said matter-of-factly, "I could eat eggs any time." He turned to me. "You like eggs?"

"Yeah," I replied, "I like just about anything."

"There's two things you gotta learn to like—three things—evangelizing," he corrected himself. "Chicken, bologna, and eggs. Everybody'll feed you either chicken or bologna."

"Or pork 'n beans or Vienna sausage," Wanda said.

"What do you do about cooking when it's just you and James?" I asked.

"Usually Mondays and Tuesdays we're in Cleveland, and I cook for us there in our mobile-home trailer," she said, "I buy groceries and cook just for two days and then usually we leave on Tuesday night or Wednesday and go to the meetings and we eat there all week long at folks' houses where we stay. They cook for us. And then we go back to Cleveland. It's kind of like a routine in a way, every week. We don't ever go out, unless we're going back to Cleveland and we might stop at McDonald's or somewhere."

Indeed the Rogerses' lives didn't include many of the simple pastimes—like picnics, county fairs, even nightly television—that many people take for granted. "It's not that we wouldn't like to go to a park or something," Wanda Rogers explained. "We just don't have time."

"Not even for a vacation?" I asked.

"No, no, all year around it's traveling, traveling, traveling, from one church to the next, one state to the next," she said, acknowledging

that, for the future, she could look no farther than the next stop on
the map. "All I can see is just staying on the road continuously."

"Do you think you'll ever have a family?"

"God hasn't blessed us with any yet," she answered.

"What would you do if you had a child, in terms of traveling?"

Mike Shreve spoke for her, "Rejoice."

A soft smile came to her lips. "Yes, I'd love it," she said. "I guess
I would travel as long as I could. Maybe that's why God hasn't blessed
us with any. It's kinda helpful in the work we're doing not having any,"
she added wistfully, "but it's a beautiful thought."

With increasing frequency, the boys poked their heads into the truck
to see if lunch was ready, banging the screen door behind them as
they retreated to the grounds, to wait. At last Wanda Rogers spread
bacon strips and sausage on paper towels to drain, and Mike Shreve
sent two boys across the road, to retrieve some jelly and a chocolate
cake baked by a local church lady. When they returned, the others
straggled in, followed by the older musicians and James Rogers. The
latter was an average-size man of twenty-six, somewhat more reserved
than his more outgoing wife and Mike Shreve. He tended not to
participate in the good-natured bantering that quieted only long enough
for the blessing and then continued throughout lunch, not ceasing until
the heaping plates of bacon and eggs were emptied and one by one
the boys wandered away from the truck.

When only James Rogers and I were left, we too headed to his car
to talk. Although I had seen him around the grounds, we had not
spoken directly. At first he seemed standoffish, but gradually he grew
talkative and relaxed, or as relaxed, I suspected, as he might ever be.
He had been raised in a strict Pentecostal home, and all the "thou
shalts" and "thou shalt nots" had left him with a self-conscious
reserve—a man who would forever be "James," never the more in-
formal "Jim." He had approached me with a certain amount of suspicion, asking about my background and guardedly answering my own
questions until our curiosities were mutually piqued by the discovery
that five years earlier I had interviewed the man he had once worked
next to in a North Carolina cotton mill, a man who was a high-ranking
leader in the Ku Klux Klan. Even then, James Rogers chose his words
carefully, often returning to comments he feared might be misinter-
preted.

Revivals had been an important part of his life—especially those of Brother Hall. He had been healed at age four by the elder evangelist, and it was, in fact, Hall's meetings that prompted the Church of God to oust the entire Rogers family after his parents refused to stop attending them. "The people put an ultimatum on us—you either cut this out or we're going to turn you out," James Rogers told me, "so they turned us out because we loved Brother Hall. And still do. We would have rather remained in the church, Mother would, and not really come out. She would have rather been able to do both, but it just didn't work that way."

In spite of the reprimand, the Rogerses remained steadfast in their faith and religious worship, and all that went with those beliefs.

"Even after Mother left the Church of God, she continually taught us in that old Church of God life-style, which kept me from a lot of things," James Rogers said. "I've never smoked. I've never drank. I've never touched beer or whiskey. I've never had a cigarette. Well, I've never had a lot of things. After I got to the point where I could have got it if I wanted it, I had so much fear of God in me until I couldn't do it."

But what James Rogers did do was sing and play the guitar in the various nondenominational churches the family attended over the years. As youngsters, he and two brothers—Steve and Joe—would harmonize while washing and drying the dishes. By the time he was fifteen they had formed a trio that performed in area churches, including the very Church of God that had expelled the family.

"Just because we had broken fellowship somewhat with the churches didn't mean we were totally ousted," he assured me. "We lived good lives. They had to admit that. We were considered clean livers, you know, clean people. We lived holy, as holy as we could."

"How did you come to join Brother Hall and Mike?" I asked.

"I was singing with our group and things were getting stale," he explained. "It was becoming boring. We were doing it only on weekends. I was what they call a cotton mill worker, a textile worker. On the weekends, and sometimes during the week, we'd do a local and then on weekends we'd try to run to Georgia or to South Carolina." Eventually the group had expanded to include a sister, and there were, he said, offers that could have led to a full-time singing career. Nevertheless, James Rogers conceded, the routine had gotten stale. "Steve who was the brother that's right under me, as far as age is concerned, one day he come and he said, I'm going with Mike Shreve. Mike hadn't even asked him to begin with. Steve says, I'm just going. It was a common thing for kids to take off and travel with Brother Hall. I figured, Well, it'll work. He'll probably let him go. So Steve started selling everything he had. So I said, Man, I'm not setting here. My brother Steve, I had sung with him for seven years and course I had been close to him all my life. He's been right next to me, and I said, I'm just not setting here and doing a seven to four, whatever. I'm tired of that."

The two brothers and their wives immediately set out to join Mike Shreve in Tampa. Steve worked with him for a year; James, for two and a half. Then, about a year and eight months ago, James Rogers left to work with his brother Ernest before stepping out on his own.

"It was just common knowledge that I felt Brother Hall would like me to work with him since I've been so close to him all this time," he said. "I'd been working with Mike for two and a half years, in and out of the office. So we talked. Very few words. He said, Yes, he'd like for me to come into the association, and I feel like God's leading me to more and more things."

For a time James Rogers sat quietly, as if sorting through what we had discussed, to make certain he had said what he really intended to say. "This is very serious," he said, to reiterate his dedication to his work. "I do it full time, but I do it full time because I love God, not because I'm trying to evade a job." He looked at me, to make certain I interpreted him correctly. "I mentioned earlier," he said, "that I was tired of an eight-to-five job, but that's not the reason. As Brother Hall has said many times, if you can't make it in the world at a job, don't expect to just take off preaching and make it. God's called me from the very beginning."

"Do you ever miss having a home?"

"I don't think there's anybody in their right mind that would say that they didn't miss it," he said. "Sometimes I go in and it feels oh, God, it's good to be home. I just don't want to move." He recalled those days of selling everything they owned and heading out in the old leaky van, and of coming in during the middle of the winter to find the bed frozen. "It's been a long hard climb, but God's leading me," he was confident. "I see some things ahead."

"Is this the first car since you had to give the other one back?" I asked.

"In actuality, this is the first nice car we've ever owned. It's brand-new. Has four thousand miles on it."

"So it took you a long time to get a nice, new car again."

"Yes," he acknowledged, "I drove hand-me-downs, you know, sec-ondhand cars."

When I asked if, like Mike Shreve and Pat Hayes, he put back into the ministry all the money he collected, keeping only enough to live on, James Rogers answered, "Yes and no. When you've been in the ministry the length of time I have, it takes about all the money people donate to run your own personal affairs. Every once in a while God blesses me enough that I can help uphold my part of the Shield of Faith. But I stay in the red most of the time." He stopped. "To answer that question in maybe a better way, I turn in as much as I can. Most of the time, nothing any at all."

"In other words," I clarified, "you don't know if two weeks from today you're going to have fifty dollars or one hundred dollars to live on?"

"No, ma'am," he said, somewhat embarrassed. "As a matter of fact, to tell you the honest truth, right now I'm five hundred dollars in debt, and I don't even have a place to preach. So this is totally on faith. If God don't work a miracle in the next couple of weeks, I'm gonna lose this automobile. And I'd never go to anybody else and ask 'em for it. Like, Hey, let me borrow the money. I believe that God's going to work it out. If He don't that'll be another one of those hardships."

"I imagine it takes a certain kind of wife," I said.

James Rogers agreed. "I don't believe there's a preacher in this whole country that's got a wife with the personality my wife has, not only in meeting other people but in stick-to-it-ness and willingness. When I first started to leave and go with Mike Shreve, she spun out of the car lot, went up the road, and came back an hour later and said, Honey, I figured it out and we can go. And after that, I've never really seen her want to turn back, though I know she desires to have a nice little house with a fence and yard, and some children. We had a miscarriage the first of the year," he said, lowering his eyes for a moment before he added, "She's behind me."

He looked across the empty grounds and studied the abandoned tent with uncharacteristic nostalgia. Tomorrow night it would come down, and he remembered all the ones he had helped raise and dismantle. Tent revivals had been an important part of his family's life, and they continued to be, even now. Two of his brothers and a nephew worked on the tent crew for Robert Ellswick, another young evangelist who had come up under Hall's ministry, and still another nephew had led the singing at Pat Hayes's services in Grundy, Virginia. James himself remembered helping erect tents—especially Brother Hall's—from the time he was a small boy.

"Do you ever get to see many of the people you meet again?" I asked.

"Many times we meet people that we never see again," he answered, "but a lot of times we frequent the area in churches such as this little church right here, and, yeah, we see a lot of the people again, and a lot of the people have seen us before is the reason they come. Course we're after new converts. That's the main thing. But not only that, the people already established in churches, they need this. They need something to keep them boosted up in the spirit and keep them excited. Aw, man, they'll be talking about this for six weeks. And then if they got healed they may be talking about it for years. So there's a lot of people blessed. It never ceases to amaze me some of the things God does. You don't see it, but it happens. It just happens—I wasn't hearing but now I'm hearing. I wasn't seeing but I'm seeing. I had a pain but it's gone. I like to see some—I don't know how to say this. I'd like to see some creative power. I'd like to see arms grow out where there was none. I'd like to see feet that were too short by that much—"

"Have you seen that?"

"No, I haven't," he was candid, "I've heard stories, but I have seen people—I saw a woman who was deaf and dumb from her birth. She could make sounds, but I couldn't understand the words. Maybe the people with her understood it 'cause they had been with her. But she was deaf and dumb. Little sounds came out of her mouth. Or at least, that's all I knew about it. And the people brought her up said she was deaf and dumb. And I saw her get healed. She was totally deaf, and she started hearing and she said Ba-bee. She was mimicking the sounds, she said, Ba-bee. Started talking see, 'cause you can't talk when you don't know what to say. That happened in Mike Shreve's services. Mike has had some beautiful miracles for a young man. And as an aspiring minister I'm reaching for that. But it's not a matter of what I can do so people can see me, it's how many people can I help, and that's the God's truth. And what's going to cause them to get healed is the fact that I feel compassion. Twelve times in the New Testament Jesus was moved with compassion, and several of those times he healed a multitude. But if I couldn't heal them, if I could heal their souls, their body, their mentality, if I could heal their attitude. The psychologist might say that's just doing their work for them. I'd say that's a good work."

Brother Hall hadn't come to a covered-dish luncheon served under the tent by the church ladies. It was almost three o'clock when the evangelist's copper-color Cadillac pulled onto the grounds and headed up the adjacent slope where he parked and waited, not coming down until time for our interview. During my stay in Sparta, he had spent little time around the tent, arriving just before each service and disappearing immediately after the benediction. Between his arrival and the start of the service, he would remain in his car, alone, in view of the people but seldom mingling among them. In Aberdeen he had also remained apart. Even when the members of his team went out for late-night suppers, he never joined them. "I have four or five hours that I'm totally involved with people," he told me during our conversations there, "The rest of my time I like to be mine with a Bible or book or just relaxation or thinking or whatever."

Now, as we talked under the tent, Hall freely acknowledged that he was a loner. "I don't mind the pulpit, and the bigger crowd the better because I like that. I really like that," he said. "My problem is one on one, talking to two or three people. I don't really like that. Don't mind to tell you, I much prefer being alone."

"Do you like to be alone to think?" I asked.

The evangelist was direct. "I don't want to give you some puffed-up something," he said. "I just like to be alone, whether it's to think or not."

As a young man, when he was state overseer for the Church of God of Prophecy in Colorado, Utah, and western Texas, he often spent long periods of time in the desert. "I'd go and stay for days," he recalled, almost nostalgically. "Nobody there but me. Drive my car out on that desert—you know you can drive as far as you want to, right across the sand, and just stay there like a hermit. Take two or three gallons of water. Some food. Build a fire at night. I really like that. Probably more than I would now," he conceded, "but I like it, I really do."

In Sparta there was another reason he spent so little time on the grounds. When he wasn't sleeping or preaching, he was on the road visiting sick members of the far-flung congregation he had accumulated over four decades. "If you're a minister in one town—say you're in Lenore or you're in Cleveland, Tennessee, or you're in Dayton, Ohio—okay, that's your charge. But a ministry like I have, can you imagine?" He shrugged to underscore the magnitude of his problem. "Maybe I was here fifteen or twenty years ago in a revival. Well, I come here now and somebody's sick over in Galax Hospital, maybe forty or fifty miles away, or down in Hickory, which is eighty-four miles—that's where I went last night—and they call my office. There's a man I'm supposed to see before I leave here in Yadkinville. That's about seventy miles from here. I feel obligated to those folks just like a pastor would feel obligated to his charge. Really these are my people. Some of them I haven't seen in fifteen years."

"It's just that your congregation is more spread out," I observed.

"Yeah, that's all, and I'm getting in a hard place that every evangelist faces—funerals. Maybe they get converted in your ministry and when they expire they want you to preach their funeral. That's becoming quite a chore for me because I have to take off and try to get back in," he said, adding "But again, if people are with you when they're well and don't need you, then where are you when they need you? I mean, that's my idea of a minister. I don't want to be somebody's friend for gain's sake. It's sort of a dilemma, but if I can, I'll go preach the funeral."

"When you're not on the highway driving, do you sleep in your car?" I asked, remembering the rod of clothes hanging across the backseat of his Cadillac.

He nodded. "Sometimes you drive into a place like this at the last minute, and usually they'll have someplace you can freshen up, take a bath, shave, and rather than beat around trying to find a room, I just make a pad somewhere a lot of times. And look, where you gonna find a room? There's a little place down there," he said, "but honest to God, sometimes I'd rather take a sleeping bag or something."

I could understand why the evangelist drove the big, expensive Cadillac: It was his transportation, his office, his home, his place to sleep and find solitude. I too had decided against the shabby tourist court and another one on Highway 20 and seriously considered sleeping in my own car before locating a nice motel twenty-five miles south of town. But with Hall, the quality of facilities usually had little bearing on his decision to sleep in his automobile. "I don't *have* to," he emphasized, "People are good to me. There's been a lot of money gone through my hands—I kid you not," he said, not boastfully, but to explain the guiding philosophy of his organization. "Our bills are about thirteen hundred dollars a day, and that isn't anything compared to some other evangelists. Nothing. So what would twenty-five dollars for a motel be? But my idea of the disciples and Jesus was altogether different from a lot of people's. And if that's the type of ministry I want, then I should make my life-style like that."

Hall insisted he was not unique. Quite a few evangelists stayed on the road continuously and lived much as he did. "I happen to believe what I preach," he said. "I really happen to believe that we can change a man's life. I don't know to what extent God is going to require, but the Bible's pretty simple. It says, If a man hears the Gospel and believes, he shall be saved. So since I believe this, I want to stay out there and speak to ever' person I can. I don't want to be a minister to receive. I want to minister to a type of people that need me. There's others that don't need my ministry. They really don't. They wouldn't appreciate it. I happen to know the type people I reach. I'm not in the dark on that. But to me that was the ministry of the disciples and Jesus—friend of the friendless and those who's in desperation, on drugs."

His ministry was also made up of folks in out-of-the-way places like this, from backgrounds not unlike his own. Geographically and economically isolated from more mainstream society, they had come to look forward to his visits in much the way their forebears anticipated those of the circuit riders. And a deep fondness developed between them. In my own travels, people, even those of different faiths, recalled memorable evenings spent at Hall's meetings. And the evangelist himself frequently sprinkled his sermons with nostalgic recollections of past revivals.

Now when I mentioned his penchant for the small towns bypassed by other evangelists, he smiled. "I love them," he said. "These people are neglected. They don't have the finances so they cannot support the larger tents and the bigger efforts," he explained, "and then also it's a little easier if you go to a small town. Lenore, North Carolina, or even Greenville, South Carolina, or if you go to Wilkesboro, we're not there twenty-four hours but what ever'body knows we're there. But go to Baltimore. You could be there a year and people two blocks away won't know you are there. So you reach the people faster."

By noon Saturday the packing had already begun. The makeshift table had been taken apart and, along with the hot plate and kitchen utensils, placed on the ground near the side entrance to the truck. Mike Shreve's Datsun was backed up to the rig, and he and James and Wanda Rogers were loading cartons of canned goods and fresh produce donated by local church members. Shreve and his team would eat that during their brief stay in Cleveland and then take what was left to Harlan, Kentucky, to tide them over until the people there began bringing their own food offerings. The practice of giving food was not unlike pioneer days when preachers regularly held what they called "poundings," requesting everyone to bring a pound of flour, sugar, coffee, vegetables, or some other produce to feed their families. The night before last, at the close of the service, Shreve too had asked the congregation to help feed the boys traveling with him, complimenting one of the ladies on an earlier dish. "That was the best macaroni salad I've ever eaten," he declared, "and by faith I see another bowl to-morrow night!"

Now, under Shreve's watchful eye, those same boys dutifully worked at clearing out the truck, to make room for the tent and the sound equipment and most of the folding chairs. They giggled and horsed around yet they never stopped working, for by nightfall the truck must be ready to receive the giant vinyl. When at last it was empty and swept clean, they turned their attention to the tent, removing the augers and loosening some of the stakes. The dismantling progressed at a relaxed but steady pace, interrupted only long enough for lunch. By late afternoon, when only those items deemed absolutely essential to conducting the night's meeting remained, Mike Shreve drove off in his car and the boys dispersed, to shower and change clothes for the service.

By seven o'clock the tent was almost filled. Extra folding chairs had been set out, and during the singing some of the heftier men and boys carried in the church pews to accommodate the overflow crowd. Many were the same folks who had shown up night after night; others— among them two families I had seen in Aberdeen, Maryland—had driven long distances for a chance to hear Brother Hall. There was a festiveness about the occasion, almost that of a family reunion, as the revivalgoers remembered the elder evangelist's past visits. Even Hall got into the spirit, introducing the people from Maryland and recalling their late pastor's funeral and the glory days as well, when Princess Margaret attended one of his services, when he owned the third largest tent on the sawdust circuit, and when Aimee Semple McPherson used to roar into her huge Angelus Temple on a motorcycle, warning "Stop! You're on your way to hell and God sent me here to stop you!" The people too testified about God mending busted hips, healing whip-lashes, rheumatic fever, and swollen feet, and twice pushing back Death's spirit.

Relieved of her kitchen responsibilities, Wanda Rogers sat next to me, relaxed and buoyant, singing and responding, along with the au-dience, to Mike Shreve's entreaties to complete a scriptural verse. A full ensemble of musical instruments—an organ, electric piano, drums, cymbals, even a saxophone and a tambourine—set the tempo and the mood, building with the crowd's emotions to a feverish pitch, until Brother Hall felt moved to pray for those with cancer, deaf ears, back trouble, and "superfluous growths." A short woman in her sixties came forward with a blind eye, and the elder evangelist stopped the music. "I don't see any reason why God shouldn't help us," he told the crowd before sternly addressing the Lord. "Now, God, I expect You to touch this woman. I expect You to do it. I'm not talking to some man," he shouted, "I'm talking to You, God, the creator of all things. Why should I brag about You for thirty-seven years and bring a little case like this to You and not get an answer? In the name of God, touch this body!" And when at last Brother Hall had prayed, the woman exclaimed, "I can see!" and the crowd, as one, shouted *Amen!*

BENEDICTION

And when the people had received their blessings, they folded their chairs and carried them to the tractor-trailer, empty now and ready to receive what had been the makings of a revival. One by one they handed the chairs to young boys who stacked them in the rear of the truck. With car headlights trained on the tent, the men and boys began packing away the musical instruments, dismantling the platform, removing the side poles. Suddenly winches squeaked, and the tent inched slowly downward—half-mast, shoulder level, waist high, until the vinyl flattened onto the ground. Then the men and boys worked in teams and as a team pulling up stakes, loosening ropes, unlacing the sections, carrying the center poles to the waiting truck. One man kneeled, neatly, lovingly folding a section of the vinyl and recalling the tents he had helped assemble. He remembered the thrill of his first one, and when as a small boy he had carried hammers and stakes and water to the older workers, eager for the day he too could help and maybe even be a tent manager. "There's a pride that goes with putting up a tent," he said. "You want a tent set up right. You want people to ride by and say That looks nice!" When the last section had been folded, he grew melancholy. "There's a sadness that comes with leaving," he explained, "but there's happiness too that you've done good, that you've helped a lot of people." In the glare of headlights, he and the others lifted and loaded into the night, until chairs and amplifiers and drums and the makings of the

tent were carefully packed in the truck. And when he could do no
more, the man stood back and smiled.

"You know," he said, "God really likes tents!"

Bibliography

Books on contemporary revivals and revivalists are surprisingly few, and many of the ones that do exist are severely lacking in objectivity and thoroughness. The best source of material can be found in secular newspapers and magazines that have carried far too many articles to include here. For those readers who wish to do further reading on the various aspects of revivals and Pentecostalism, I offer this abbreviated list of some of the publications I found most helpful:

Alford, Delton L. *Music in the Pentecostal Church*. Cleveland, Tennessee: Pathway Press, 1967.

Allen, Asa Alonzo, with Wagner, Walter. *Born to Lose, Bound to Win*. New York: Doubleday, 1970.

Blackwell, Lois S. *The Wings of the Dove: The Story of Gospel Music in America*. Norfolk, Virginia: Conning Co., 1978.

Bloch-Hoell, Nils. *The Pentecostal Movement: Its Origins, Development, and Distinctive Character*. New York: Humanities Press, 1964.

Carden, Karen W., and Pelton, Robert W. *The Persecuted Prophets*. South Brunswick: A. S. Barnes, 1976.

Clements, William M. "The Rhetoric of the Radio Ministry." *Journal of American Folklore*, October 1974, pp. 318–27.

Coles, Robert. "God and the Rural Poor." *Psychology Today*, January 1972, pp. 33–40.

Conn, Charles W. *Like a Mighty Army: A History of the Church of God*. Cleveland, Tennessee: Pathway Press, 1977.

Daugherty, Mary Lee. "Serpent-Handling as Sacrament." *Psychology Today*, October 1976, pp. 232–43.

Dickinson, Eleanor, and Benziger, Barbara. *Revival!* New York: Harper & Row, 1974.

Flake, Carol. *Redemptorama: Culture, Politics, and the New Evangelicalism.* Garden City, New York: Anchor Press, 1984.

Flynt, J. Wayne. *Dixie's Forgotten People: The South's Poor Whites.* Bloomington: Indiana University Press, 1979.

Frady, Marshall. *Billy Graham: A Parable of American Righteousness.* Boston: Little, Brown and Co., 1979.

Frank, Jerome. *Persuasion and Healing: A Comparative Study of Psychotherapy.* Baltimore: Johns Hopkins Press, 1961.

Gaines, Steven S. *Marjoe: The Life of Marjoe Gortner.* New York: Harper & Row, 1973.

Hadden, Jeffrey K., and Swann, Charles E. *Prime Time Preachers: The Rising Power of Televangelism.* Reading, Massachusetts: Addison-Wesley, 1981.

Harrell, David Edwin, Jr. *All Things Are Possible: The Healing and Charismatic Revivals in Modern America.* Bloomington: Indiana University Press, 1975.

Jones, Loyal. "Mountain Religion: The Outsider's View," in *Religion in Appalachia*, pp. 401–07. John D. Photiadis, ed. Morgantown: West Virginia University Center for Extension and Continuing Education, 1978.

Kane, Steven M. "Holiness Fire Handling in Southern Appalachia: A Psychophysiological Analysis," in *Religion in Appalachia*, pp. 113–24. John D. Photiadis, ed. Morgantown: West Virginia University Center for Extension and Continuing Education, 1978.

———. "Holy Ghost People: The Snake-Handlers of Southern Appalachia." *Appalachian Journal*, Spring 1974, pp. 255–62.

———. "Ritual Possession in a Southern Appalachian Sect." *Journal of American Folklore*, October-December 1974, pp. 293–302.

La Barre, Weston. *They Shall Take Up Serpents: Psychology of the Southern Snake-Handling Cult.* New York: Shocken Books, 1969.

McLoughlin, William Gerald, Jr. *Billy Graham: Revivalist in a Secular Age.* New York: Ronald Press Co., 1960.

———. *Billy Sunday Was His Real Name.* Chicago: University of Chicago Press, 1955.

Morris, James. *The Preachers.* New York: St. Martin's Press, 1973.

Pelton, Robert W., and Carden, Karen W. *Snake-Handlers: Godfearers or Fanatics?* Nashville: Thomas Nelson, 1974.

Poloma, Margaret. *The Charismatic Movement: Is There a New Pentecost?* Boston: Twayne Publishers, 1982.

Rosenberg, Bruce A. *The Art of the American Folk Preacher.* New York: Oxford Press, 1970.

Samarin, William J. *Tongues of Men and Angels: The Religious Language of Pentecostalism.* New York: Macmillan, 1972.

Sherrill, John L. *They Speak With Other Tongues.* New York: McGraw-Hill, 1964.

Synan, Vinson. *The Holiness-Pentecostal Movement in the United States.* Grand Rapids, Michigan: Eerdmans, 1971.

Tifton, Jeff, and George, Ken. "Testimonies." *Alcheringera/Ethnopoetics,* vol. 4, no. 1, 1978, pp. 69–71.

Titon, Jeff, and George, Ken. "Dressed in the Armor of God." *Alcheringa/ Ethnopoetics,* vol. 3, no. 2, 1977, pp. 10–13.

Weisberger, Bernard A. *They Gathered at the River: The Story of the Great Revivalists and Their Impact Upon Religion in America.* New York: Octagon Books, 1979.